Interactive Web Development With Three.js and A-Frame

Create Captivating Visualizations and Projects in Immersive Creative Technology for 3D, WebAR, and WebVR Using Three.js and A-Frame

Alessandro Straccia

www.orangeava.com

First published: April 2024
Published by: Orange Education Pvt Ltd, AVA™
Address: 9, Daryaganj, Delhi, 110002, India

275 New North Road Islington Suite 1314 London,
N1 7AA, United Kingdom

ISBN: 978-81-97223-96-9

www.orangeava.com

Dedicated To

*My Mom and Dad, Who Taught Me How to Be the Person
I Turned Into*

*And to My Kids, Victor and Lucca, Who Teach Me How
to Be the Person I Am Becoming*

About the Author

Alessandro Straccia holds a bachelor's degree in Advertising and Marketing from Methodist University of São Paulo and a Technical Degree in Computer Science from ETE Lauro Gomes of São Bernardo, Brazil. He began developing an interest in Creative Development at a very young age, using his dad's Apple II to create 2D graphics using the Logo language and adding some interactivity using BASIC language. Some years later, Alessandro took his first steps in 3D using 3D Studio and POV-Ray, and began working with more professional languages such as C and Pascal.

His professional experience started in 1998, where he gathered all his knowledge to build multimedia applications with Macromedia Director and rich content websites with Adobe Flash for Brazilian advertising agencies. At these agencies, Alessandro earned several important awards, such as the Merit at One Show Interactive, two shortlists at the Cannes Advertising Festival, and two WSA Mobile prizes. In 2011, he started his own studio to help clients and advertising agencies in building Creative Tech and digital projects.

In 2020, Alessandro moved to the UK to work for a game studio, using his creative skills to lead the Marketing Art team. However, his passion for the Creative Tech area spoke louder, and he decided to focus on AR and VR areas, building projects for studios such as Unit9, Eyekandy, Globant, Treatment Studio, Nexus, Blippar, among others. He also started to work as a consultant for companies and studios interested in utilizing Creative Tech in their projects. More recently, he has started to explore Unreal Engine Fortnite to build playable content for educational and entertainment purposes.

He is currently working as a Creative Technologist for many creative studios in the US, UK, Europe, and Brazil, building interactive applications using web 3D and web AR/VR experiences for big brands. He also gives lectures about Creative Technology and immersive technologies for universities, startups, and private companies.

When not working on Creative Tech projects, Alessandro enjoys traveling, cooking, and playing video games with his kids.

About the Technical Reviewer

Anderson Mancini is a visionary creative developer from Brazil, specializing in three.js and WebGL development. He has delivered over 100 projects that showcase his expertise. As a three.js specialist, he is renowned for creating free components and helpers for the community, accessible on his GitHub page.

In addition to his prolific project portfolio, Anderson is a dedicated teacher, offering courses on three.js that share his deep knowledge with aspiring developers. His global reach extends beyond the Brazilian market, reflecting his commitment to shaping the future of creative development on a global scale.

Currently focused on empowering organizations with his creative prowess, he is known for infusing strategic and visually compelling solutions into the digital landscape. As an advisor to emerging creative startups, he plays a pivotal role in shaping the industry's future. His passion extends to various publications where he shares insights, emphasizing the importance of robust design principles and user-centric experiences.

He not only excels in tackling design challenges but also plays a pivotal role in shaping the forefront of cutting-edge and sustainable creative platforms. Whether through his project contributions, educational initiatives, or global collaborations, Anderson emerges as a key influencer in the dynamic realm of creative development.

Acknowledgements

Interactive Web Development With Three.js and A-Frame is the result of 10 years of study and professional work with these amazing technologies. However, it would not have been possible without the amazing initiative and work of the founders and maintainers of Three.js and A-Frame.

First and foremost, I extend my gratitude to Ricardo Cabello (aka Mr. Doob - https://mrdoob.com) for creating the amazing 3D web library called Three.js. He is revolutionizing the way we build interactive and rich content for the web, helping creative developers like me to make a living and encouraging new developers to try different development pathways, including mobile and desktop apps, CRUD, and other "normal" development areas.

I also thank the Mozilla team for creating A-Frame, and its current maintainers Diego Marcos, Kevin Ngo, and Don McCurdy.

To the Three.js and A-Frame community spread across Stack Overflow posts, Discord, and Slack channels, I extend my sincere thanks. Let's continue to help both beginners and experienced creative developers.

I would also like to express my gratitude to my family, especially my mom, who has always supported me, and my dad, who gave me the opportunity to start exploring CGI on his Apple II computer with BASIC and Logo languages. To my kids, Victor and Lucca, who always amaze me with their creativity and enthusiasm, and who helped me test some of the code examples from this book. And to my fiancée, Aline, who encouraged me to start this project and supported me until the end, despite all the challenges I faced during this period.

I extend my appreciation to the collaborators of this book - the entire AVA team, editors, and reviewers. A special thanks to Anderson Mancini, the technical reviewer who provided precious ideas on how to improve the content flow and understanding, and to Felipe Matos, who helped me revise and write some code examples for this book.

Finally, to the readers, thank you for choosing this book as your first step - or maybe not the first - on creative development. It's a wonderful journey, and I'll be your guide on the next pages.

Preface

Creative Development is a relatively lesser-known area in software development. It involves various creative tools glued together with coding languages. While you don't need to be a master in 3D, design, or even sound design to be a good creative developer, it's important to know the basics of all these areas and, especially, understand how to put them together to build amazing Creative Dev apps.

This book focuses on web tools – specifically Three.js and A-Frame – due to their popularity and relatively low learning curve, basically relying on HTML, CSS, and JavaScript.

This book is organized into nine chapters to guide you from the basics of Three.js to more complex and specialized lessons. By the end of this book, you will be able to build Creative Development apps based on the web, both for desktop and mobile platforms. You will learn to interact with rich content such as 3D assets, videos, and more. Even if you are an experienced Three.js developer, this book contains useful examples and templates that will help you enhance your own projects.

Chapter 1. Getting Started with Three.js: This chapter covers the foundations of Three.js, providing context about the library, how to make it work on your computer, and the basic tools needed to get started with it.

Chapter 2. Our First Scene: This chapter delves into the concepts of 3D primitives, materials, lights, and shadows. Learn how to use Three.js cameras and set up the animation loop to deliver the final result: our first Three.js scene.

Chapter 3. Interacting with Our Scene: This chapter teaches you how to interact with the scene using keyboard, mouse, and mobile phone data. Uncover the basic concepts of raycasting and learn how to click and interact with scene objects. Finally, we will dive into camera controls to move the camera around and put everything together to build a simple first-person shooter game.

Chapter 4. Adding Some Realism: This chapter explores ways to add more realism to the scene, including adding third-party 3D objects, setting up realistic materials and textures, and adding a physics engine to build a more interesting 3D scene.

Chapter 5. Post Processing: This chapter guides you a step further in scene realism by adding post-processing effects to give your scene sophisticated features such as glow and bloom, depth of field, and more.

Chapter 6. Introduction to WebAR and WebVR: This chapter introduces you to the concepts of WebAR and WebVR and provides the basics of the A-Frame 3D framework.

Chapter 7. Creating Your First WebAR Experience: This chapter takes you into the world of WebAR, adding more A-Frame knowledge and explaining how to build 3DoF, Image Tracking, and Face Tracking AR scenes.

Chapter 8. Creating Your First WebVR Experience: This chapter guides you through the WebVR world, explaining the basics of VR interaction and delivering a virtual exhibition in VR.

Chapter 9. Useful Boilerplates to Start Your Projects: This chapter presents you with Creative Development best practices and gathers all the book's lessons packed in seven useful boilerplates that you can use and adapt to build your own projects.

This book is filled with practical and real-world examples that will help you to start and improve your Creative Development skills with Three.js and A-Frame. We hope this book empowers you to build your own Creative Development projects and gives you more curiosity and excitement about this incredible development area. Happy coding!

Downloading the code bundles and colored images

Please follow the links or scan the QR codes to download the
Code Bundles and Images of the book:

https://github.com/OrangeAVA/Interactive-Web-Development-With-Three.js-and-A-Frame

The code bundles and images of the book are also hosted on
https://rebrand.ly/b84ca5

In case there's an update to the code, it will be updated on the existing
GitHub repository.

Errata

We take immense pride in our work at **Orange Education Pvt Ltd,** and follow best practices to ensure the accuracy of our content to provide an indulging reading experience to our subscribers. Our readers are our mirrors, and we use their inputs to reflect and improve upon human errors, if any, that may have occurred during the publishing processes involved. To let us maintain the quality and help us reach out to any readers who might be having difficulties due to any unforeseen errors, please write to us at :

errata@orangeava.com

Your support, suggestions, and feedback are highly appreciated.

DID YOU KNOW

Did you know that Orange Education Pvt Ltd offers eBook versions of every book published, with PDF and ePub files available? You can upgrade to the eBook version at **www.orangeava.com** and as a print book customer, you are entitled to a discount on the eBook copy. Get in touch with us at: **info@orangeava.com** for more details.

At **www.orangeava.com**, you can also read a collection of free technical articles, sign up for a range of free newsletters, and receive exclusive discounts and offers on AVA™ Books and eBooks.

PIRACY

If you come across any illegal copies of our works in any form on the internet, we would be grateful if you would provide us with the location address or website name. Please contact us at **info@orangeava.com** with a link to the material.

ARE YOU INTERESTED IN AUTHORING WITH US?

If there is a topic that you have expertise in, and you are interested in either writing or contributing to a book, please write to us at **business@orangeava.com**. We are on a journey to help developers and tech professionals to gain insights on the present technological advancements and innovations happening across the globe and build a community that believes Knowledge is best acquired by sharing and learning with others. Please reach out to us to learn what our audience demands and how you can be part of this educational reform. We also welcome ideas from tech experts and help them build learning and development content for their domains.

REVIEWS

Please leave a review. Once you have read and used this book, why not leave a review on the site that you purchased it from? Potential readers can then see and use your unbiased opinion to make purchase decisions. We at Orange Education would love to know what you think about our products, and our authors can learn from your feedback. Thank you!

For more information about Orange Education, please visit **www.orangeava.com**.

Table of Contents

CHAPTER 1
Getting Started with Three.js

Introduction

This chapter outlines the foundations of Three.js, giving you a bit of context of the Javascript library and explain why we cannot use 3D directly in the web browser. We will also discuss HTML <canvas> and WebGL and cover some other Three.js alternatives and spin-offs. You will learn about the tools required to build your Three.js scenes and how to make them work in your web browser. In the end, we will provide you with the Three.js useful links to download the library, examples, and documentation, and build our first Three.js boilerplate.

Structure

In this chapter, we will discuss the following topics:

- Introduction to WebGl
- Three.js History
- Three.js Alternatives
- Extending Three.js
- Tools and Requisites to Start Developing
- Downloading and Installing Three.js
- How to Use This Book
- Project Structure

Introduction to WebGL

If the subject of Three.js generated some interest in you, we suspect you know a bit about HTML, CSS, and JavaScript. These are the Holy Trinity of web development. With these pillars, you can do almost everything on your web or mobile browser—create graphics and animations, for example. Using HTML and CSS you can draw simple shapes and add simple animations to them. However, if you need to draw more complex graphics or animations, only HTML and CSS will not be enough.

This is why the tag `<canvas>` was introduced by Apple to JavaScript language in 2004. With this magic tag, you can draw 2D shapes and bitmaps over a defined area of your browser. You can draw circles, polygons, and more but no 3D shapes, complex textures, and sophisticated animations at all. The remedy to this was found in 2009 by the Khronos Group, along with Apple, Google, Mozilla, and Opera, who introduced the WebGL technology-Web Graphics Library, a way to render complex 3D graphics to web browsers.

TIP: If you are interested in <canvas> resources and 2D drawing, check **FabricJS** (http://fabricjs.com). It is a very powerful JavaScript library that helps you with drawing and animating 2D content on <canvas>. You can even use a dynamic canvas element as a texture for your 3D materials!

WebGL allows GPU-accelerated usage of physics, image processing, and effects as part of the web page canvas, without the use of plug-ins. This was a huge evolution for developers and designers who have been struggling to create more interesting designs and interactions on web pages.

Pure WebGL operates at a basic level—you need to code some GLSL stuff (C++) to define your materials and even your 3D objects need to be defined vertex by vertex—so it is not practical in any sense. This is why, around 2009, the first web 3D libraries were created. This is all about Three.js: it is a WebGL library that allows the developer to use advanced graphic features only with the knowledge of JavaScript without the more complex WebGL/GLSL languages.

Three.js History

The first decade of the 21st century was the age of Flash, the incredible graphic + animation + interactive development software that brought to us rich and (very) animated websites that would never exist if dependent only on HTML + JavaScript technologies. Flash came up with an interesting script language called ActionScript, and you could do loads of things while using it but it could not help with 3D.

In this scenario, **Ricardo Cabello**, AKA **mrdoob** developed Three.js, initially in Flash ActionScript, and then ported to JavaScript. Three.js had its first official version launched in 2010 entirely as a cross-browser with no plugin needed. Under an MIT license, Three.js was rapidly adopted by designers, creative developers, and 3D artists, gathering a huge community of enthusiasts and contributors. Nowadays, Three.js is the most used 3D library and has been used by freelancers, big digital studios, architecture offices, AR and VR companies. Even NASA now uses it on some mini sites and interactive animations. However, you have other options to do 3D stuff on your web browser.

If you are not so familiar with 3D graphics concepts, we need to explain an important thing: the render concept. By render, we mean the tasks executed by a computer to transform Maths formulas into viewable graphics, and this is what WebGL does (and Three.js through WebGL). For a computer, a 3D scene is a series of geometry points, materials, textures and lights that means nothing to us, but a render engine transforms all of this into a beautiful image that we can understand and appreciate.

The 3D rendering task is very complex, and it gets more complex depending on your scene parameters, the number of objects, lights, rendered image resolution, render quality, and other factors. So, we use 3D software (like Blender, 3D Max, Maya, Cinema4D, Houdini, and so on) to be able to draw objects and scenes in 3D space. These software render the 3D scenes into high-quality images, and sometimes rendering just one frame can take hours. We call these renders as **offline renders**.

In contrast to offline renders, we have **real-time renders**, such as proprietary game engines, Unity, Unreal Engine, and Three.js. They render 3D scenes in real time, using different techniques that allow the computer GPU to deliver complex 3D graphics in real time. Unfortunately, it is not possible to have the same level of quality of offline renders on real-time renders, but nowadays they are good enough to be used in game productions and even on movies and TV shows. If you search for **virtual production** on the internet, a plethora of productions that use game technology to deliver high-quality 3D content will come up.

So, Three.js is a real-time render engine, which means that it uses different techniques to be able to render complex 3D scenes on your browser screen. Unlike Unity and Unreal Engine, which are standalone softwares and can use the computer GPU directly (so they can use powerful graphic resources at a very fast speed), Three.js uses WebGL, which is limited by the browser resources and speed. This is why it is very hard to have Three.js scenes with a render quality comparable to Unity or UE scenes. But we are making every effort to resolve it. Nowadays we have dozens of techniques and shaders that can improve Three.js render quality very dramatically.

There are benefits and caveats to using different renders, and the best benefit by far of using Three.js is the possibility to have a 3D scene ready to run on (almost) any browser and device, without any need to download or install anything and without any compatibility concerns. We call this **friction**, and depending on what you want to deliver to your user, this factor is crucial. The users can wait a bit more to download and install a game or a mobile app that they will play for months, but they will not wait for long to open a website with 3D graphics or an AR/VR scene on their mobile phone.

We will discuss in more detail about some techniques to improve your render quality with Three.js further in this book.

Three.js Alternatives

Three.js is considered the most used 3D library available for the web, with more than 34k repositories on GitHub and more than 20k topics on StackOverflow. However, this is not the only 3D library available for the web. Following are the main Three.js alternatives:

Babylon.js: It is probably the best alternative to Three.js, has the same basic features of Three.js, but has some interesting features embedded in the core, such as physics engine and some nice visual improvements as **SSR (screen space reflections)** and **AO (ambient occlusion)**. Babylon has a good GUI editor and a powerful web 3D inspector too:

Unity WebGL: Unity is one of the most powerful game engines in the market. Thousands of game studios and indie game developers use it to deliver not only games but interactive and rich experiences. Unity can export to WebGL and run on browsers but in a very limited (and heavy) way. Also, Unity is not an open-source tool, so you need to buy a license to use it on bigger projects.

PlayCanvas: This is a full game engine focused on the web. It has a very powerful GUI editor and allows the user to build complex interactions without any line of code. PlayCanvas offers a free subscription for smaller projects, but as Unity does, you need to buy a license to use it for more robust projects:

There are other interesting alternatives, but they are not real 3D libraries or engines for the web. D3.js, for example, renders 3D graphics on web browsers but it is specific for data visualization. Blend4web has good 3D features (and very good integration with Blender), but it is not as popular as Three.js and Babylon.

Apart from the competitors that use completely different web 3D render engines, there are some libraries that use Three.js as a render engine but have different development approaches.

Extending Three.js

You can use Three.js on its *pure* version, but you have some interesting spin-offs that can increase your productivity or be more friendly to your tech stack:

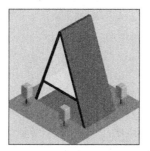

A-frame: This is a HTML framework based on Three.js. It uses HTML tags and components to allow the developer to build 3D scenes with less code and less complexity. It is largely used for web AR and VR applications, and you can use pure Three.js code along with A-frame code. We will focus on A-frame in later chapters that are dedicated to web AR and VR.

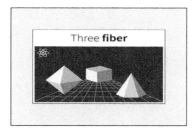

React Three Fiber, or R3F: This is a React framework based on Three.js. It allows React developers to use Three.js with re-usable components and fully integrated into React core. R3F has a good number of native components and allows the user to use pure Three.js code if needed.

So now that you know a bit more about Three.js history and some other web 3D alternatives, it is time to stretch your fingers and start doing some code.

Tools and Requisites to Start Developing

As a developer, you probably have your own tech stack and tools to develop, but it is always good to remember some basic stuff. So, basically, you will need:

- A good **code editor**, such as Sublime, Notepad++, VSCode, and so on.
- **Local server software**, such as Xampp or Wamp, or you can use Node.js and Webpack to automate your code compiling and web serving. In this chapter, we will keep it simple and use a local server software. All the examples and boilerplates presented in this book have been tested with Xampp.
- And, of course, a web browser. Chrome and Firefox have the best performance and WebGL compatibility.

All the examples and boilerplates from this book used **Xampp (**https://www. apachefriends.org/download.html**)** local server to run, so to be able to run these files you will need (after installing Xampp of course) to start the local server. You just need to open it and, in the same line of Apache, click the `Start` button. Now you need to open your file explorer and find the Xampp install folder (generally `c:/xampp`). Inside this folder you will find the folder `htdocs`. Everything you add here will be used for Xampp to run as a web page, just like on a non-local web server, the only difference is that they will be accessible by the URL `http://localhost/foldername`.

We recommend that you to create a folder inside `htdocs` to add your code and GIT push all the book boilerplates to another folder for reference and experiment:

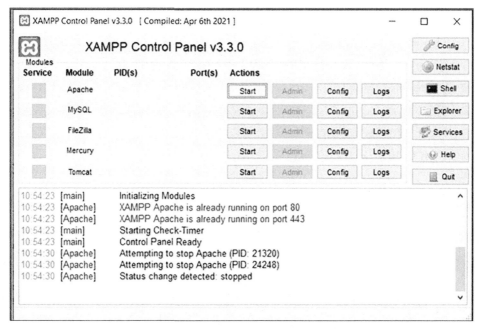

Figure 1.1: *Xampp control panel*

If you use VSCode, just create the projects on it and run the LiveServer extension in order to make the web pages work properly. We advise you that all the examples from this book and the provided boilerplates will not work if you just open the pages in your web browser.

Downloading and Installing Three.js

You are probably aware that Three.js is available at https://threejs.org. In this link you will find the core code, documentation, and good examples of Three.js features and applications.

There are some other useful links:

- **Documentation**: https://threejs.org/docs:

  You will find all `Three.js` classes and explanations about each one here. Unfortunately there are not too many code examples in the Documentation, so maybe you will need to look further on StackOverflow to find better examples on how to use the classes.

- **Examples**: https://threejs.org/examples

  You will find excellent examples of what you can do using `Three.js`, with code sources.

- **GitHub**: https://github.com/mrdoob/three.js

   The main GitHub source of `Three.js`. You can clone the repository and start tweaking the examples and see what happens.

- **StackOverflow**: https://stackoverflow.com/questions/tagged/three.js

   The Three.js section on StackOverflow is huge – this is a good thermometer to know how popular `Three.js` is.

- **Web Forum**: https://discourse.threejs.org

   A good place to find answers for your issues.

- **Discord server**: https://discord.com/invite/56GBJwAnUS

There is no need to install anything, really. You can just call Three.js library directly from this link: https://unpkg.com/three@0.153.0/build/three.module.js. But you can download it from Three.js or GitHub websites and run it locally.

Also, you can use NPM to install Three.js into your project. NPM stands for **Node Package Manager** and it is a package manager based on Node.js that adds more functionalities to JavaScript projects. To use it, first you need to install Node.js (https://nodejs.org) and after that you can install Three.js and any other third-party package via Terminal, CMD or PowerShell:

```
npm install --save three
```

Our choice in this chapter is to keep it as simple as possible, so the examples you will find here will call the JavaScript libraries directly from the CDN.

The current Three.js version when this book is being written is **R153**, so for compatibility reasons, we will use only libraries compatible with this version. Also, we decided to use the Three.js **module** version, which uses modern JavaScript and simplifies loads of things in the code work. If you are unfamiliar with JavaScript modules, please take a look on this good guide on Mozilla website: https://developer.mozilla.org/en-US/docs/Web/JavaScript/Guide/Modules.

Using this book

In this book, you will find hundreds of code examples with rich explanations about each part of the code. To make it easier to follow and not fill up the book with hundreds of lines of code that you will probably not write down on your computer, we are sharing with you the GitHub repository with code examples and boilerplates for each lesson of this book. It is a good idea to clone this repository before starting to follow the lessons: https://github.com/OrangeAVA/Creative-Technology-with-Three.js.

This repository is organized by chapters and sections, but not all sections have code examples. In the beginning of each chapter or section that uses a new file example, you will find this gray box:

You can find the code of this section in the folder: https://github.com/OrangeAVA/ Creative-Technology-with-Three.js/tree/main/...

Just go to the folder and open it on your code editor.

In the beginning of each code example, we added the example **file name** we talk about, but please note that we only mention it in the first appearance of the code. If the next code example does not have the file name it is because we are still using the same file.

The code examples use a different **font family**, to make it clear that it is about code. And finally, we add **line numbers** in front of each code example line, so you just need to look for the mentioned line number on your code editor to find the mentioned code:

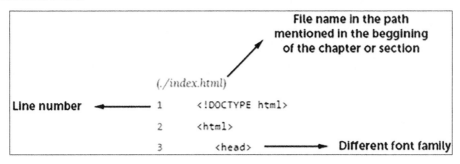

Figure 1.2: *How to use the code examples*

If you do not find a line number in front of the code example, it is because this respective part is not present in the code example file.

Project Structure

To keep things simple and organized, we suggest this project structure for the examples you will find in this chapter:

```
index.html
styles.css
— js
—— main.js
— assets
—— images
—— models
```

Simple as that. For more complex examples, it is interesting to break your main JavaScript file into more specific parts, but for now, let us keep it this way. In the `index.html` file, you will have all the UI elements you need to add to interact with your scene. In the main.js you will add all JavaScript code and the Three.js code too, they basically mix together. It is a good idea to create an `assets` folder to store UI image elements, and the 3D assets too. You can do the same for videos, sound effects, and so on.

That said, let us see what we need for our first Three.js boilerplate.

You can find the code of this section in the folder: https://github.com/OrangeAVA/Creative-Technology-with-Three.js/tree/main/chapter01/boilerplate

(./index.html)

```
1    <!DOCTYPE html>
2    <html>
3      <head>
4        <title>Chapter 1</title>
5        <meta charset="utf-8">
6        <meta name="viewport" content="width=device-width, initial-scale=1.0,
         maximum-scale=1.0, user-scalable=no, viewport-fit=cover">
10       <link rel="stylesheet" type="text/css" href="styles.css" media="all"/>
12       <script type="importmap">
13       {
14         "imports": {
15           "three": "https://unpkg.com/three@0.153.0/build/three.module.js"
16         }
17       }
18       </script>
19       <script type="module" src="js/main.js"></script>
20      </head>
22      <body style="touch-action: none;">
23        <div id="threejsContainer"></div>
24      </body>
25    </html>
```

In this part, we load `Three.js` main JS file as module:

```
12              <script type="importmap">
13              {
14                "imports": {
15                  "three": "https://unpkg.com/three@0.153.0/build/
                    three.module.js"
16                }
17              }
18              </script>
```

Here, we added a `<div>` element that will be our Three.js scene container:

```
23              <div id="threejsContainer"></div>
```

Note that it is not the `Three.js` `<canvas>` element yet. You will see in the next chapter that we are going to create it on the fly before the Three.js scene definition, but you can create the `<canvas>` element in HTML and simply point the `<canvas>` DOM element to `Three.js` scene.

And for our `main.js` file:

(`./js/main.js`)

```
1   import * as THREE from 'three';

3   window.addEventListener('load', function() {
4       start();
5   });


7   async function start() {
8     document.write('Hello world!');
9     console.log(THREE);
10  }
```

The famous Hello world sentence.

Please note that we are importing all `Three.js` classes (*) under the THREE definition, so every time we use THREE in our code, that means we are looking for something inside `Three.js` library.

Now we have everything in place to start adding `Three.js` code!

Conclusion

In this chapter, we delved deeper into the history and foundations of Three.js. We understood Three.js alternatives and other useful tools to start building your projects. You are now ready to start the development of your first Three.js scene.

In the next chapter, we are going to create a 3D scene with basic 3D elements – we call them **primitives** – like cylinder, sphere, torus, and so on. We will introduce the light and shadow concepts. We will discuss the differences between different kinds of lights and shadows, and how they affect the 3D scene. Also, we will talk about Three.js materials and textures and finally, put everything together to present your first Three.js scene.

Points to Remember

- Normal web/mobile browsers are not capable of rendering 3D elements natively, this is why we need to use WebGL–a graphics library created to use complex resources of 3D, lighting, and textures.

- WebGL is basic level and needs a good knowledge of GLSL C++ code to manipulate geometry, textures, and materials.

- Three.js is a library that simplifies complex WebGL development on web/ mobile browsers.

- We need a local server software to be able to run the Three.js code correctly.

- After loading the Three.js library, we are ready to start coding.

Multiple Choice Questions

1. Three.js is...

    a. A development language.

    b. A framework to draw 3D graphics directly to HTML.

    c. A library that uses WebGL to draw 3D graphics to <canvas> element.

    d. A 3D operating system.

2. To code in Three.js you will need to know...

    a. Javascript classes to draw and manipulate 3D elements.

    b. Low-level code to manipulate WebGL classes directly.

    c. GLSL and C++ code.

    d. Low-level WebGL classes and GLSL C++ code.

3. Why should we use the modules version of Three.js?

    a. It uses modern JavaScript.

    b. It is more organized and easier to use.

    c. Avoids code clutter on more complex projects.

    d. All of the alternatives above.

4. Three.js was born...

    a. In 2015, from new HTML5 graphic resources.

    b. In 2009 as a Javascript framework.

    c. In 2009, first in Flash ActionScript, then ported to JavaScript.

    d. None of the previous alternatives.

5. Aframe and React Three Fiber are:

    a. Independent web 3D frameworks.

    b. Web 3D development languages.

    c. Tweaks of Three.js to do different things.

    d. 3D frameworks built on top of Three.js to simplify web 3D development.

Answers

1. c

2. a

3. d

4. c

5. d

Questions

1. Why are pure HTML, CSS, and Javascript not capable of drawing complex 3D graphics on web browsers?

2. What are the differences between a development language, a library, and a framework?

3. Why does rendering complex 3D graphics on web browsers need a special library?

4. Why is Flash/ActionScript not used anymore?

5. Why do you need local server software to run Three.js pages correctly?

6. What are the advantages and disadvantages of using a Three.js framework such as Aframe or R3F?

7. Why does one use Javascript modules instead of pure Javascript functions/classes?

8. What are the benefits of using the CDN version of a Javascript library such as Three.js? What are the caveats?

9. Do you prefer to develop using pure HTML/CSS/JavaScript code or work under a package manager/builder tool?

10. What are the advantages and disadvantages of Three.js and Babylon?

Key Terms

- **Library**: It is a set of routines for a particular language or operating system. It simplifies and adds extra functionality and features to your application. Specifically for Three.js, it is a bridge between 'normal' JavaScript code and low-level WebGL classes and GLSL shaders.

- **Framework**: A framework is a pre-built structure used for development in a certain programming language. It gathers common tasks and classes to simplify and save time when developing. In the case of Three.js, Aframe is an HTML framework, and R3F is a React framework.

- **Low-level development**: A low-level language or API is generally a way to interact directly with machine code—in our case, the browser machine code. It means you will deal directly with memory allocation and other 'machine friendly' tasks. In your case, WebGL is a low-level API/library that talks directly to the computer GPU.

- **Local server**: It is a software that mimics a web server behavior, but on your local environment/computer. Instead of publishing your files to a web server, you can publish a local folder and make it work exactly how it would be published on a web server. Software like Xampp and Wampp, or some Node.js applications are local server applications.

- **JavaScript module syntax**: The first JavaScript applications were a bit small and not too complex, but as soon as the language started to get more popular, large and complex applications started to be built in JavaScript. The module syntax organizes and simplifies big and complex architectures, allowing you to import parts of the code (modules) as needed. Modern browsers allow the use of this functionality natively, without the need to use any other JavaScript library or framework.

- **GPU, or Graphics Processing Unit**: In contrast to the CPU (Computer Processing Unit), the GPU is a computer processor that specializes in graphics processing. It can deal with tons of data and calculations simultaneously, allowing the computer to deliver high-quality 2D and 3D graphics. It has been popularly used to allow computers to run complex games and 3D software, but it has also been used for Artificial Intelligence.

CHAPTER 2

Our First Scene

Introduction

Now that you have a bit more knowledge about WebGL and Three.js, and you are more familiar with the tools and resources needed to start developing Three.js, it's time to put your hands in the code. In the last chapter, we built the boilerplate structure and added the necessary libraries. In this chapter, we'll start adding the proper Three.js code.

We'll introduce the concept of 3D primitives such as cylinders, spheres, torus, and more. In addition, we'll talk about lights and shadows, and put some volume to our scene. We'll discuss the differences between point, direct, spotlight, and ambient lights, and understand how shadows work. After adding some lights to our scene, we'll explain different kinds of materials and texture parameters. Finally, we'll talk about cameras and the animation loop, and show the final result: our first scene.

Structure

In this chapter, we will discuss the following topics:

- Basic Scene Setup
- Creating the Renderer
- Creating the Camera
- Creating our First 3D Mesh
- Rendering our Scene
- 3D Primitives
- Materials
- Texture Maps
- Special Textures
- Lights, Shadows, and Three-Point Lighting Concept

- Cameras
- Animation Loop
- Animating a Texture

Basic Scene Setup

You can find the code of this section in the folder: https://github.com/OrangeAVA/ Creative-Technology-with-Three.js/tree/main/chapter02/section01_green_cube

We ended the last chapter with a working HTML + CSS + JS structure and added the Three.js library using modules. Our main JS file looks like this, with a Hello World code:

```
(./js/main.js)
7  async function start() {
8    document.write('Hello world!');
9  }
```

So, let's delete this part:

```
9 document.write('Hello world!');
```

So, let's delete this part:

```
  document.write('Hello world!');
```

And start adding the proper Three.js code.

Creating the Renderer

First of all, we need to tell Three.js where to create the 3D viewport. If you remember in the last chapter, we added this `<div>` element to the `index.html` file:

```
index.html:
```

```
23  <div id="threejsContainer"></div>
```

This will be our viewport container. Going back to the `./js/main.js` file, right after importing the `Three.js` library, let's add this line right in the beginning of the code:

```
5  let renderer, scene, container, camera;
```

And inside the `start()` function, we need to add the `Three.js` renderer and scene definitions:

```
20  renderer = new THREE.WebGLRenderer({ antialias: true });
```

The parameter `antialias` smooths the lines and edges of the 3D objects, improving the render quality. Now, we need to tell `Three.js` renderer the size of our 3D viewport:

```
21   renderer.setSize( window.innerWidth, window.innerHeight );
```

In this case, we are telling Three.js that our 3D viewport will fill the browser's window `innerWidth` and `innerHeight` sizes, filling up our entire screen. Now we need to point the previously created `threejsContainer` div to the Three.js container:

```
24   container = document.querySelector( '#threejsContainer' );
```

```
25   container.appendChild( renderer.domElement );
```

`renderer.domElement` is the <canvas> element Three.js creates when we run the following command: `new THREE.WebGLRenderer()`.

You can simply add `renderer.domElement` into your body by using `document.body.appendChild( renderer.domElement )`, however, we prefer to add it into a <div> element so it's easier to interact with it if needed. In this case, the `#threejsContainer` div.

Finally, let's create the Three.js scene that will contain all the 3D elements:

```
28   scene = new THREE.Scene();
```

Creating the Camera

Now, it's time to create the camera, which represents the viewpoint of the scene:

```
31   camera = new THREE.PerspectiveCamera( 60, window.innerWidth / window.innerHeight, 0.1, 1000 );
```

We'll discuss cameras in depth later in this chapter.

Now that we know how to add a camera to the scene, it's a good idea to move it somewhere, because the default position of any created object in Three.js is always 0,0,0 (the same goes for rotation, and the default value for scale is 1,1,1). For now, you won't be able to see any difference, but we want to make sure that the scene will work from the beginning. So, let's move the camera a bit back in order to be able to see the center of the scene:

```
37   camera.position.z = 5;
```

You can do the same for the other two axis: `camera.position.x` and `camera.position.y`, or you can move the three axis simultaneously this way: `camera.position.set(0,0,5);`

Rotation and scale have the same code syntax, with the exception that scale won't work for cameras because, obviously, scaling cameras doesn't make sense. You can rotate the camera the same way as you moved it, but if you are using camera controls, things will work a bit differently. We'll talk about this in depth in *Chapter 3, Interacting with Our Scene,* in the section **camera controls**.

Creating Our First 3D Mesh

It's time to add our first 3D object to our Three.js scene. 3D objects in Three.js are made from two components: *geometry* and *material*. The geometry part is the 3D shape of the object, made from 3D vertices connected by edges and faces. The material part is the color (and the other material properties such as transparency, reflection, and so on) and the texture of the object. Here's how it works:

```
40  const geometry = new THREE.BoxGeometry( 1, 1, 1 );
41  const material = new THREE.MeshBasicMaterial( { color: 0x00ff00 } );
```

In the first line, we created a `THREE.BoxGeometry`, which is a cube *primitive*. By primitives, we understand that they are the most basic 3D forms you can have in the 3D space. We'll talk more about 3D primitives later in this chapter. The numbers inside the ( ) are the dimensions of the cube: width (x), height (y), and depth (z) sizes. A `THREE.BoxGeometry` can have additional parameters such as `widthSegments`, `heightSegments`, and `depthSegments`, which are, basically, the number of segments of each axis. So a value of 2 on `widthSegments` will result in a cube with a section in the middle of the face in the x-axis. It's basically to increase the mesh's "resolution" in case you need to deform the object or do something else on the cube's geometry. It works the same way for `heightSegments` and `depthSegments`.

The second line is the material definition: `THREE.MeshBasicMaterial`. We have other kinds of materials (which we'll see in more detail later), and the `THREE.MeshBasicMaterial` is the most basic kind of material you can have in `Three.js`. On the material parameters, we have only one, the `color` parameter, with the value of `0x00ff00`, which is the hexadecimal value of `00ff00`. In `Three.js`, instead of using `#00ff00` as we are used to do in HTML, we tell `Three.s` that the value is a hexadecimal number by using `0x` - zero x - plus the hex value, with no quotation marks. In this case, we told `Three.js` that we want a bright green color for our cube.

We have the geometry and the material already defined, so now we need to create a proper object putting both together, and we do this in the following line of code:

```
42  const cube = new THREE.Mesh( geometry, material );
```

By the way, *mesh* in 3D terminology is the definition of a collection of 3D vertices and polygons. In Three.js, it considers the material too. Finally, to add the cube mesh in the scene:

```
48  scene.add( cube );
```

Rendering Our Scene

In order to see the 3D scene, we need to tell Three.js to render the scene:

```
51  renderer.render( scene, camera );
```

This will tell Three.js to render the scene using the camera we created earlier. Save the code and refresh your browser, and you will get output as shown in *Figure 2.1*:

Figure 2.1: *A green cube*

It's our recently created cube with a bright green material applied to it. However, it looks like a 2D shape. This is because the cube is right in front of the camera, so we are only seeing the face that is closer to it. To fix that, we can do a couple of things: move/rotate the camera or move/rotate the object. Let's rotate the object a bit:

```
45  cube.rotation.set(0, Math.PI / 4, 0);
```

Three.js use radians in the angles, so `Math.PI`/4 is 45 or 0.7854 in the y axis. And now we can see the scene as shown in *Figure 2.2*:

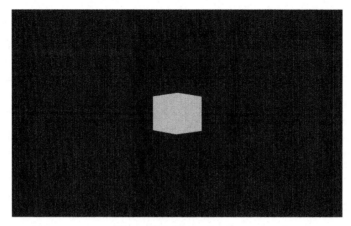

Figure 2.2: *Rotated cube*

You can notice that the cube is slightly rotated, but still very flat. We will explain this in the Lights and Materials section later in this chapter. For now, let's celebrate it's your first full Three.js scene!

3D Primitives

You can find the code of this section in the folder: https://github.com/OrangeAVA/Creative-Technology-with-Three.js/tree/main/chapter02/section02_primitives

In the previous section, we created a green cube. The cube is one of the most basic and common 3D primitives:

```
28   const geometryCube = new THREE.BoxGeometry(0.5, 0.5, 0.5);
```

However, we have other primitives too, and these are the most common:

```
PlaneGeometry
```

width:Float, height:Float, widthSegments Integer, heightSegments: Integer

It's a 3D plane that you can use for building floors, walls, and ceilings.

For example:

```
36   const geometryPlane = new THREE.PlaneGeometry(0.5, 0.5);
```

```
SphereGeometry:
```

```
radius : Float, widthSegments : Integer, heightSegments : Integer, phiStart : Float, phiLength : Float, thetaStart : Float, thetaLength : Float
```

It's, obviously, a sphere:

```
43   const geometrySphere = new THREE.SphereGeometry(0.35, 16, 16);
```

Where `phiStart` and `phiLength` define the horizontal angle and horizontal size of the sphere, and `thetaStart` and `thetaLength` do the same but for the vertical orientation. You can use these parameters to draw only a part of the sphere, such as a sphere slice or a half-sphere.

`CylinderGeometry`:

```
radiusTop : Float, radiusBottom : Float, height : Float, radialSegments
: Integer, heightSegments : Integer, openEnded : Boolean, thetaStart :
Float, thetaLength : Float
```

It's a cylindrical object:

```
50  const geometryCylinder = new THREE.CylinderGeometry(0.35, 0.35,
0.75);
```

Where `radiusTop` and `radiusBottom` are the radii of the top and bottom of the cylinder, respectively. If you set one of these parameters as zero, you will get a pyramidal cylinder. `Height` is the height of the cylinder, while `radialSegments` and `heightSegments` are the number of faces on the height or on the top/bottom caps; `openEnded` removes the 'cap' of the cylinder (transforming it into a very thin tube), and `thetaStart`/`thetaLength` cuts the cylinder and transform it into a slice.

`TorusGeometry`:

```
radius : Float, tube : Float, radialSegments : Integer, tubularSegments
: Integer, arc : Float
```

A torus is like a donut or a tire:

```
57  const geometryTorus = new THREE.TorusGeometry(0.4, 0.1, 16, 32);
```

Where `radius` is the external radius of the torus, `tube` is the thickness, `radialSegments` and `tubularSegments` are the number of faces (in radius direction and in tube direction, respectively), and `arc` cuts the torus, with 0.1 is the minimum 'slice', and Math.PI*2 is a full torus.

`CapsuleGeometry`

```
radius : Float, length : Float, capSegments : Integer, radialSegments :
Integer
```

It's a cylinder with rounded extremes:

```
    const geometryCapsule = new THREE.CapsuleGeometry(0.25, 0.5, 4, 8);
```

`CircleGeometry` :

```
radius : Float, segments : Integer, thetaStart : Float, thetaLength : Float
```

A 3D mesh of a 2D circle shape:

```
71  const geometryCircle = new THREE.CircleGeometry(0.5, 64);
```

ConeGeometry:

radius : Float, height : Float, radialSegments : Integer, heightSegments : Integer, openEnded : Boolean, thetaStart : Float, thetaLength : Float

A cone 3D shape where you can decrease the number of radial segments to create pyramids and other conical meshes:

```
78  const geometryCone = new THREE.ConeGeometry(0.5, 1, 32);
```

RingGeometry:

innerRadius : Float, outerRadius : Float, thetaSegments : Integer, phiSegments : Integer, thetaStart : Float, thetaLength : Float

A 3D mesh of a 2D ring shape:

```
85  const geometryRing = new THREE.RingGeometry(0.2, 0.5, 32);
```

TorusKnotGeometry:

radius : Float, tube : Float, tubularSegments : Integer, radialSegments : Integer, p : Integer, q : Integer

It's a continuous shape that twists and turns around the surface of a torus. The number of twists and turns are determined by the parameters p and q:

```
92   const geometryTorusKnot = new THREE.TorusKnotGeometry(0.25, 0.075, 64, 16);
```

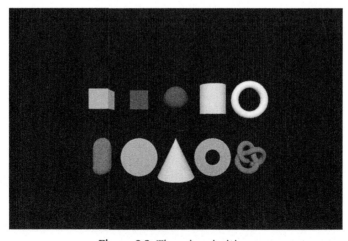

Figure 2.3: *Three.js primitives*

Materials

You can find the code of this section in the folder: https://github.com/OrangeAVA/ Creative-Technology-with-Three.js/tree/main/chapter02/section03_materials

Earlier in this chapter, we created our first Three.js material:

```
const material = new THREE.MeshBasicMaterial( { color: 0x00ff00 } );
```

`MeshBasicMaterial` is, as the name says, the most basic material available in Three.js. We call it a flat material, a material that doesn't show any shadows and is not affected by lights. Generally, `MeshBasicMaterial` is good for debug and code examples, but it's not so useful for creating real 3D scenes, unless you are looking for this flat appearance.

Before moving on to the other kinds of materials, let's explain a bit about shading models. We have basically two types of shading models: the simple (non-physical) shading models, and the physical shading models:

- **Simple shading models:** These models use a simplified algorithm to get to the material colors. It's very fast but doesn't consider the real physical properties of the material, resulting in a not truly photorealistic render.

- **Physically based shading models:** These models use an algorithm that considers the physical principles of the material to get the material colors and properties, just like in real life. It results in photorealistic rendered images, but it's much harder for the GPU to render. However, modern desktop and mobile GPUs can handle it, so nowadays, we use physically based shading models as default in both offline and real-time renderers. We generally call it **PBR** or **Physically Based Rendering,** and you will see loads of references for PBR materials from now on:

```
45   const materialSphere01 = new THREE.MeshBasicMaterial({ col-
     or: 0x00ff00 });
46   const sphere01 = new THREE.Mesh(geometrySphere, material-
     Sphere01);
47   sphere01.position.set(-3, 1.5, 0);
48   scene.add(sphere01);


// Create a sphere with a Mesh Standard Material
68   const materialSphere04a = new THREE.MeshStandardMaterial({
     color: 0x0000ff, metalness: 1, roughness: 0 });
69   const sphere04a = new THREE.Mesh(geometrySphere,
     materialSphere04a);
```

```
70  sphere04a.position.set(0, 2.5, 0);
71  scene.add(sphere04a);


    // Create two light sources (required for Mesh Physical Material)
132 const light01 = new THREE.PointLight(0xffffff, 1, 500, 50);
133 light01.position.set(4, 5, 5);
134 scene.add(light01);


136 const light02 = new THREE.PointLight(0xffffff, 1, 500, 50);
137 light02.position.set(-4, 3, 5);
138 scene.add(light02);
```

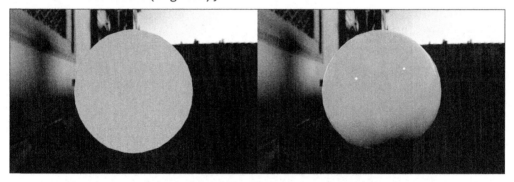

Figure 2.4: *MeshBasicMaterial (simple shading model) in comparison with MeshStandardMaterial (physically based shading model)*

Here are some other kinds of materials that we commonly use in Three.js:

- **MeshPhongMaterial:** It uses a Blinn-Phong shading model to calculate the reflections and the brightness of the surface. It's one of the first shading models used on 3D software, although it's gradually losing space for physical-based shading models.

- **MeshLambertMaterial:** It also uses a simple shading model based on the Lambertian reflectance model. It's good for non-shiny surfaces and is very cheap for GPU processing.

- **MeshStandardMaterial:** It is a physically based material that uses Metallic-Roughness workflow and PBR approach. Basically, the metallic parameter controls whether the material looks like a metal or not. A lower value gives you a plastic look, while a higher value gives you a metallic look. The roughness parameter controls how rough your material looks, or visually speaking, how blurred are the reflections. In practical terms, a lower value gives you a very bright shiny look with very detailed reflection, while a higher value blurs the reflection and the highlights, resulting in an opaque look.

- **MeshPhysicalMaterial**: It is a more advanced version of **MeshStandard Material**. It has the same parameters as MeshStandardMaterial and more: **Clearcoat** simulates an extra layer of reflection found in some materials (such as car paint materials). **Advanced transparency** allows the user to add more reflectiveness to transparent materials. **Advanced reflectivity** increases the flexibility of reflective materials. **Sheen** simulates the soft shininess of some materials like velvet.

- **MeshToonMaterial**: A cell shader that renders a cartoon-like material.

- **SpriteMaterial**: Renders the texture in a way that it's always facing the camera - it's particularly useful for HUD elements, labels, and informative texts over 3D objects. It should be used along with THREE.Sprite() geometry, as you can see between the lines 121 and 129 of the boilerplate of this section:

Figure 2.5: *Example of each kind of material*

By the way, in this boilerplate you will see some advanced resources, such as RGBELoader() and TextureLoader(). Don't worry, we'll talk about them soon.

Each kind of material has common properties (that are shared among almost all material kinds), and some specific material properties, but they are applied in the same way:

```
const material = new THREE.MeshPhysicalMaterial(parameter1: value,
parameter2: value, parameter3: value, …);
```

or:

```
const material = new THREE.MeshPhysicalMaterial();

material.parameter1 = value;

material.parameter2 = value;

material.parameter3 = value;
```

In the *Additional Information section* of this chapter, you will find a complete explanation about each parameter.

Texture Maps

You can find the code of this section in the folder: https://github.com/OrangeAVA/ Creative-Technology-with-Three.js/tree/main/chapter02/section04_textures

By texture map, we mean an image that will be applied to a material parameter. For parameters that use texture maps, you need to load the texture first. You can simply load it and apply the texture to the material afterwards:

```
const texture = new THREE.TextureLoader().load('./assets/images/texture.
jpg');
  const materialCube = new THREE.MeshStandardMaterial({ color: 0xffffff,
  map: texture });
```

However, we strongly recommend you wait for the texture to be loaded using the TextureLoader() callback: on slow internet connections, the texture can take some seconds to load, and your material will look ugly until the texture is fully loaded. In the callback function, you can apply the texture to the object and add it to the scene:

```
28  const map01 = new THREE.TextureLoader().load('./assets/images/
texture01.jpg',
29       function ( texture ) {
30           materialCube = new THREE.MeshStandardMaterial({ color:
0xffffff, map: texture });
31      cube = new THREE.Mesh(geometryCube, materialCube);
32      cube.position.set(-1.5, 1, 0);
33      cube.rotation.set(Math.PI/8, Math.PI/4, 0);
34      scene.add(cube);
35      render();
36  }
37  );
```

Texture maps have some special parameters to change the look of the texture applied to the material. You can find all parameters in the *Appendix 2* of this chapter.

Special Textures

We have some special needs textures that require a different texture loading method. Let's examine some of them.

Cube Maps

You can find the code of this section in the folder: https://github.com/OrangeAVA/ Creative-Technology-with-Three.js/tree/main/chapter02/section05_textures_ cubemap

Cubemap is a special way that 3D software uses to draw 360 images for environments, for example. It requires six images that represent each side of a cube, as follows:

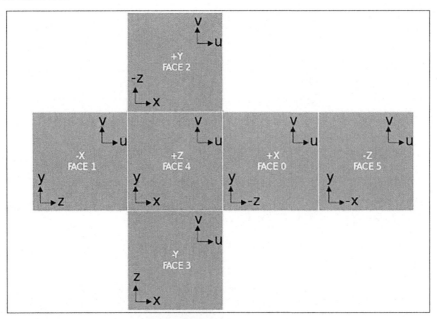

Figure 2.6: *Cube Map*

```
26  background = new THREE.CubeTextureLoader().setPath('./assets/images/
cubeMap/')
27     .load(['px.jpg','nx.jpg','py.jpg','ny.jpg','pz.jpg','nz.jpg'],
28       function(texture) {
```

```
29              scene.background = texture;
30              scene.environment = texture;
31          render();
32          }
33      );
```

Where px = positive x-axis, py = positive y-axis, pz = positive z-axis, nx = negative x-axis, and so on.

Three.js uses it on environment maps and backgrounds to "surround" the scene with an image. It's a full 360-degree background, so when you rotate the camera, you will see different parts of the background. You can convert "normal" images into cubemaps using some graphic software like Photoshop, or you can do it online here: https://jaxry.github.io/panorama-to-cubemap.

RGBE

You can find the code of this section in the folder: https://github.com/OrangeAVA/ Creative-Technology-with-Three.js/tree/main/chapter02/section06_textures_ rgbe

You can use it for loading RGBE images (RGB - Red, Green, Blue + E, or RGB + exposure). It's especially useful if you want to load HDR (High Dynamic Range) images for your environments. It makes ALL the difference when you are trying to create a photorealistic scene, since an HDR image can tint your scene and objects with the background image colors, just like in real life. We'll discuss more about this topic in *Chapter 4, Adding some Realism.*

First of all, you need to import the RGBE loader at the beginning of the code:

```
2   import { RGBELoader } from 'https://unpkg.com/three@0.153.0/examples/
jsm/loaders/RGBELoader.js';
```

Then, import the texture:

```
26  background = new RGBELoader().load(
27      "./assets/images/pisa.hdr",
28      function (texture) {
29          texture.mapping = THREE.EquirectangularReflectionMapping;
30          scene.background = texture;
31          scene.environment = texture;
32          renderer.toneMapping = THREE.LinearToneMapping;
```

```
33          renderer.toneMappingExposure = 1;
34          renderer.outputEncoding = THREE.sRGBEncoding;
35          render();
36      },
37    );
```

Where:

```
29          texture.mapping = THREE.EquirectangularReflectionMapping;
```

Is used to tell Three.js that the image we are importing has an `equirectangular` image (a spherical 3D shape converted to a rectangular 2D shape, such as a world map), as the default texture mapping type in Three.js is `THREE.UVMapping`:

Figure 2.7: *Example of an equirectangular image*

An equirectangular image looks a bit stretched, but if you project it into a sphere, it will look perfect just like in the following example:

Figure 2.8: *The same image applied to a sphere*

And:

```
30        scene.background = texture;
31        scene.environment = texture;
```

We will tell Three.js that we want the texture for both the scene background and the scene environment. If you only use `scene.environment`, the scene background will stay untouched, but all the objects with some reflective material will use it as the reflection map (unless you have already set some material `environmentMap` parameter).

The other three parameters make all the difference on RGBE environments:

```
32        renderer.toneMapping = THREE.LinearToneMapping;
33        renderer.toneMappingExposure = 1;
34        renderer.outputColorSpace = THREE.SRGBColorSpace;
```

As the RGBE format contains the image exposure data, you can tweak it to darken or lighten the scene:

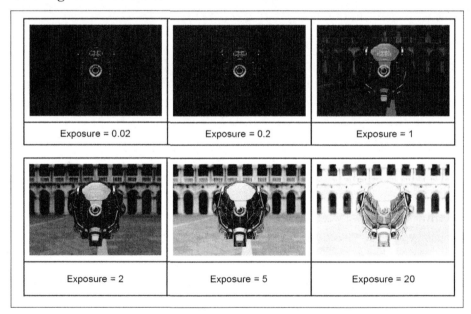

Figure 2.9: *Image exposure in RGBE format*

Canvas Texture

You can find the code of this section in the folder: https://github.com/OrangeAVA/ Creative-Technology-with-Three.js/tree/main/chapter02/section07_textures_ canvas

What if you could have a 2D canvas as a texture? Let's say you want to build a simple HTML drawing board using `<canvas>` element, you can use a `CanvasTexture` for it. It's very straightforward: first, you create the <canvas> element and do whatever you want with it. In the following example, we are creating a 512×512 canvas element, filling the background with #ffffff color, and drawing a black square inside it:

```
40   const canvasElement = document.createElement("canvas");
41   canvasElement.id = "canvasElement";
42   canvasElement.width = 512;
43   canvasElement.height = 512;
44   const canvasContext = canvasElement.getContext("2d");
45   canvasContext.fillStyle = "#ffffff";
46   canvasContext.fillRect(0, 0, canvasElement.width, canvasElement.
height);
47   canvasContext.fillStyle = "#000000";
48   canvasContext.fillRect(64, 64, 384, 384);
49   document.body.appendChild(canvasElement)
```

Note that you don't necessarily add the <canvas> element to DOM, since Three.js will get the canvas data directly. We added it in line 49 just for better scene understanding. Now you need to set the canvas element as a map for the material we are creating:

```
51   const materialCanvas = new THREE.MeshStandardMaterial();
52   materialCanvas.map = new THREE.CanvasTexture(canvasElement);
53   materialCanvas.map.needsUpdate = true;
```

The last line is necessary only if you are updating the canvas element dynamically. Otherwise, you can leave it as it is.

And that's it, very simple. You can even use the regular `texture` parameters (such as `wrapS`, `wrapT`, `repeat`, and so on) to customize your canvas texture.

Video Texture

You can find the code of this section in the folder: https://github.com/OrangeAVA/ Creative-Technology-with-Three.js/tree/main/chapter02/section08_textures_ video

Last but certainly not least important, we have the `VideoTexture` type. It's self-explanatory: it applies a video to your material texture, just like `CanvasTexture` does. First of all, you need a regular <video> element added to your HTML, and a button to play the video:

(index.html):

```
24  <video id="videoElement" loop crossorigin="anonymous" playsinline
        src="./assets/videos/flower.mp4"></video>

26  <div id="ui">
27      <button id="videoPlayBtn">PLAY</button>
28  </div>
```

Unlike CanvasTexture, you need to have the video element added to your HTML, but it doesn't need to be visible (in this case, we hid it via CSS). To play the video, we created an HTML button, and now we need to add an Event Listener to it:

(./js/main.js):

```
16  document.querySelector("#videoPlayBtn").addEventListener("click",
    function () {
17      videoElement.currentTime = 0;
18      videoElement.play();
19  });
```

And finally, to apply the video to the texture map:

```
48  const materialVideo = new THREE.MeshStandardMaterial();
49  const videoTexture = new THREE.VideoTexture(videoElement);
50  materialVideo.map = videoTexture;
```

But there's a trick here: if you just add this code to your boilerplate, you won't see the video applied to the cube. This happens because you need to update your renderer frame by frame to be able to see the video applied to the 3D object. So, remove the current renderer.render(scene, camera) line and add it in the same place:

```
68  animate();

69  function animate() {
70      renderer.render(scene, camera);
71      requestAnimationFrame(animate);
72  }
```

We will learn more about the render loop in the upcoming chapters.

Dealing with video (and audio) is a bit tricky because modern browsers are very picky about playing multimedia content without user interaction. For example, you can't play a video without a user click (there are some workarounds, but they are... workarounds!). On mobile browsers (especially on iOS), the restrictions are much worse: you can only play a video with sound if the user clicks on an HTML element.

Lights and Shadows

You can find the code of this section in the folder: https://github.com/OrangeAVA/ Creative-Technology-with-Three.js/tree/main/chapter02/section09_lights_ and_shadows

We have talked a lot about materials and textures, and it's an endless subject: you can spend hours researching all materials and textures properties, workflows, and methods. However, without lighting, you simply can't see your 3D object. Moreover, bad lighting can ruin a material that you have spent hours tweaking and embellishing. So, let's start this section by introducing the concept of lighting on 3D software.

Similar to the real world, it's impossible to see anything in a 3D scene without a light source. The light sources emit light rays that reach the objects in the scene and interact with their material properties. In addition to the reflected colors, the light rays cast shadows on objects too. Unlike offline renders, Three.js uses a "shadow map" approach, which is a much more simplified (and fast) way to calculate shadows in 3D scenes. The other way to do it is using the Raytracing technique, which consists of calculating every single light ray (and the bounced rays too), so you can imagine how heavy this approach is for the GPU, especially for a real-time web-based render engine like Three.js.

Now that we understand the concepts of lights and shadows in 3D software, it's easier to explain the differences between the different kinds of lights of Three. js as follows:

- **AmbientLight:** It basically tints the scene with color or, if the color is white or gray, lights up the scene equally. It's used to fine-tune the lighting of a scene, and it doesn't cast shadows:

```
73  const ambientLight = new THREE.AmbientLight(0xffffff, 0.25);
74  scene.add(ambientLight);
```

- **PointLight:** It emits light rays in all directions, such as a light bulb. The parameters are `color` (hex), `intensity` (float, default: 1), `distance` (float, the range distance the light can reach, default: 0, which means infinite distance), and `decay` (float, the distance decay of the light source):

```
76    const pointLight = new THREE.PointLight(0xffffff, 0.5, 500, 50);

77    pointLight.castShadow = true;

78    pointLight.position.set(6, 5, 5);

79    scene.add(pointLight);
```

- **SpotLight:** It emits light rays in one direction, limited by a frustum, such as a lamp. The parameters are the same as `pointLight`, with these additional ones: `angle` (float, the size of the frustum, a small value gives you a very tiny light spot) and `penumbra` (float, the gradient where the light source starts to dim - it basically blurs the borders of the light spot). It requires a `target` to point the light in some direction. Anything outside the light frustum is dark, so it works like a lantern:

```
81    const spotLight = new THREE.SpotLight(0xffffff, 0.5, 500, 50);

82    spotLight.castShadow = true;

83    spotLight.target = sphere02;

84    spotLight.position.set(-2, 5, 5);

85    scene.add(spotLight);
```

- **DirectionalLight:** It works like `SpotLight`, emitting light rays in one direction, with the difference that on `DirectionalLight` the light rays are parallel, such as a distant light source like the Sun, and there's no light spot. The parameters are the same as `SpotLight`:

```
87    const directionalLight = new THREE.Directional-
      Light(0xffffff, 0.5);

88    directionalLight.castShadow = true;

89    directionalLight.target = sphere03;

90    directionalLight.position.set(-4, 5, 5);

91    scene.add(directionalLight);
```

In addition to these ones, there are other kinds of lights that are very specific, and we won't go deep into them: `RectAreaLight`, `HemisphereLight`, and `LightProbe`.

The parameters are basically the same for all the light types: color, intensity, distance, and decay. For `SpotLight` and `DirectionalLight`, you need to add a target to them in order to point the light source towards the target - if you simply try to use the `.rotate.set` method on these light sources, it won't work:

```
89     directionalLight.target = sphere03;
```

The target can be another object (for example, the sphere) or a point in space. In this case, just move the `targetObject` to a desired position:

```
const targetObject = new THREE.Object3D();

targetObject.position.set(5, 0, 0);

scene.add(targetObject);

light.target = targetObject;
```

Casting Shadows

Now that you have added light sources to the scene, you may have noticed that they are just lighting it and no trace of shadows at all. This is because you need to tell Three.js that you want the light sources to cast shadows. Here's how to do this:

```
77  pointLight.castShadow = true;
```

Now, we need to set the scene to compute the shadows too. So, go back to the renderer definition and add it:

```
19  renderer.shadowMap.enabled = true;
```

```
20  renderer.shadowMap.type = THREE.PCFSoftShadowMap;
```

Where `shadowMap.type` parameter is the algorithm used to filter the shadow maps. The options are `BasicShadowMap`, `PCFShadowMap`, `PCFSoftShadowMap` and `VSMShadowMap`.

Where `THREE.BasicShadowMap` is the simplest (and faster) one, with no filtering, and the last two have more sophisticated filtering algorithms, resulting in more smooth shadows. The default is `THREE.PCFShadowMap`, which is a middle-ground result that works well for most of the 3D scenes. You can set the shadow resolution too, as follows:

```
100  directionalLight.shadow.mapSize.width = 512;
```

```
101  directionalLight.shadow.mapSize.height = 512;
```

The lower the resolution of the shadow maps, the blurrier and less defined the shadows will be. A higher shadow map resolution impacts the scene performance too. In the boilerplate scene you will be able to notice the quality difference between each shadow map value.

Now, you need to tell Three.js that you want the objects to cast (and receive too if you want) shadows. Then:

```
55  sphere01.castShadow = true;
```

And, finally, you need a floor that will receive the shadows:

```
46  plane.receiveShadow = true;
```

And the scene will look like this:

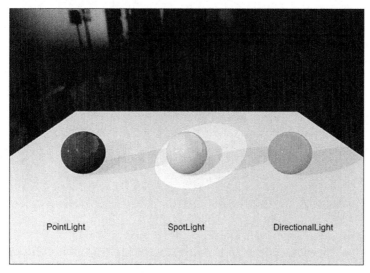

Figure 2.10: *Complete 3D scene*

It's a good start, for sure! We have a complete 3D scene, with a 3D object, materials, light, and shadow. However, we can improve it.

Three-Point Lighting Concept

Our scene has only one light source, which is located at the right of the object, a bit up and in the middle position between the cube and the camera, so you can see very clearly the right face of the cube, while at the same time the left and top faces are a bit dark. To make 3D scenes look more realistic, we will apply an approach that is used by real-world photographers and cinematographers: the **Three-Point Lighting** concept:

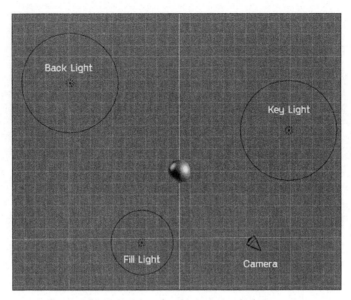

Figure 2.11: *Top view of a three-point lighting setup*

The *Three-Point Lighting* concept is a lighting setup that gives the photographer (or in our case, YOU) more control over the scene and focus on the main aspect of the scene without hiding the parts that are not so important. It's composed of three parts:

- **Key Light**: It's the main light that should illuminate the main subject and be positioned in front of it, slightly to the left or right and at an upper position from it. The light intensity should be higher than the other lights. The key light defines the overall look and feel of the scene.

- **Fill Light:** It balances the lighting, adding some light to the shaded surfaces. It's generally located on the opposite side (in the x-axis) of the Key Light, at the same level (y-axis) of the main subject, and sometimes a bit up.

- **Back Light:** It's located behind the main subject and serves to detach it from the background, highlighting the object contours.

There are different lighting setups used in photo and film studios; for example, four-point lighting, which uses a light source to illuminate the background and reduce the shadow cast by foreground objects, or even a two-point lighting setup, which uses only key and fill lights:

Figure 2.12: *Scene result*

Now that you know the concept, feel free to build your lighting setup as you wish.

Cameras

The last element of our first scene setup is the camera: it's the scene viewpoint. The camera element in Three.js (and on most of all 3D software) works pretty much like a real-world photo or video camera and lenses.

We introduced the camera subject at the beginning of this chapter:

```
camera = new THREE.PerspectiveCamera( 60, window.innerWidth / window.innerHeight, 0.1, 1000 );
```

So, let's break up the Three.js camera definition:

`new THREE.PerspectiveCamera` is the camera type definition. The available camera types are as follows:

- **THREE.PerspectiveCamera**: As the name says, a camera with a perspective projection. It uses the FoV (Field of View), other camera parameters, and the object position to render the scene. So, objects closer to the camera will look bigger and more distorted, and objects more distant will look smaller and less distorted. It's the way human eyes see.

- **THREE.OrthographicCamera**: It uses a parallel projection, so the faces of a cube will show up parallel to each other, regardless of the camera and object position. In the same way, objects closer or farther to the camera will appear at the same size. It's used for architecture visualization and in some isometric games.

There are other specific camera types (such as `THREE.CubeCamera` and `THREE. StereoCamera`), but they are used in very specific cases. and we won't discuss them in detail at this time.

The camera parameters are as follows:

- The first parameter (60) is the FoV (**Field of View**) parameter. It refers to the vertical field of view of what the camera is seeing. Smaller numbers will 'see' less of the scene (let's say, more zoomed in), and higher numbers will see more of the scene (less zoomed in). However, as we are not moving the camera forth or back, the FoV number distorts the perspective too. Small FoV numbers will present less perspective distortion (more straight lines), and high FoV will present more perspective distortion. Compared to real cameras, small FoVs are like telephoto lenses and high FoVs are like wide-angle lenses. For normal camera use (such as first-person shooter games or architecture visualization scenes), a number between 60 and 90 is recommended.

- The second parameter (`window.innerWidth/window.innerHeight`) is the aspect ratio of the camera. Let's say, if your browser window size is 1280×750 pixels (remember that it is the inner size of the window, excluding the browser's toolbars, and so on), the aspect ratio will be 1.706. By default, Three.js sets the aspect ratio value to 1, so it considers a square pixel. However, if you set a square pixel (1×1) and your canvas size is 1280x750, you will see a stretched look. So, you need to tell Three.js to compensate the pixel size by dividing the canvas width by the canvas height and get the correct aspect ratio. It's a good idea to update your camera's aspect ratio if the canvas or the browser window size changes; otherwise, you will get a distorted scene look.

- The third parameter (`0.1`) is the `near` parameter, which means that everything closer from this point to the camera won't be visible.

- The fourth parameter (`1000`) is the `far` parameter. Similar to the `near` parameter, everything from the far point won't be visible to the camera. We generally cap the camera view range to save computational resources in case of big and crowded scenes, exactly the way game developers used to do in the past (actually they are still doing it in some games nowadays!). It's all about cost × benefit.

To move and rotate the camera, it's pretty much the same as we did on 3D primitives:

```
26  camera.position.set(0, 6, 10);
```

```
27  camera.rotation.set(THREE.MathUtils.degToRad(-25), 0, 0); //rotates
20 deg down
```

By the way, this method is very useful if you want to use degrees instead of radians:

```
THREE.MathUtils.degToRad(value in degrees)
```

Or the other way round:

```
THREE.MathUtils.radToDeg(value in radians)
```

The camera element is quite simple and doesn't have too many parameters or caveats. In the next chapters, we'll see how to add more sophisticated controls to it to make the camera behave like a first-person shooter game camera or an Aeroplan camera.

Animation Loop

You can find the code of this section in the folder: https://github.com/OrangeAVA/ Creative-Technology-with-Three.js/tree/main/chapter02/section10_ animation_loop

The scene we have created so far is basically a static scene. We have set all scene parameters (objects, lights, camera positioning and rotation, lights, and shadows parameters, and so on), but nothing happens on the scene after you refresh your browser window. This is because Three.js runs the scene only once, and it's done. So, if we want to add some movement to the scene, we need to create an **animation loop**.

We briefly discussed this topic in the section *video textures*, and it works the following way:

```
animate();
function animate() {
        renderer.render(scene, camera);
        requestAnimationFrame(animate);
}
```

Basically, we create a function called `animate()`, and at the end of the function, we call it again, and again, and again... This is known as a *recursive* function, or a function that calls itself. So, inside the `animate()` function, we can add anything that we want to have movement in the scene:

- An object that we want to move or rotate
- A camera movement

- The render method itself (for example, to advance one frame of the video and update the material texture)
- A user input

The method `window.requestAnimationFrame()` is the JavaScript method that advances one frame of the browser clock and calls the `animate()` function again. It runs usually at 60 frames per second, but it will depend on your scene complexity, computer load, browser load, GPU power, and so on.

That said, let's add some movement to the scene. Let's say, if we want the cube to rotate slowly along the y-axis, you just need to add it to the beginning of the `animate()` function:

```
81  cube.rotation.y += 0.01;
```

Now let's move our camera a bit:

```
camera.position.z += 0.01;
```

This one will move your camera slowly out the scene. However, we can make things even more interesting by rotating the camera around the cube. Remove the last line you added, and add the following variables to the beginning of the code:

```
7  let angle = 0;
8  let radius = 5;
```

And the following two lines inside the animation loop:

```
85  camera.position.x = radius * Math.cos(angle);
86  camera.position.z = radius * Math.sin(angle);
87  angle += 0.01;
```

Now your camera is rotating around the cube! Here's a brief explanation: This little formula increases the position in the *x*-axis using the cosine of the current angle (that is increased by 0.01 each frame), starting from 5 (the radius) and going to -5, and going this way on and on. At the same time, the *z*-axis is increased by the sine of the current angle, starting from 0, growing until 5, decreasing to -5, and going this way on and on. The result is a 2D circle-like movement that you are seeing on your computer screen.

However, there's something unusual: the camera is always facing the front. It's an interesting movement but we want to rotate the camera around the cube for real: the cube needs to be the target of the camera. To fix that, just add the following line after the last line we added previously:

```
90  camera.lookAt(cube.position);
```

The `lookAt` method points the first object (in this case, the camera) to a given Vector3 value (in this case, the x, y, and z position of the cube). You could do this way too:

```
camera.lookAt(new THREE.Vector3(0, 0, 0));
```

The full animation loop will look like this:

```
// Created a animation loop
78  function animate() {

      // Rotates the cube
81    cube.rotation.y += 0.01;


      // Rotate the camera around the scene
85    camera.position.x = radius * Math.cos(angle);
86    camera.position.z = radius * Math.sin(angle);
87    angle += 0.01;

      // points the camera to the cube
90    camera.lookAt(cube.position);

      // Renders the scene
93    renderer.render(scene, camera);
94    requestAnimationFrame(animate);
95  }


   // Call the animation method
98  animate();
```

As we are talking about the animation loop, it's a good idea to add a trick to fix the camera aspect ratio we mentioned some lines ago. It basically detects if the browser window changes its sizes and tells Three.js to recalculate the camera aspect ratio and the canvas size:

```
104  function onWindowResize() {
105      camera.aspect = window.innerWidth / window.innerHeight;
```

```
106        camera.updateProjectionMatrix();
107        renderer.setSize(window.innerWidth, window.innerHeight);
108    }
109    window.addEventListener("resize", onWindowResize);
```

This way we make sure the Three.js canvas will always fill the browser window up 100% and the correct aspect ratio will be preserved. We added it to the next examples from now on.

Animating a Texture

You can find the code of this section in the folder: https://github.com/OrangeAVA/ Creative-Technology-with-Three.js/tree/main/chapter02/section11_texture_ animation

Our last experiment will be on a material texture: let's animate a texture using the offset parameter. We created two cubes, each one with a different texture map.

```
70   const map01 = new THREE.TextureLoader().load('./assets/images/tex-
     ture01.jpg',
71       function ( texture ) {
72           materialCube01 = new THREE.MeshStandardMaterial({color: 0xffffff,
                 metalness: 0.1, roughness: 0, map: texture });
73           materialCube01.map.wrapS = THREE.MirroredRepeatWrapping;
74           materialCube01.map.wrapT = THREE.MirroredRepeatWrapping;
75           cube01 = new THREE.Mesh(geometryCube, materialCube01);
76           cube01.position.set(-2, 1, 0);
77           cube01.rotation.set(0, Math.PI/4, 0);
78           cube01.castShadow = true;
79           spotLight02.target = cube01;
80           scene.add(cube01);
81       }
82   );


85   const map02 = new THREE.TextureLoader().load('./assets/images/
     texture02.jpg',
86       function ( texture ) {
```

```
87      materialCube02 = new THREE.MeshStandardMaterial({color: 0xffffff,
                  metalness: 0.1, roughness: 0, map: texture });
88      materialCube02.map.wrapS = THREE.MirroredRepeatWrapping;
89      materialCube02.map.wrapT = THREE.MirroredRepeatWrapping;
90      cube02 = new THREE.Mesh(geometryCube, materialCube02);
91      cube02.position.set(2, 1, 0);
92      cube02.rotation.set(0, Math.PI/4, 0);
93      cube02.castShadow = true;
94      spotLight01.target = cube02;
95      scene.add(cube02);
96        }
97      );
```

This line tells Three.js to repeat the mirrored image in the edges - the default setting would just copy the last column infinitely, and we don't want that:

```
73          materialCube01.map.wrapS = THREE.MirroredRepeatWrapping;
74          materialCube01.map.wrapT = THREE.MirroredRepeatWrapping;
```

And finally let's add the following lines to the animation loop:

```
106  if (materialCube01) materialCube01.map.offset.x += 0.01;
109  if (materialCube02) materialCube02.map.offset.y -= 0.01;
```

It will increase the x offset of the image by 0.01 in each frame, which will give the impression that the image is sliding in the left direction. For the other cube, we are decreasing 0.01 the y offset, this way it looks like it's sliding up.

You can use it with sprite sheets to simulate the movement of 2D elements (in case, you can't use a video due to file size restrictions), or animate parts of the textures of your 3D object. The possibilities are endless!

Conclusion

In this chapter, we discussed the elements that create a 3D scene in Three.js: 3D primitives, materials, textures, lights, shadows, and cameras. We went a bit further explaining about animations and the animation loop. You are now able to build a scene from scratch, using 100% Three.js content, and have the knowledge to increase your scene quality by using image and video textures. You gained an understanding of the foundations of light design on a 3D scene, as well as how to create a realistic 3D material using the PBR workflow.

In the next chapter, you will learn how to add user interaction to the scene using a keyboard, a mouse, or a touch device. By the end of the chapter, you will be able to put everything together and build a simple game with user input.

Points to Remember

- You need at least a camera, a 3D primitive, and a light source to be able to see a Three.js scene.

- Don't forget to run `renderer.render(scene, camera)` at the end of your script or in the animation loop in case the scene has some animation.

- 3D primitives are the most basic way to build 3D objects: generally, in sophisticated 3D software, we use primitives as the starting point for any modeling work, such as extruding and beveling faces, pushing vertices, subdividing surfaces to increase details, sculpting, doing boolean operations, and more. However, we don't have these resources in Three.js. In *Chapter 4: Adding Some Realism*, we'll explain in detail how to import 3D models and deal with them.

- Always use `MeshStandardMaterial` or `MeshPhysicalMaterial` material types. Even though they cost a bit more of GPU processing, the flexibility and the render quality always pay off!

- To be able to apply an image or a video into a material texture, you need to use a proper loader for it: `THREE.TextureLoader().load` for images or `THREE.VideoTexture()` for videos. Remember that the texture takes some time to load, and the callback function inside these methods is exactly for it: do whatever you want to do with the texture AFTER it is completely loaded; otherwise, the console will throw errors about the texture not existing.

- Try not to load textures that are not on your own server: some servers (most of all actually) have strict CORS (Cross-Origin Resource Sharing) policies and don't allow other websites to load their content externally.

- If your lights are not casting any shadows, always check if the `renderer.shadowMap.enabled` is `true`, if the lights are set with `castShadow = true`, if your objects are casting and receiving shadows, and if the lights are placed on a position that can cast visible shadows. Furthermore, we always forget some of these details when we are building a 3D scene!

- `DirectionalLight` and `SpotLight` can't be rotated as normal 3D objects. Don't forget to use the `.target` parameter to point these kinds of light sources toward the desired subject.

- Don't forget to add anything that moves or needs to be updated in real time into the animation loop.

Multiple Choice Questions

1. 3D primitives are...

    a. The most basic methods of Three.js library.

    b. The most basic and simple 3D models.

    c. Pure WebGL 3D models.

    d. 3D objects that are imported into a Three.js scene.

2. A material simple shading model is:

    a. A kind of material that can be applied only to simple 3D primitives.

    b. A complex shading algorithm that considers the physical properties of the material.

    c. The only kind of material available on Three.js.

    d. A simplified shading algorithm to calculate colors, lights, and reflections over a 3D material.

3. PBR is:

    a. A way to make the materials render faster.

    b. An old material algorithm that is not used anymore.

    c. A physical-based shading approach that considers the physical properties of the material to render high-quality scenes.

    d. A very complex shading model only available on offline renderers.

4. Which one is correct about material textures:

    a. You need a callback inside the loader function if you need to deal with the texture after it is fully loaded.

    b. You can use the same loader method for any kind of texture (image, video, and so on)

    c. They are loaded immediately when you call the texture loader.

    d. You can load textures from any website over the internet.

5. Which of the following is true about Three.js lights:

    a. You can scale and rotate lights freely.

    b. They have the `castShadows` parameter `true` by default.

    c. Ambient lights produce highlights and cast shadows.

    d. `SpotLight` and `DirectionalLight` need a .target parameter to point the light source towards a direction; otherwise, they will point to [0,0,0] point.

Answers

1. b

2. d

3. c

4. a

5. d

Questions

1. What are the differences between simple shading models and physically based shading models?

2. Why does the PBR workflow use the Packed Texture approach?

3. Why does Three.js not have a way to model complex 3D models (subdivision surfaces, boolean operations, and more) as the 3D software does?

4. Why do servers have this CORS policy to prevent other websites from loading their content?

5. In your opinion, what's the best way to add an environment texture to your scene? Why?

6. What are the advantages and disadvantages of using a simple shading model and a physically based shading model on Three.js materials?

7. How can you use THREE.MeshBasicMaterial on a scene to improve the realism?

8. You need to render a ball bouncing on a floor using the animation loop. How could you do it?

9. How can you create an array of objects (let's say, 100 cubes), modifying slightly their position and rotation?

10. Your scene has two different cameras in different positions. How can you switch the active camera every 5 seconds?

Key Terms

- **RGBA**: Image format that has four channels: Red, Green, Blue, and Alpha, which means an RGB image with transparency (usually a PNG image format).

- **RGBE (or Radiance HDR)**: Image format that has four channels: Red, Green, Blue, and Exponent, where the E channel stores high dynamic range information, so the image can have different exposure values. The file format for RGBE images is the HDR file format.

- **Exposure:** In photography, the exposure is the amount of light that reaches the camera film or sensor. Images with a low exposure capture very low lighting and get dark. In opposition, a higher exposure captures a lot of light, and the image gets very bright and washed, with a lot of highlights.

- **PBR:** It stands for **Physically Based Rendering**, a material shading model that considers the physical material properties to calculate its colors, highlights, reflections, and so on. The most used material shading model nowadays.

- **Equirectangular projection:** In cartography, it converts a spherical 3D image into a rectangular 2D image. We use equirectangular projection to apply 360-degree images (captured from 360-degree cameras) to environment maps and create realistic 3D scenes.

- **Mesh normals:** By normals, we mean the orientation of a 3D polygon, and it's used to tell the 3D render if the face is visible or not from the camera. By default, the normals can be visible from one side only, which means the 3D polygons that are facing the camera are visible, and the 3D polygons that have the opposite orientation won't be rendered.

- **Normal map**: It is a way to add more details to materials, without adding more complexity to the mesh. It works by faking the light bounce direction depending on the color of the normal map that the light ray hits.

- **Ambient Occlusion**: It's a rendering technique that calculates the soft shadows on the inner corners of 3D objects, adding more realism to 3D scenes. Three.js can do it using Post Processing or using AO Maps. It's called *Contact Shadows* too.

- **AO Map (or Ambient Occlusion Map)**: To avoid using Post Processing (which increases the scene complexity and render time), you can render the Ambient Occlusion Map in your favorite 3D software and export it. You can learn more about *texture baking* in *Chapter 4: Adding some Realism.*

- **Metalness:** It's a property of PBR materials that tells the render how metallic the object is. In physics, a material with a high metalness parameter is a *conductive* material, which means that it conducts energy well. Visually speaking, a metallic material has a high reflection with no diffuse. In opposition, a material with a low metalness parameter is a *dielectric* material, which means it doesn't conduct energy well, like wood, rubber, fabric, and so on.

- **Roughness**: It's a PBR material property that tells the render how rough or smooth a material is. Visually speaking, it blurs the reflection of reflective materials.

- **Sheen**: It works as a soft shininess effect found in some materials such as velvet.

- **Clearcoat**: It works as a second reflectivity layer found in materials such as car paint.

- **CORS (Cross-Origin Resource Sharing)**: It's a server-side policy that blocks other websites from loading their content externally. It's used to prevent third-party websites from loading or copying their content, due to copyright concerns or server load limitations.

- **UV Mapping**: It's the process of projecting a 2D texture onto a 3D model's surface. Three.js defaults consider the UV map channel of imported 3D files, but you can tell Three.js to use different mapping types like `THREE.EquirectangularReflectionMapping` or `THREE.CubeReflectionMapping`. You can generate UV maps from your favorite 3D software and export them along with the exported 3D model. Three.js can interpret up to three UV maps on each 3D model.

- **Refraction**: In physics, it's the bending of a light ray when it passes through a non-opaque object. This is why you see a distorted spoon when you see it inside a glass full of water. The amount of bending is defined by the **IoR (Index of Refraction)**. The IoR of water is 1.333, and the diamond is 2.418.

- **FPS**: It stands for frames per second. It's the number of frames that are rendered per second. In cinema, the regular fps is 24. In games, it varies from 30 to 60fps, where 60fps is recommended for very fast-moving games, such as racing or first-person shooter games. The JavaScript method `window.requestAnimationFrame()` can deliver up to 60fps.

Additional Information

Material Parameters

Parameters available for all material types (except the special kinds such as `MeshToonMaterial`, `SpriteMaterial`, and more):

- `color` (hex): It is the color of the material in Hexadecimal (0xff0000).
- `map` (texture): It is the decal texture of the object. On 3D software, it's called *Albedo Map* or *Diffuse Map* too.
- `transparent` (boolean): It tells Three.js if the material is transparent or not (`true` or `false`) and should be used along with the `opacity` parameter.
- `opacity` (float 0 to 1): If the `transparent` parameter of the material is `true`, it controls the opacity of it.
- `side`: It tells Three.js how to render the mesh *normals*. The default value is `THREE.FrontSide`, where the normals facing the camera will be rendered, and the ones that have an opposite orientation won't. `THREE.BackSide` is the other way round, and `THREE.DoubleSide` will render the normals that are and aren't facing the camera.
- `emissive` (hex): It defines the color (in Hexadecimal) of the object emissive (glow). Be aware that it's not an object glow effect, which can only be achieved in Three.js using *Post Effects*.
- `specular` (hex): It defines the color (in Hexadecimal) of the object's shininess.
- `shininess` (float 0 to 1): It controls the intensity of the specular color.
- `bumpMap` (texture): It's a grayscale texture that adds a fake bump to your material. It doesn't affect the mesh geometry but plays with the light to present this bump effect. It's quite deprecated, since we now have `normalMaps` that are much more precise.
- `normalMap` (texture): Unlike `bumpMap`, it's a full RGB texture that distorts how the normal map affects the lighting. We use normal maps to add more details to 3D objects without increasing the mesh complexity.
- `alphaMap` (texture): It's a grayscale texture that controls the material transparency. The white color is fully opaque, while the black color is fully transparent.

- aoMap (texture): It's a texture that controls the Ambient Occlusion of the material. Ambient Occlusion is an effect that simulates soft shadows in the inner corners of 3D objects. It's a fake approach that can increase the material realism without impacting render time. Three.js uses only the **red channel** of the image, and it requires a secondary UV to work as expected.

- envMap (texture): It's the texture that will 'surround' the object that has this material applied to. You can use it to simulate fake reflections, since Three.js render doesn't have a true reflection capability (for example, *raytraced* reflections).

- emissiveMap (texture): It's an RGB texture that tells Three.js render how glowing a material is. It's not a physical property, so it won't affect other materials and won't add a glowing effect to your object (for this effect, take a look at the fifth chapter).

- specularMap (texture): It controls the material's shininess and the shine color.

- lightMap (texture): A light map is a grayscale texture that tells Three.js render which parts of the object are more or less affected by the scene lighting. Black means no lighting, and white means very bright. As the aoMap, it requires a secondary UV map to work.

- displacementMap (texture): It's a grayscale texture that distorts the mesh geometry. To have an effective result, your mesh needs to be quite detailed (with a lot of vertices); otherwise, the distortion won't be visible.

- aoMapIntensity (float 0 to 1): It increases/decreases the aoMap effect.

- lightMapIntensity (float 0 to 1): It controls the intensity of the lightMap.

- emissiveIntensity (float 0 to 1): It controls how intense the emissive (map or color) of a material is.

- displacementScale (float 0 to 1): It controls the intensity of the displacement of a displacementMap.

- normalScale (vector2): It controls the intensity of a normalMap applied to the material. It works on U and V, so it's a vector2 parameter.

- reflectivity (float 0 to 1): It tells Three.js render how much the material is reflective. In this case, the environment map will be used as the reflection image, and it won't consider objects that surround the current object (not a true reflection).

- refractionRatio (float): It shows how much a transparent object distorts the background. Air has an IoR (Index of Refraction) = 1 (approximately), water has an IoR = 1.333, and diamond is 2.418. The material refraction will work along with the Environment Map.

- `combine`: It calculates how the material color interacts with the Environment Map. It works like Photoshop Blending Modes: `THREE.MultiplyOperation` (default), `THREE.MixOperation`, and `THREE.AddOperation`.

- `fog` (boolean): It tells Three.js render if the material is affected or not by the scene's fog parameter, and can be either true or false.

- `wireframe` (float 0 to 1): A wireframe material will show the geometry mesh as lines, such as a grid.

- `wireframeLinewidth` (float 0 to 1): It defines the thickness of the wireframe lines.

Parameters available for `MeshStandardMaterial` and `MeshPhysicalMaterial`:

- `metalness` (float 0 to 1): This property controls how much the material looks like a metal, where zero is non-metallic, while 1 is fully metallic.

- `roughness` (float 0 to 1): This property controls how rough a material is. In practical terms, it blurs the reflections and the specular of the material. A material with both high metalness and high roughness will look like brushed metal, with a very blurred reflection. At the same time, high metalness and low roughness will present a material that has very defined reflections, such as a polished metal plate.

- `metalnessMap` (texture): It's an RGB texture that controls the metalness on different parts of the material. On PBR materials, Black color is non-metallic, and white is fully metallic. Three.js uses only the **blue channel** of the RGB texture.

- `roughnessMap` (texture): It's an RGBA texture that controls the roughness on different parts of the material. Three.js uses only the **green channel** of the RGB texture.

Parameters available only for `MeshPhysicalMaterial`:

- `clearcoat` (float 0 to 1): As previously discussed, it's a second layer of reflectivity found in materials such as car paint. It should be used along with `clearcoatMap`.

- `clearcoatRoughness` (float 0 to 1): It blurs the reflection on clearcoat maps.

- `clearcoatNormalScale` (vector2): When using a clearcoatNormalMap, it controls the amount of normals distortion intensity on U and V. It's a vector2 parameter.

- `sheen` (float 0 to 1): As previously discussed, it's a soft shininess effect found in some materials like velvet. It should be used with `sheenMap`.
- `sheenColor` (hex): It tints the sheen effect with an RGB color.
- `sheenRoughness` (float 0 to 1): It blurs the reflection on sheen maps.
- `specularColor` (hex): It adds an RGB color to the specular reflection.
- `specularIntensity` (float 0 to 1): It controls the amount of specular reflection on a material.
- `transmission` (float 0 to 1): It's a special parameter that allows advanced transparency on non-opaque materials. It's different from `transparent` and `opacity` parameters and uses other parameters such as `thickness` and `ior` to present a more realistic transparent object. Be aware that advanced transparency is very heavy for GPU rendering, so use it with caution.
- `thickness` (float 0 to 1): It controls the thickness of transparent objects. Picture it as a non-solid glass ball, where the parameter controls the thickness of the glass layer (and the glass ball interior is filled with air, for example).
- `ior` (float): It's used along with thickness parameters, and it controls the amount of background distortion on refractive materials. Unlike the `refractionRatio` parameter, it will distort the actual 3D scene behind the transparent object, not just the `environmentMap` applied to it.
- `clearcoatMap` (texture): An RGBA texture where the red channel controls the amount of clearcoat intensity of the material.
- `clearcoatRoughnessMap` (texture): An RGBA texture where the green channel controls the roughness on a clearcoat layer.
- `clearcoatNormalMap` (texture): An RGBA texture that controls the normal distortion of a clearcoat layer.
- `sheenRoughnessMap` (texture): An RGBA texture where the alpha channel controls the roughness of the sheen effect.
- `sheenColorMap` (texture): An RGB texture that tells the colors that Three.js will use for the sheen effect.
- `specularIntensityMap` (texture): An RGBA texture where the alpha channel tells which parts of the material have more or less specular reflection.
- `specularColorMap` (texture): An RGB texture that controls the specular colors of the material.
- `thicknessMap` (texture): An RGBA texture where the green channel controls the thickness of a transparent (used along with the transmission, and no transparent + opacity parameters).

- `transmissionMap` (texture): An RGBA texture where the red channel controls the transmission transparency.

Texture Parameters

- `offset` (vector2): It offsets the texture on both the x- and y-axis. Using it along with `needsUpdate`, you can animate textures by shifting the x- or y-axis with `window.requestAnimationFrame()` method.

- `wrapS` **and** `wrapT`: It tells Three.js how to repeat an image texture. `THREE.RepeatWrapping` will repeat the texture indefinitely, `THREE.ClampToEdgeWrapping` will copy the last line or column of the texture indefinitely, and `THREE.MirroredRepeatWrapping` will repeat the full texture indefinitely but mirror it either on the x- or y-axis.

- `repeat` (vector2): It tells Three.js the amount of repetitions of the image texture. The default is (1,1), which means that you will see only one instance of the texture by UV. Numbers higher than 1 will compress the texture on each axis (a value of 2 will double it, 3 will copy it 3 times, and so on), and numbers smaller than 1 will stretch the texture (cutting it in the edge of the UV).

- `rotation` (float radians): It will rotate the image texture.

- `center` (vector2): Using it along with the `rotation` parameter, it will tell Three.js the center of the rotation. Starts with (0,0), which means the center of the UV.

- `channel` (int 0, 1, or 2): For materials that need different UV sets (such as `aoMap` and `lightMap`), you can generate more than one UV in your favorite 3D software. So, channel 0 is UV1, channel 1 is UV2, and channel 2 is UV3.

- `flipY` (boolean): Due to a WebGL particularity (that processes the images flipped up), Three.js added this parameter to unflip it. The default parameter is true, so sometimes, when you dynamically load image textures, you may need to set `flipY: false` to fix it. In case, you need to flip the texture in the x-axis, just use `texture.repeat.x = - 1` to do the trick.

- `needsUpdate` (boolean): If you need to change the textures dynamically (for example, changing a material texture when the user clicks on a button), you need to set this `needsUpdate` parameter as `true`.

CHAPTER 3

Interacting with Our Scene

Introduction

You have, at this point, a fully working Three.js scene with 3D objects, lights, shadows, a camera, and even an animation loop. Now we will show you how to interact with the scene using a keyboard, a mouse, and mobile phone data. We will learn the basic concepts of raycasting–setting up the scene to allow clicking and interacting on the scene objects, glowing and showing a label when it has been clicked. After that, we will introduce you to Three.js camera controls to move the camera around and interact with it. Finally, we will put everything together to build a simple game using all the concepts learned in this chapter.

Structure

In this chapter, we will discuss the following topics:

- Introducing Scene Interaction
- Keyboard Interaction
- Mouse/Touch Interaction
- Raycasting
- Mobile Phone Interaction
- Camera Controls
- A Step Further
- Basic Game Concepts

Introducing Scene Interaction

Our scene looks pretty good so far– it has everything a 3D scene should have, even some animated elements. However, if we want to build visually impressive websites, AR/VR experiences, games and product configurators, we need to go a bit further. We need to add some interaction to it.

By interaction we mean any user input that can produce results in the computer or mobile phone screen. The input can be anything– a pressed key on the keyboard, a mouse movement or a mouse button clicks, an input from mobile phone data. Even the camera image can produce some kind of interaction– nowadays we have technologies capable of capturing your face via webcam or mobile phone camera and reacting to eye blinks, mouth movements, and so on. It can even be a microphone audio input where you can control the 3D scene using your voice. But let us start from the basics– the keyboard.

Keyboard Interaction

You can find the code of this section in the folder: https://github.com/OrangeAVA/ Creative-Technology-with-Three.js/tree/main/chapter03/section01a_ keyboard_interaction

In earlier times, we used to use the keyboard to play games– even on very sophisticated racing games where the keyboard action was just about steering left/right, full press on gas or the brakes. No smooth transitions, and no analogic controls, and we used to play these games very well!

The keyboard interaction in JavaScript is very basic – we just need to create event listeners to detect if a key is pressed or released. The basic syntax of the keyboard listeners looks like this:

```
document.addEventListener(
"keydown", (event) => {
const keyName = event.key;
console.log("key down:", keyName);
},
false,
);
```

```
document.addEventListener(
"keyup", (event) => {
const keyName = event.key;
console.log("key up:", keyName);
},
false,
);
```

In this example, we are just reading the keyboard down (press) and up (release) and logging the results. If you run this code, it throws the following messages as you press the keyboard arrows:

```
key down: ArrowUp / key up: ArrowUp
key down: ArrowDown / key up: ArrowDown
key down: ArrowRight / key up: ArrowRight
key down: ArrowLeft / key up: ArrowLeft
```

Now that we know the names of the keys we want to map, let us move on– add some code to make the cube move from the keyboard arrows press. To start, let us create some variables at the beginning of the script to act as axis increment and read the status of the keys:

(./js/main.js)

```
let arrowPressed = { left: false, right: false, up: false, down: false };
let increment = 0.025;
```

And in the keyboard listeners, from the line 56 onwards:

```
56  document.addEventListener(
57      "keydown", (event) => {
58          const keyName = event.key;
59          switch (keyName) {
60            case "ArrowUp":
61              arrowPressed.up = true;
62              break;
63            case "ArrowDown":
64              arrowPressed.down = true;
65              break;
66            case "ArrowRight":
```

```
67                arrowPressed.right = true;
68                break;
69              case "ArrowLeft":
70                arrowPressed.left = true;
71                break;
72          }
73        },
74      false,
75  );
```

Depending on the pressed key (keydown), we change the status of the corresponding variable object. We can do the same thing for the release (keyup) event listener, but wait— any key the user releases will disable the key's status, so we can simplify it a bit:

```
77  document.addEventListener(
78      "keyup", (event) => {
79          arrowPressed.up = false;
80          arrowPressed.down = false;
81          arrowPressed.right = false;
82          arrowPressed.left = false;
83        },
84      false,
85  );
```

(of course, if you need more sophisticated movement, it's a good idea to disable the keys status individually, but for this example we don't need to do it).

Finally, we need to move the cube according to the values of the increment variable and the keys status. So, we add this line to the animation loop (you need the cube position to be updated in real time):

```
89  function animate() {
90      if (arrowPressed.left) cube.position.x -= increment;
91      if (arrowPressed.right) cube.position.x += increment;
92      if (arrowPressed.up) cube.position.z -= increment;
93      if (arrowPressed.down) cube.position.z += increment;
        ...
```

And voilá! Our cube is moving when you press a key on the keyboard. You can change the speed of the movement by changing the `increment` variable value. But why not make things more interesting? We can make the interactivity richer by adding an inertia effect on the cube movement.

Adding Some Inertia

You can find the code of this section in the folder: https://github.com/OrangeAVA/ Creative-Technology-with-Three.js/tree/main/chapter03/section02a_ keyboard_interaction_inertia

For this, we need to change the code a bit. First of all, we need to add more variables to the beginning of the script:

(./js/main.js)

```
5  let vel = new THREE.Vector3(0, 0, 0);
6  let acceleration = 0.001;
7  let damping = 0.96;
8  let increment = new THREE.Vector3();
```

If we want to modify the speed value of the cube, we do not want to deal with it directly. This is why we created the variable `vel` – to store the velocity value that will be modified by the other parameters, such as `acceleration` and `damping`. The `acceleration` parameter will be increased by the key press in the corresponding direction, and the `damping` value will slow down the cube movement when you are not pressing any key, serving as an inertia effect. Now, let us add this in the beginning of the `animate()` function:

```
96   if (arrowPressed.left) increment.x -= acceleration;
97   if (arrowPressed.right) increment.x += acceleration;
98   if (arrowPressed.up) increment.z -= acceleration;
99   if (arrowPressed.down) increment.z += acceleration;

101  vel.x += increment.x;
102  vel.z += increment.z;

104  if (!arrowPressed.left && !arrowPressed.right) {
105    vel.x *= damping;
106  }
```

```
107  if (!arrowPressed.up && !arrowPressed.down) {
108    vel.z *= damping;
109  }
```

Previously, in the beginning of the code, we changed the `increment` variable to a `Vector3` value (actually it could be a `Vector2`, since we are dealing only with two axes, but let us make it a `Vector3` to not change the axes orders), and depending on the key press, it is increased/decreased by the `acceleration` value, so the more you keep the key pressed, the more acceleration you will apply to the velocity.

In the other way, if there is no key pressed, the `damping` parameter will decrease the cube velocity until it gets to zero (stops). And finally, let us update the cube position with the corresponding `vel` values:

```
111  cube.position.x += vel.x;
112  cube.position.z += vel.z;
```

And now you have a cube that reacts from a keyboard key press, with some interesting inertia effect! You can apply this acceleration/damping technique to any other object movement, making any user interaction richer and more fun! But let us move on to the next subject– mouse/touch interaction.

Mouse/Touch Interaction

You can find the code of this section in the folder: https://github.com/OrangeAVA/ Creative-Technology-with-Three.js/tree/main/chapter03/section02a_mouse_ interaction

In the previous section, we learnt how to interact with a Three.js scene using the keyboard. Reading the mouse and touch input is pretty much the same– just add event listeners to the right events. There are specific listeners for mouse and touch devices, but JavaScript allows us to use one that will read both inputs: the pointer listeners. We will need three pointer listeners: one for the left click press, one for the left click release, and one for the pointer movement:

```
document.body.addEventListener("pointerdown", function (event) {});

document.body.addEventListener("pointerup", function (event) {});

document.body.addEventListener("pointermove", function (event) {});
```

Please note the pointerdown/pointerup events are by default related to the left pointer button. To read other pointer buttons you need to deal with the `event. button` *parameter too.*

Before adding the code to do the proper cube movement, we need to add some variables to the beginning of the script:

```
9   let dragFlag = false;
10  let prevMousePos = { x: 0, y: 0 };
```

The variable `dragFlag` will be updated by the left pointer button press and will turn on/off the rotation movement, and the variable `prevMousePos` will store the temporary pointer x and y positions, in a way we can calculate the pointer movement (delta x and delta y). We will not use the y (vertical movement) value because we want just a single rotation on the cube y-axis, so the pointer movement on the x-axis seems more logical.

In the `pointerdown` event, let us add the following code:

```
94  document.body.addEventListener("pointerdown", function (event) {
95      dragFlag = true;
96      prevMousePos.x = event.clientX;
97  });
```

This code instructs the browser to activate the `dragFlag` parameter when the left pointer button is pressed and stores the current value x of the pointer (`event.clientX`) to the `prevMousePos` variable. In the same way, we want to stop the movement when the left pointer button is released, so:

```
99   document.body.addEventListener("pointerup", function () {
100      dragFlag = false;
101  });
```

And finally, where the magic happens: the `pointermove` event:

```
103  document.body.addEventListener("pointermove", function (event) {
104      if (!dragFlag) return;
106      var deltaX = event.clientX - prevMousePos.x;
107      cube.rotation.y += deltaX * 0.01;
108      prevMousePos.x = event.clientX;
109  });
```

This event is triggered when a pointer movement happens, and we want to apply the `deltaX` value (*previous x position* minus the *current x position*) to the cube as a rotation in the y-axis. We want that this happens only when the left pointer button is pressed, so we have added this line to ignore the rest of the function if the left pointer button is not pressed:

```
104   if (!dragFlag) return;
```

But if the left pointer button is pressed, we need to calculate the deltaX and apply it to an arbitrary rotation of the cube:

```
106   var deltaX = event.clientX - prevMousePos.x;
107   cube.rotation.y += deltaX * 0.01;
```

The value 0.01 is a decent rotation value (in radians) that is neither slow nor fast, but feel free to tweak this value as you wish. A positive deltaX value (that means the pointer walked from left to right) will rotate the cube in a positive y axis rotation (anticlockwise direction), and a negative deltaX (pointer walked from right to left) will rotate the cube in the clockwise direction. And finally:

```
108   prevMousePos.x = event.clientX;
```

prevMousePos can be updated with the current value so that we can continue to calculate the deltaX in the next loop cycle. That's it, you can even move the cube with the keyboard and rotate it using the pointer!

Adding Inertia to the Pointer Movement

You can find the code of this section in the folder: https://github.com/OrangeAVA/ Creative-Technology-with-Three.js/tree/main/chapter03/section02b_mouse_ interaction_inertia

Like keyboard interaction, let us add some inertia to the movement of the pointer. We are basically doing the same thing we did for the position, but for rotation. So add this in the beginning of the script:

```
12   let angVel = { x: 0, y: 0 };
13   let angAcceleration = { x: 0, y: 0 };
14   let angDamping = 0.06;
```

We are keeping them as Vector2 values in case you need in the future to use the y-axis pointer movement too. Now our pointerdown event will look like this:

```
98   document.body.addEventListener("pointerdown", function (event) {
99     dragFlag = true;
100    prevMousePos.x = event.clientX;
101    angVel.x = 0;
102    angVel.y = 0;
```

```
103    angAcceleration.x = 0;
104    angAcceleration.y = 0;
105  });
```

It means that when you press the left pointer button, the angular velocity and angular acceleration are zero, and the values start to increase from this point. In the pointermove event, add an angVel.x object to the end of the function, which will look like this:

```
112  document.body.addEventListener("pointermove", function (event) {
113    if (!dragFlag) return;
115    let deltaX = event.clientX - prevMousePos.x;
116    cube.rotation.y += deltaX * 0.01;
117    prevMousePos.x = event.clientX;
118    angVel.x = deltaX * 0.01;
119  });
```

This is to increase (or decrease) the angular velocity depending on the pointer movement (actually, the deltaX value). Finally, in the animation loop, right after the cube position increment part:

```
144  if (!dragFlag) {
145    angAcceleration.x = -angVel.x * angDamping;
146    angVel.x += angAcceleration.x;
147    cube.rotation.y += angVel.x;
148  }
```

If the left pointer button is pressed, it does nothing because we are already changing the cube y rotation on the pointermove event. But as soon as you release the button, there is no added movement to the cube rotation and it starts to calculate the rotation damping, frame by frame, to slow down the cube rotation. It gives the cube rotation this nice effect of inertia, just like we did with the position. Cool, huh?

Raycasting

You can find the code of this section in the folder: https://github.com/OrangeAVA/ Creative-Technology-with-Three.js/tree/main/chapter03/section03_raycasting

Raycast is a concept from the interactive 3D world that is used for detecting interactive 3D objects clicked (or tapped) on a 2D screen. The name of this concept could be a bit confusing because it is very similar to **raytracing** and, in fact, they are pretty much similar. You can cast (or trace) rays on a 3D scene to do loads of things. A raytracing algorithm can trace rays to calculate the colors and properties of a material on a certain 3D object, or calculate the projected shadow over a surface, among other things. A raycasting algorithm casts rays on a 3D scene to detect if a ray is intercepting some 3D object, and in this way, we can detect if an object is being clicked. In Three.js, we use this method:

```
raycaster.setFromCamera( screenPoint, camera );
```

The `raycaster` translates the `screenPoint` parameter (a `vector2` number, the coordinates of a clicked point on a 2D screen) to a `vector3` number (the corresponding 3D space coordinate) and casts a ray from the camera to this 3D point. If the ray intersects an object, it returns the intersected object and the 3D position of the intersected point, among other useful data.

So, how to implement it? In the previous section, we ended up by moving the cube on keyboard arrows keypress and rotating it by a pointer drag. Now we need to add some scripts to read the pointer position and cast the rays. First of all, let us add these variables to the beginning of the script, to make them available through all the code, and initialize the `raycaster` object:

```
25  let raycaster = new THREE.Raycaster();
26  const cursorPos = new THREE.Vector2();
```

For the raycasting method itself, let us create a function for it:

```
187  function updateRaycaster(event) {
188    cursorPos.x = (event.clientX / window.innerWidth) * 2 - 1;
189    cursorPos.y = -(event.clientY / window.innerHeight) * 2 + 1;
191    raycaster.setFromCamera(cursorPos, camera);
192    const intersects = raycaster.intersectObjects(scene.children, false);
```

And calls it into the `pointermove` event listener:

```
136  updateRaycaster(event);
```

This part of the code normalizes the cursor position, transforming the values from screen pixels to numbers between zero and one. It also normalizes the coordinates making the central point of the screen as (0,0), so a far-left point will be -1 on the x-axis, a far-right point will be 1, a far-top point will be -1 on the y-axis and a far bottom point will be 1:

```
188  cursorPos.x = (event.clientX / window.innerWidth) * 2 - 1;
189  cursorPos.y = -(event.clientY / window.innerHeight) * 2 + 1;
```

Here we make the raycasting work:

```
191   raycaster.setFromCamera(cursorPos, camera);
192   const intersects = raycaster.intersectObjects(scene.children, false);
```

It gets the camera position and casts rays to the normalized `cursorPos` point. The `intersectObjects` method will test among all the objects inside the `scene.children` (in this case, all objects present in the scene, but you could specify a group of 3D objects and the raycast will consider only them). The second parameter is the `recursive` parameter— if it is true, it will cast rays to the objects and their children in case you have sub-objects too. Generally, we just want to get the main (parent) object, so let us keep it as *false*. This operation will result in the data inside the variable `intersects` and if you *console.log* this variable, you will see something like this when the pointer is over some 3D object:

```
194   console.log(intersects);
```

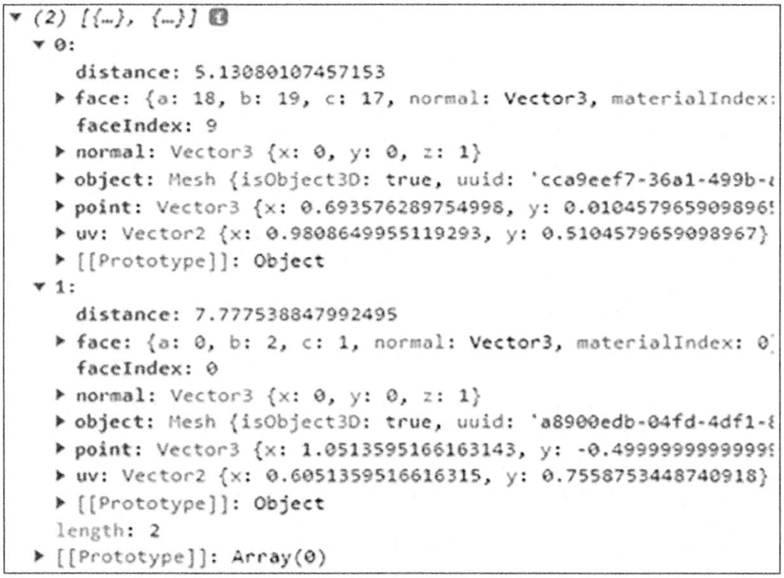

```
▼ (2) [{…}, {…}] ⓘ
  ▼ 0:
      distance: 5.130801107457153
    ▶ face: {a: 18, b: 19, c: 17, normal: Vector3, materialIndex:
      faceIndex: 9
    ▶ normal: Vector3 {x: 0, y: 0, z: 1}
    ▶ object: Mesh {isObject3D: true, uuid: 'cca9eef7-36a1-499b-ⵊ
    ▶ point: Vector3 {x: 0.693576289754998, y: 0.010457965909896!
    ▶ uv: Vector2 {x: 0.9808649955119293, y: 0.5104579659098967}
    ▶ [[Prototype]]: Object
  ▼ 1:
      distance: 7.777538847992495
    ▶ face: {a: 0, b: 2, c: 1, normal: Vector3, materialIndex: 0ʼ
      faceIndex: 0
    ▶ normal: Vector3 {x: 0, y: 0, z: 1}
    ▶ object: Mesh {isObject3D: true, uuid: 'a8900edb-04fd-4df1-ⵊ
    ▶ point: Vector3 {x: 1.0513595166163143, y: -0.49999999999999!
    ▶ uv: Vector2 {x: 0.6051359516616315, y: 0.7558753448740918}
    ▶ [[Prototype]]: Object
    length: 2
  ▶ [[Prototype]]: Array(0)
```

Figure 3.1: *Content of the raycasting object*

It returns an array of objects of all the 3D objects that have been intercepted by a camera ray on that specific pointer cursor position. It returns more than one object because the ray does not stop on the first object— it continues until the end of the scene (but you can specify the range of the ray using `.near` and `.far` parameters, pretty much like you did with the camera object). The object order in the array corresponds to the order of the objects that have been intercepted, so the first one (index `[0]`) will be the cube, and the second one (index `[1]`) will be the plane floor. We usually want to detect only the first intersected object, and if there is no intersection (no object under the pointer cursor), we do nothing. So let us add it to the function:

```
198  if (intersects.length > 0) {
199    console.log(intersects[0].object);
```

It will *console.log* the first object of the `intersects` list, the object that is right under the pointer cursor. And what can we do with it? Using this very same code, we can add a label that shows up on a pointer hover. To do this, we first need to add names to the objects. So let us add it in the cube and the plane floor definitions:

```
66  cube.name = 'Cube';
75  plane.name = 'Floor';
```

We need to create the label HTML element and stylize it too:

```
(index.html, after threejsContainer div)
23  <div id="label">value</div>
```

```
(styles.css)
9   #label {
10      display: none;
11      position: absolute;
12      z-index: 99;
13      background-color: #fff;
14      width: auto;
15      padding: 5px 15px;
16      top: 0;
17      left: 0;
18      border-radius: 5px;
19      transform: translate(-50%, -115%);
20  }
```

It will create a nice HTML label over the Three.js canvas container but hidden at this time. In the `pointermove` event listener, let us add this right after the `updateRaycaster` function call, to update the label html position when the pointer moves:

`(./js/main.js)`

```
138   document.querySelector("#label").style.left = event.clientX + "px";
139   document.querySelector("#label").style.top = event.clientY + "px";
```

And inside the **updateRaycaster** function, let us add this line:

```
196   document.querySelector("#label").style.display = "none";
198   if (intersects.length > 0) {
201       document.querySelector("#label").style.display = "block";
202       document.querySelector("#label").innerHTML = intersects[0].
          object.name;
203   }
```

It forces the label to be hidden all the time, but if there is an intersected object, let us show the label and add the object name to the label container. And that's it, we have a dynamic label system for our 3D scene!

To finish this section, let us interact with the cube changing its colour by clicking it. To start, let us add this colour array to the beginning of the script:

```
28    const cubeColours = [0xff0000, 0xffff00, 0x0000ff, 0xf0f0f0];
```

And now let us create a function to be triggered in the pointer down (click) event listener:

```
206   function clickRaycaster(objectName, callback = null) {
207       raycaster.setFromCamera(cursorPos, camera);
208       const intersects = raycaster.intersectObjects(scene.children,
          false);

210       if (intersects.length > 0) {
211         if (intersects[0].object.name === objectName) {
212           if (callback) callback();
213         }
214       }
215   }
```

In this function, we are passing two parameters− the object name we want to click and a callback function to be executed after the click is detected. And finally, add this to the end of the `pointerdown` event listener:

```
124    clickRaycaster("Cube", function () {
125    const randomColour =
          cubeColours[Math.floor(Math.random() * cubeColours.length)];
126    cube.material.color.setHex(randomColour);
127  });
```

We call the `clickRaycaster` function with the `Cube` parameter (the name of the cube object), and a callback function that chooses randomly a colour from the `cubeColours` array and applies it to the cube material color. Note that we are using the method `new THREE.Color` to define the color of the cube material, and not the hexadecimal value directly, but you can use this method too:

```
126  cube.material.color.setHex(randomColour);
```

If you want to extend these methods to change the floor color, or to make the cube jump on a pointer click, feel free to experiment! The possibilities are endless.

Mobile Phone Interaction

You can find the code of this section in the folder: https://github.com/OrangeAVA/Creative-Technology-with-Three.js/tree/main/chapter03/section04_mobile_interaction

We will now switch between your computer screen and your mobile phone, and to do this we need to make sure you can access your local server (your computer) from your mobile phone. We presume you are currently accessing the exercises this way:

```
http://localhost/some_local_folder/exercise
```

Or if you are using Node.js to serve the pages, it probably appears something like this:

```
http://localhost:3000
```

If you try to access this URL on your mobile phone browser, it will obviously fail– there is no local server running on your phone, so **http://localhost** will not work at all. However, if your phone is connected to the same network as your computer (the webserver), it becomes easy to access it– you just need to find out the local IP address of your computer. Depending on the way you serve the project using Node.js, it will publish the web page to the right IP, so the next step is not necessary. However, if you are using any other kind of web server that publishes to *localhost*, you will need to open the computer Console (Windows) or Terminal (Mac) and type:

ipconfig (on Windows computers)

ifconfig (on Mac computers)

You will see something like this:

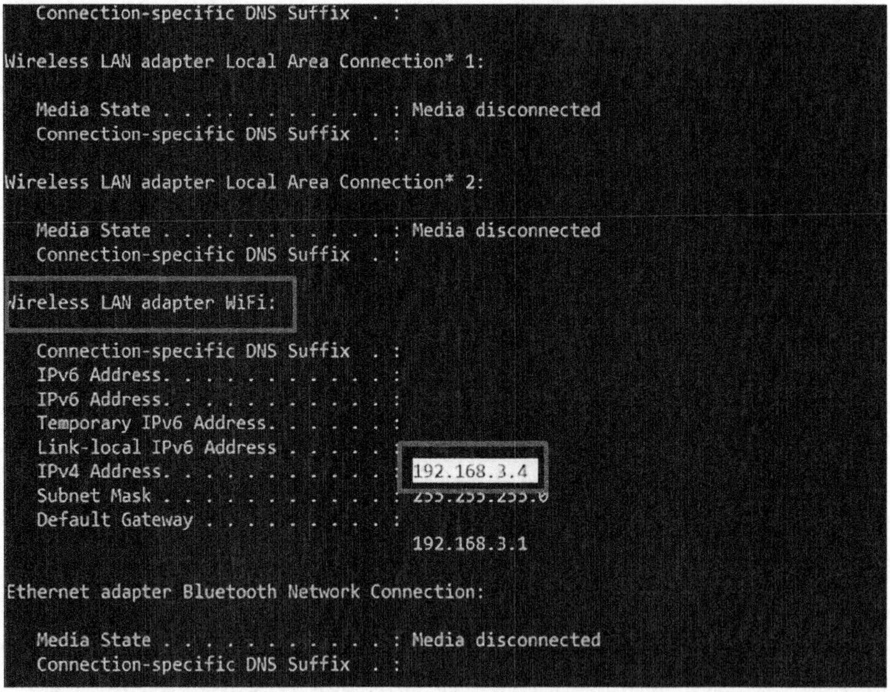

Figure 3.2: *Network settings*

In this case, the computer's local IP is 192.168.3.4, so all you have to do is open the phone mobile browser and type http://192.168.3.4/folder_of_the_project. If it does not work, double check if your phone is connected to the same network as your computer (web server) and if there is no firewall or antivirus blocking an external access.

There is one more detail– as we previously mentioned, mobile browsers are very picky due user's privacy restrictions, and we cannot use the mobile device gyroscope (camera and microphone as well) on http (no-SSL) servers. This means that you need to run it over https to be able to read deviceMotion data. If you are using some local web server such as Xampp or Wampp, the things are simpler: just type https://your_ip/project_folder on your mobile browser. It will complain about the lack of a SSL certificate, but you can just ignore it and click **Visit Website**, and you will be able to open the page with no more issues:

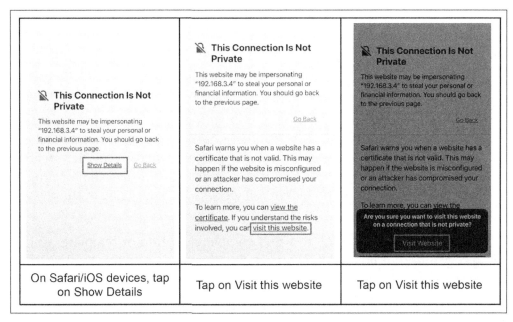

Figure 3.3: *Page privacy settings*

On Chrome and/or Android phones, you will see this screen:

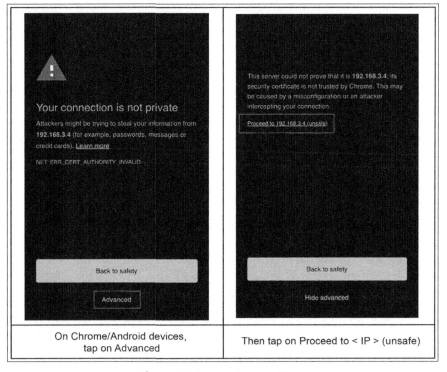

Figure 3.4: *Page privacy settings*

If you are using a Node.js local web server, there are specific (and more complicated) configurations, and you will probably need to generate a SSL certificate and use it along with a NPM configuration. For more details, you can check here: https://www.geeksforgeeks.org/how-to-create-https-server-with-node-js/

Note: If you are deploying the project files to a proper web server (not your local computer), it needs to have a SSL certificate anyway. It is not a good idea to deploy a commercial (or even a personal) project where your client will see these privacy errors. Please note that these details are equally valid for projects that use camera and microphone. We will discuss AR once again in the relevant chapter.

For this section, we are going to use a completely different template, since it uses a very different boilerplate. You can find this project on this book's GitHub repository, under the folder:

https://github.com/OrangeAVA/Creative-Technology-with-Three.js/tree/main/chapter03/section04_mobile_interaction

But we will explain the main details of this project here.

First of all, we need to ask for user's permission to access the mobile phone `deviceMotion` data. So, we added this button in the HTML file (we added some CSS styles too, but we will not show it here):

`(index.html)`

```
24   <button id="permissionButton">Tap to allow device permissions</button>
```

In the `main.js` file, we need to add an `eventListener` to this button and attach to it to the code to trigger the `deviceMotion` permission (it will not work if you just call the `DeviceMotionEvent.requestPermission()` function – you need a user interaction to trigger it).

`(./js/main.js)`

```
16   function deviceMotionStart() {
17     if (typeof DeviceMotionEvent.requestPermission === "function") {
18       DeviceMotionEvent.requestPermission().then((response) => {
19         if (window.DeviceOrientationEvent) {
20           window.addEventListener("deviceorientation", (event) => {
21             gyroscopeData = event;
22             gyroscopeEnabled = true;
```

```
23              document.querySelector("#permissionButton").remove();
24              start();
25            });
26          } else {
27            alert("Gyroscope not supported on this device.");
28          }
29        });
30    }
31  }
```

```
33  window.addEventListener("load", function () {
34    documentquerySelector("#permissionButton").addEventListener("-
click",
      function () {
35      deviceMotionStart();
36    });
37  });
```

So, when the user taps on the button, the mobile OS triggers the deviceMotion native prompt. The user needs to tap on the **Allow** button to give permission to the web page to read the deviceMotion data. Only after that, we can start the proper code:

Figure 3.5: *Gyro permissions*

One detail– the permission persists until the user keeps the mobile browser open (even in the second plane). If the user closes it, the mobile browser will ask for permissions again when you open the page.

Moving on, we added some global variables in the beginning of the script:

```
6   let ball;
7   let gyroscopeData = { alpha: 0, beta: 0, gamma: 0 };
8   let gyroscopeEnabled = false;
9   const ballVel = new THREE.Vector3(0, 0, 0);
10  const bounciness = -0.7;
11  const minBounds = new THREE.Vector3(-1.25, 0, -2.25);
12  const maxBounds = new THREE.Vector3(1.25, 0, 2.25);
```

The variable **gyroscopeData** stores the data from the mobile phone *gyroscope* (that reads the mobile phone rotation), as you can see in the following image:

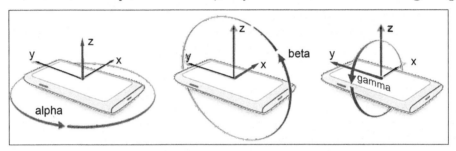

Figure 3.6: *Image source: newnow.co*

To play this **game**, your phone should be positioned just like in the preceding image, like it is placed over a table, and not upwards (facing you, as we usually hold a phone). It could be a bit confusing because the 3D coordinates will consider that the scene is visible from the top of the screen– so the ball movement from left to right of the phone screen is the x-axis, and ball movement from top to bottom of the screen are actually the z-axis. The y-axis is the height of the scene that we will not consider in this example.

The variable **ballVel** will store the ball velocity in the three axes (but we will not use the y-axis because your phone will always face up, so the height will not be considered). The variable **bounciness** is the factor that calculates the ball velocity when it reaches the border of the mobile phone, and the variables **minBounds** and **maxBounds** are the coordinates (in Three.js units, not screen pixels) of the bounds of the screen. We are considering just arbitrary values that cover most of the mobile phones screen sizes, but maybe the ball would bounce before or after the phone screen on your phone– the calculation of real phone screen sizes would be quite complicated and would take a lot of paragraphs, and it is not our main objective in this chapter.

The Three.js scene setup is basically our main boilerplate, with a white surface and a very reflective blue ball. We also have two light sources and the camera is right up the scene, looking down towards the centre of the scene. Finally, we added a debug window that shows in real time the alpha, beta, and gamma phone data values. The scene will look like this image here:

Figure 3.7: *Preview of the ball game*

In the animation loop, we are calling the updateBallPosition() function that calculates the ball position depending on the gyroscope data:

```
107   function updateBallPosition() {

108       if (gyroscopeEnabled) {

109         const alpha = gyroscopeData.alpha;

110         const beta = gyroscopeData.beta;

111         const gamma = gyroscopeData.gamma;


113         debugDiv.innerHTML = `alpha: ${gyroscopeData.alpha}<br>beta:
      ${gyroscopeData.beta}<br>gamma: ${gyroscopeData.gamma}`;


115         const acceleration = new THREE.Vector3( Math.sin((gamma *
      (Math.PI / 180)) / 1000), 0, Math.sin((beta * (Math.PI / 180)) /
1000));
```

```
117        ballVel.add(acceleration);


119        ball.position.add(ballVel);


121        if (ball.position.x < minBounds.x || ball.position.x > max-
Bounds.x) {
122       ballVel.x *= bounciness;
123       ball.position.x = THREE.MathUtils.clamp(
     ball.position.x, minBounds.x, maxBounds.x);
124     }


126    if (ball.position.z < minBounds.z || ball.position.z > max-
Bounds.z) {
127       ballVel.z *= bounciness;
128       ball.position.z = THREE.MathUtils.clamp(
     ball.position.z, minBounds.z, maxBounds.z);
129     }
130      }
131  }
```

What is going on here? Firstly, we get the alpha, beta and gamma data and calculates the acceleration depending on the amount of each value – so when your phone is facing up, if you rotate it a bit in the y-gamma-axis, the acceleration in the y direction (of the phone, not of the 3D scene) will be low, if you rotate it a lot, the acceleration will be high:

```
115  const acceleration = new THREE.Vector3(Math.sin((gamma *
     (Math.PI / 180)) / 1000), 0, Math.sin((beta * (Math.PI / 180)) / 1000));
```

As in the previous examples (keyboard and pointer interaction), we are using Sine functions to act as a friction effect and smooth out the movement. The first value of the Vector3 (*x*) will read the gamma value (*y* rotation of the phone), the second value (*y*-axis of the 3D scene) is zero because we are not considering the scene height, and the third value is the *z*-axis, that considers the beta value of the gyroscope. In the next lines, we add the acceleration values to the current `ballVel` value and apply it to the ball position, making the ball moves depending on your phone rotation:

```
117  ballVel.add(acceleration);
119  ball.position.add(ballVel);
```

The method add, unlike what we did for adding objects into the scene, just sum up to two Vector3 coordinates. And finally, to calculate the ball collision on the phone borders, we have this:

```
121  if (ball.position.x < minBounds.x || ball.position.x > maxBounds.x)
     {
122      ballVel.x *= bounciness;
123      ball.position.x = THREE.MathUtils.clamp(ball.position.x,
         minBounds.x, maxBounds.x );
124  }

126  if (ball.position.z < minBounds.z || ball.position.z > maxBounds.z)
     {
127      ballVel.z *= bounciness;
121      ball.position.z = THREE.MathUtils.clamp(ball.position.z,
         minBounds.z, maxBounds.z);
129  }
```

It detects if the ball is off the bounds (on x-and z-axis) and applies the bounciness factor to the ball position to make it bounce back when it hits the borders. The method THREE.MathUtils.clamp just makes sure the ball will not go through the border values, clamping the values to minBounds and maxBounds.

And now you have a simple but interesting game that considers your phone rotation to play! But why don't you make this little game more interesting by adding a new axis (the y-axis we are not using now) on it? You can add an eventListener for touchstart/touchend and make the ball jump a bit by tapping on the screen.

Camera Controls

We learned in the last chapter how to move and rotate the camera around to build a cool animation with Three.js. In this chapter, we are talking specifically about interaction, and Three.js has very specific ways to interact with cameras. Actually, it has specific methods to deal with cameras depending on the kind of interaction you want. They are called **Camera controls** and these are the most important ones.

OrbitControls

You can find the code of this section in the folder: https://github.com/OrangeAVA/ Creative-Technology-with-Three.js/tree/main/chapter03/section05a_orbit_ controls

As the name indicates, it allows the user to use the camera to orbit the scene, or basically rotate the camera around a target. The main parameters are:

- **domElement**: The canvas element Three.js is attached to. Usually renderer. domElement.

- **target**: The Vector3 coordinate the camera will orbit around to.

- **enabled**: Turns the orbit camera control on/off. It is on by default.

- **enableDamping** and **dampingFactor**: Controls the inertia movement effect of the camera. It is false by default, and when it is on by default, the value is 0.05.

- **enablePan** and **panSpeed**: Allows the user to pan (slide the camera left and right) with the keyboard. The default is true, but you need to add controls.listenToKeyEvents(window); to make it work. The pan keys are defined by the parameter keys:

```
keys = {
    LEFT: 'ArrowLeft', //left arrow
    UP: 'ArrowUp', // up arrow
    RIGHT: 'ArrowRight', // right arrow
    BOTTOM: 'ArrowDown' // down arrow
}
```

- **enableRotate** and **rotateSpeed**: Allows the user to rotate the camera horizontally or vertically around the target (it is on by default) and sets the rotation speed.

- **minDistance** and **maxDistance**: Minimum and maximum distance in the z-axis the camera can move. Gets closer or farther from the target.

- **minAzimuthAngle** and **maxAzimuthAngle**: Limits the horizontal rotation around the target.

- **minPolarAngle** and **maxPolarAngle**: Limits the vertical rotation (up/down) around the target. For example, if you do not want the camera to go below the floor, just use controls.maxPolarAngle = Math.PI / 2;

Usage:

```
55  controls = new OrbitControls(camera, renderer.domElement);
56  controls.target = new THREE.Vector3(0, 0, 0);
61  controls.update();
```

Remember: you need to call controls.update() in the animation loop to make OrbitControls to work.

PointerLockControls

You can find the code of this section in the folder: https://github.com/OrangeAVA/Creative-Technology-with-Three.js/tree/main/chapter03/section05b_pointer_lock_controls

This is a funny one– it makes the camera react like a First Person Shooter game camera. As soon as you start interacting with the scene (by clicking a button or on the canvas element), the camera rotation is locked to your pointer and `PointerLockControls` starts to listen to the keyboard events. The commands are basically to move forward (towards the direction the camera is pointing) or to move right (90 degrees clockwise). Keep in mind that you need to set up all these listeners and make the camera move manually, but in this section lesson you have everything you need to start playing around with the `PointerLockControls`.

- **domElement:** The documents element you are attaching the keyboard events to. If you are using `document.addEventListener("keydown"...`, the DOM element will be `document.body`.
- **minPolarAngle** and **maxPolarAngle**: Limits the horizontal rotation of the camera.
- **pointerSpeed**: Controls the speed of the camera rotation that is controlled by the pointer. A smaller value will slow down the camera movement.

Usage:

```
61  controls = new PointerLockControls(camera, document.body);


64  document.body.addEventListener("click", function () {
65      controls.lock();
66  });


68  controls.addEventListener("lock", function () {
69      ///do something after the pointer is locked
70  });


72  controls.addEventListener("unlock", function () {
73      ///do something after the pointer is unlocked
74  });
```

```
76  document.addEventListener("keydown", function (event) {
77    switch (event.code) {
78       case "KeyW":
79      moveForward = true;
80      break;
81       case "KeyA":
82      moveLeft = true;
83      break;
84       case "KeyS":
85      moveBackward = true;
86      break;
87       case "KeyD":
88      moveRight = true;
89      break;
90         }
91  });


93  document.addEventListener("keyup", function () {
94    switch (event.code) {
95       case "KeyW":
96      moveForward = false;
97      break;
98       case "KeyA":
99      moveLeft = false;
100      break;
101        case "KeyS":
102      moveBackward = false;
103      break;
104       case "KeyD":
105      moveRight = false;
106      break;
107         }
108  });
```

```
112  function animate() {
113      if (moveForward) {
114          controls.moveForward(increment);
115      } else if (moveBackward) {
116          controls.moveForward(-increment);
117      }

119      if (moveRight) {
130          controls.moveRight(increment);
122      } else if (moveLeft) {
123          controls.moveRight(-increment);
123      }

125      renderer.render(scene, camera);
126      requestAnimationFrame(animate);
127  }
```

You need to read the pointer/keyboard events to start interacting with the scene and move the camera. For it, you need to use `controls.moveForward` and `controls.moveRight` methods (for a backward movement, you need to set `controls.moveForward` to a negative value, the same for a left movement). In the provided boilerplate project, you can use the keys W (forward), S (backwards), A (left) and D (right) to move the camera, and the pointer to rotate it. You do not need to update the camera every frame as on `OrbitControls`, but you need to use the animation loop to move the camera according to the pressed key.

FlyControls

You can find the code of this section in the folder: https://github.com/OrangeAVA/Creative-Technology-with-Three.js/tree/main/chapter03/section05c_fly_controls

It uses the pointer and the keyboard to give the camera a kind of *flight simulator* behavior. With your pointer you can control the camera direction, and with the keys W/A/S/D (move forward, left, back, and right, respectively), arrow left/

right (left and right yaw), arrow up/down (up and down pitch) and Q/E (roll left and right) you can move the camera freely in the scene. The parameters are:

- **domElement**: The canvas element Three.js is attached to. Unlike `PointerLockControls`, you do not need to set the keyboard and pointer listeners up to make it work.

- **movementSpeed** and **rollSpeed**: Controls the movement speed in the directions and the roll speed respectively.

- **autoForward**: If it is `true`, the camera will move forward (using `movementSpeed` value) automatically.

- **dragToLook**: If it is `true`, you need to drag the pointer over the scene to change the camera direction.

Usage:

```
56   controls = new FlyControls(camera, renderer.domElement);
```

The controller `FlyControls` needs to be updated every frame to work, but you need to add a *delta time* parameter in order to update the control correctly. So, in the beginning of the script you need to initialize the `clock` method:

```
5   const clock = new THREE.Clock();
```

And inside the animation loop:

```
64   const delta = clock.getDelta();
65   controls.update(delta);
```

The method `getDelta()` calculates the time difference between the current frame and the previous frame, and you can use it to update `FlyControls` controls parameter.

TransformControls

You can find the code of this section in the folder: https://github.com/OrangeAVA/ Creative-Technology-with-Three.js/tree/main/chapter03/section05c_ transform_controls

It is not a camera control *per se*, but it is more a tool to transform scene objects. When attached to a scene object, it makes it behave just like in some 3D software such as Blender, 3D Max or Maya– when an object is selected, a set of controls are added to it and you can transform the object freely. In the provided boilerplate, you can use the keys W/E/R to switch between translate/rotate/ scale modes just like you would do on 3D Max or Maya (these are the same keyboard shortcuts by the way):

- **domElement**: The document element you are attaching the keyboard events to.

- **showX/showY/showZ**: Boolean value that indicates whether the respective axis controller is visible or not. The default value is *true* for all three axes.

- **setSize**: Sets the size of the UI controllers.

- **setSpace**: Sets the coordinate space the current object is being modified on– **world** means world coordinate space (you will translate/rotate/scale using world coordinates, which means that the controls will work using the original scene x, y and z-axes). If it is **local**, it will use local coordinates, and it will keep the object orientation to perform the transforms– if your object is rotated 45 degrees in the y-axis, when you move it, it will be moved respecting the 45 degrees rotation. In the provided boilerplate, use the key **'q'** to see how it works.

- **setMode**: Changes the mode (**translate/rotate/scale**) of the UI controller. In the provided boilerplate, the keys are w/e/r respectively.

- **attach / detach**: Adds/removes an object to the **TransformControls**, which means if you attach an object to **TransformControls**, it will show the UI controllers over it and you will be able to move/rotate/translate it.

Usage:

```
58  transformControls = new TransformControls(camera, renderer.domEle-
ment);
59  transformControls.attach(cube);
60  scene.add(transformControls);
```

Do not forget you need to attach objects to **TransformControls** to add UI controllers to them, and you need to add the **TransformControls** object to the main scene, otherwise you will not be able to see the controllers. And, don't get confused by the two controllers (**OrbitControls** and **TransformControls,** since both use the pointer controller), you need to add a **dragging-changed** listener to **TransformControls** in order to disable **OrbitControls** temporarily when the pointer is interacting with some object:

```
62  transformControls.addEventListener("dragging-changed", function
    (event) {
63    orbitControls.enabled = !event.value;
64  });
```

And finally, to give **TransformControls** more utility, you can set some key listeners:

```
66   window.addEventListener("keydown", function (event) {
67       switch (event.keyCode) {
68         case 87: // W
69             transformControls.setMode("translate");
70             break;

72         case 69: // E
73             transformControls.setMode("rotate");
74             break;

76         case 82: // R
77             transformControls.setMode("scale");
78             break;

80         case 81: // Q
81             transformControls.setSpace(
82               transformControls.space === "local" ? "world" : "local",
83             );
84             break;
85       }
86   });
```

In the current example, the keys **w/e/r** will **translate/rotate/scale** the object, and the key **q** will switch between **world** and **local** coordinates. You can set key listeners to snap the object into the grid when transforming it, increase/decrease the UI size, enable/disable the UI, show/hide specific transform axis, and so on.

These are the most useful controllers, but Three.js provides other interesting options, including ArcballControls, DragControls, MapControls and TrackballControls.

Basic Game Concept

You can find the code of this section in the folder: https://github.com/OrangeAVA/ Creative-Technology-with-Three.js/tree/main/chapter03/section06_game_ concepts

Now we have a good understanding of how to interact with scene objects and the camera, it is time to put everything together building a simple game using the basic interaction concepts. In this simple game, we are going to use camera controls, pointer interaction, keyboard interaction, and raycasting.

About the game: It is a very simplified first-person shooter game, where you can walk around the scene and shoot bullets to kill enemies. We decided not to use any physics library just to stick to this chapter's lessons, but we will talk more about physics libs (such as `cannon.js` or `ammo.js`) in further chapters.

Our starting point is the `PointLockControls` boilerplate, it has pretty much what we need to make this game work. First, let us add some variables to the beginning of the script, so we can use them further:

```
6   const clock = new THREE.Clock();
7   const velocity = new THREE.Vector3();
8   const direction = new THREE.Vector3();
9   const vertex = new THREE.Vector3();
10  const increment = 100;

12  const raycaster = new THREE.Raycaster();
13  let raycasterOrigin = new THREE.Vector3();
14  let raycasterDirection = new THREE.Vector3();

16  let moveForward = false;
17  let moveBackward = false;
18  let moveLeft = false;
19  let moveRight = false;

21  const bulletArray = [];
22  const enemyArray = [];
23  let bulletObject, enemyObject;

25  const hexColors = [
26      0xff5733, 0x7d3c98, 0x3498db, 0xf1c40f, 0xe74c3c, 0x2ecc71,
0x9b59b6,
27      0x1abc9c, 0xf39c12, 0xc0392b,
```

```
28   ];
```

```
30   let isReady = false;
```

Inside the **start()** function we added a light to be attached to the camera, in a way that it will work as a flashlight and illuminate the scene better depending on the player's position:

```
51   scene.add(camera);
```

```
53   const lightCam = new THREE.SpotLight(0xffffff, 1, 0, Math.PI / 10,
     0.25, 10);
54   lightCam.castShadow = true;
55   camera.add(lightCam);
56   lightCam.position.set(0, 1, 0);
```

```
58   const targetObject = new THREE.Object3D();
59   targetObject.position.set(0, 1, -2);
60   camera.add(targetObject);
61   lightCam.target = targetObject;
```

Add it right after the camera definition, since we want to attach the light to the camera, so it needs to be previously created. Note, in the first line, scene. add(camera) – we usually do not need to add the camera object to the scene, Three.js will not complain about it – but in this case we need the camera object to be attached to the scene in order to parent other objects (lightCam and lightCam target) to it.

We did some small changes in the floor surface, to give it a decent size for the game. We also renamed it for better code understanding:

```
73   const floorGeo = new THREE.PlaneGeometry(100, 100);
74   const floorMaterial = new THREE.MeshStandardMaterial({ color: 0xffffff
     });
75   const floor = new THREE.Mesh(floorGeo, floorMaterial);
76   floor.position.set(0, -0.5, 0);
77   floor.rotation.set(-Math.PI / 2, 0, 0);
78   floor.receiveShadow = true;
79   scene.add(floor);
```

The `PointerLockControls` remains the same, and instead of our well know green cube from the past lessons, we added two *reference objects*– the enemy (which is a cousin of our green cube) and the bullet:

```
85   const bulletGeo = new THREE.SphereGeometry(0.15, 16, 16);
86   const bulletMaterial = new THREE.MeshStandardMaterial({ color:
     0xff0000 });
87   bulletObject = new THREE.Mesh(bulletGeo, bulletMaterial);
88   bulletObject.castShadow = true;
89   bulletObject.receiveShadow = true;


92   const enemyGeo = new THREE.BoxGeometry(1, 1, 1);
93   const enemyMaterial = new THREE.MeshStandardMaterial({ color:
     0x00ff00 });
94   enemyObject = new THREE.Mesh(enemyGeo, enemyMaterial);
95   enemyObject.castShadow = true;
96   enemyObject.receiveShadow = true;
```

We call them *reference objects* because they will not be added to the scene when it is being created, but dynamically afterwards. So, instead of creating a new geometry and a new material for each new enemy/bullet, we create them only once and clone it.

Moving on, we call a function createEnemies(), that will create the enemies, of course! You can change the number of enemies as you wish but do not add too many enemies or your scene will get very crowded.

```
192  function createEnemies(amount) {
193    for (let i = 0; i <= amount - 1; i++) {


195      const enemyInstance = enemyObject.clone();
196      enemyInstance.bBox = new THREE.Box3(new THREE.Vector3(),new
         THREE.Vector3());


198      const randomColour = hexColors[Math.floor(Math.random() *
         hexColors.length)];
199      enemyInstance.material=new THREE.MeshStandardMaterial
         ({color:randomColour});
```

```
201      enemyInstance.position.set( THREE.MathUtils.randFloat(-50, 50), 0,
      THREE.MathUtils.randFloat(-50, 50) );
```

```
202      enemyInstance.rotation.set(0,THREE.MathUtils.randFloat(-Math.
      PI,Math.PI),0);
```

```
203      enemyInstance.bBox.setFromObject(enemyInstance);
```

```
205      scene.add(enemyInstance);
```

```
206      enemyArray.push(enemyInstance);
```

```
207    }
```

```
208  }
```

This function will multiply the enemies over the scene, on random x and z positions (the floor dimensions) and apply a random rotation to them. We also added some random colors to them. In the following part, we create a *bounding box* to each one, which is, in game terminology, a box created around the object to work as a collision detector– we will talk more about it in the game loop part. First, we create an empty bounding box using `THREE.Box3`, then we use `setFromObject` to make the bounding box size the same size as the recently cloned enemy:

```
196  enemyInstance.bBox = new THREE.Box3(new THREE.Vector3(),new THREE.
Vector3());
```

```
203  enemyInstance.bBox.setFromObject(enemyInstance);
```

Then, we add the new enemy to the scene, and add it to the `enemyArray` array, which will be used to calculate the collisions in the animation loop:

```
205  scene.add(enemyInstance);
```

```
206  enemyArray.push(enemyInstance);
```

The next step is creating all the scene listeners. We grouped them in the function `createListeners()`. Here we will set up the keyboard and pointer listeners to make the `PointerLockControls` work properly. Additionally, we added a `pointerdown` event listener to make the player shoot a bullet, we also added the variable `isReady` that will allow the game to start only if the pointer is locked to the screen after the first click. The function to shoot bullets is as follows:

```
210  function shoot() {
```

```
211      const bullet = bulletObject.clone();
```

```
213      bullet.geometry.computeBoundingSphere();
```

```
214      bullet.sphereBBox = new THREE.Sphere( bullet.position,
```

```
        bullet.geometry.boundingSphere.radius );
215     scene.add(bullet);


218     camera.getWorldPosition(bullet.position);

219     camera.getWorldQuaternion(bullet.quaternion);


221     bulletArray.push(bullet);

222   }
```

We did exactly what we should do with the enemies— cloned the bullet reference we created previously in the scene definition, then created the bounding box (in this case, bounding sphere). And here, we position the new bullet exactly in the same place as the camera and with the same rotation too and add it to the bulletArray array in order to be calculated in the animation loop:

```
218   camera.getWorldPosition(bullet.position);

219   camera.getWorldQuaternion(bullet.quaternion);

221   bulletArray.push(bullet);
```

Here, we are using quaternions instead of rotation angles (*Euler angles*) to get a more precise rotation. More about it in the *Key Terms* section at the end of this chapter.

Moving on in our game, we need to add some functions to remove bullets and enemies after the collision. It is a good idea to remove bullets after some time too, or they will still be updated (either the position or the collision) even if they are off the stage:

```
224   function removeBullet(bullet) {

225     bullet.removeFromParent();

226     bulletArray.splice(bulletArray.indexOf(bullet), 1);

227   }


229   function removeEnemy(enemy) {

230     enemy.removeFromParent();

231     enemyArray.splice(enemyArray.indexOf(enemy), 1);

232   }
```

Both functions work the same way— with removeFromParent method, we remove the 3D object from the scene, and the next line will remove the bullet or the enemy from the respective array. This way we avoid calculating their positions or collisions after they are not on the scene anymore.

We have to add some changes into the `animate()` function, as follows:

```
104  function animate() {
105      const delta = clock.getDelta();

107      velocity.x -= velocity.x * 10.0 * delta;
108      velocity.z -= velocity.z * 10.0 * delta;

110      direction.z = Number(moveForward) - Number(moveBackward);
111      direction.x = Number(moveRight) - Number(moveLeft);
112      direction.normalize();

114      if (moveForward || moveBackward) {
115        velocity.z -= direction.z * increment * delta;
116      }
117      if (moveLeft || moveRight) {
118        velocity.x -= direction.x * increment * delta
119      };

121      controls.moveRight(-velocity.x * delta);
122      controls.moveForward(-velocity.z * delta);

124      updateBullets();

126      renderer.render(scene, camera);
127      requestAnimationFrame(animate);
128  }
129  }
```

We added some inertia to the camera movement to make it smoother, and we are running the `updateBullets()` function every frame to update the bullet positions and the collisions between bullets and enemies:

```
237  function updateBullets() {
238    if (!isReady) return;

240    [...bulletArray].forEach((bullet) => {
241      bullet.getWorldPosition(raycasterOrigin);
242      bullet.getWorldDirection(raycasterDirection);

244      bullet.position.add(raycasterDirection.multiplyScalar(-0.5));

246      if ( bullet.position.x < -50 || bullet.position.x > 50 ||
    bullet.position.z < -50 || bullet.position.z > 50 ) {
247        removeBullet(bullet);
248      }

250      enemyArray.forEach(function (enemy, index) {
251        if (bullet.sphereBBox.intersectsBox(enemy.bBox)) {
252          removeBullet(bullet);
253          removeEnemy(enemy);
254        }
255      });
256    });
257  }
```

The updateBullets() is not as complex as it looks– it runs through the two arrays: bulletArray and enemyArray. For each bullet, it calculates the bullet position and rotation (getting the initial point from the camera position and orientation) and calculates the new position using the method multiplyScalar– it updates the position of the bullet moving it -0.5 units into the bullet direction, that is, forward. So, if you want to make the bullet faster or slower, just change this value. Also, this function monitors the bullet position and removes it from the scene if it is out of the scene bounds. And finally, it calculates the collision here:

```
250      enemyArray.forEach(function (enemy, index) {
251        if (bullet.sphereBBox.intersectsBox(enemy.bBox)) {
252          removeBullet(bullet);
253          removeEnemy(enemy);
```

```
254        }
255      });
```

So, for each bullet, it runs through `enemyArray` to find every enemy in the scene. Then it calculates the collision between the two bounding boxes– bullet and enemy bounding boxes, using the method `intersectsBox`. If it detects a collision, it removes the bullet and the enemy from the scene. Cool, huh?

Figure 3.8: *This is how the first person shooter game looks*

As said, it is a very basic game with the basic concepts we learned in this chapter. But now you have the foundations, why not improve it with some cool features? You can add a score or do some cool animation when an enemy is hit. You can even make the enemies walk around the scene randomly!

A Step Further

We learned the most common ways to interact with a 3D scene: keyboard and pointer and using mobile phone data too. But we have some other useful ways to read the user input– camera and microphone. We will not talk about them in this book because it is very specific subject but there are some cool possibilities on using camera and microphone input:

- You can use the desktop/mobile camera to read the user's head position and change the camera position accordingly, to create an effect of a window or a hole.

- You can read the user's expressions to control objects in the scene– a mouth openness can control the scale of a 3D object.

- You can attach 3D objects to the user's facial landmarks like head, nose, chin, and more. You can use Google's MediaPipe for it: https://developers. google.com/mediapipe

- You can read the user's facial landmarks to apply these data to a 3D character and make it mimic your expressions.

- You can use microphone audio volume or other audio properties to make 3D objects react to them using *Web Audio API*.

Conclusion

This chapter was all about user interaction– you learned how to use the pointer, keyboard and even mobile data to control a 3D scene. We also learned how to interact directly with 3D objects by clicking, and how to control and interact with Three.js camera. Finally, you were able to put everything together by creating a simple first-person shooter game.

In the next chapter, you will learn how to improve the realism of your scenes by using high-quality 3D assets and the Blender to Three.js 3D assets workflow, and more!

Points to Remember

- You need to add event listeners in order to be able to watch for keyboard key press, mouse/touch movement or pointer button click.

- Do not forget to listen for **out/up** events to disable the functions that were activated by **in/down** events.

- Some keyboard keys have different codes depending on the OS and the browser. On Mac computers, for example, when you type the letter **a**, you can get 65 as keycode on keydown and 97 on keypress.

- Adding inertia/gravity effects to interactive objects can bring your 3D scene to an upper level, adding more realism and fun.

- When doing raycasting, be aware that Three.js has two methods for reading the intersected objects– `intersectObject` and `intersectObjects`. The first one only returns the first intersected object, and the second returns an array of intersected objects. It is very subtle and you can spend hours trying to debug a code where using `intersectObject` instead of `intersectObjects` went unnoticed for a long time.

- Old but gold– if you are trying to apply a color to a material after it was created, use `.material.color.setHex(hex_color)` instead of use. `material.color = hex_color`.

- To be able to allow your mobile phone to access your computer's local server, you need to know the local server IP and need to be able to run it as https connection on your mobile phone browser. If you try to run it using non-secure http, you will not be able to access your mobile phone data. It works the same way if you try to access your camera or microphone. Do not forget to check if your computer's firewall allows external connections too.

- Use DeviceMotionEvent.requestPermission() method to ask for the user's permission to access mobile device motion data. It should be triggered by a user interaction, as a button click.

- OrbitControls and FlyControls need to be updated every frame. FlyControls needs an additional parameter– delta time between the current and the previous frame.

- TransformControls is not a camera control, but it is an interesting way to interact with scene objects by transforming them (position/rotation/scale) using UI helpers.

Multiple Choice Questions

1. You can interact with a Three.js scene using:

   a. Keyboard and mouse/touch

   b. Mobile data

   c. Data from camera and microphone

   d. All of the alternatives above

2. To be able to read keyboard and pointer data:

   a. You need to create event listeners for each one

   b. Just need to create a function for these kinds of inputs

   c. It is only possible to do it using pure WebGL methods

   d. None of the alternatives above

3. Raycasting is:

   a. An alternative approach to Raytracing

   b. A WebGL method to render a 3D scene

    c. A way to detect interaction with 3D objects on a 2D screen

    d. A technique to move 3D objects using code

4. To be able to read mobile phone data:

    a. You do not need to do anything; it will work straightaway

    b. You need to ask for user's permission, but it will work on secure or insecure connections

    c. It is not possible to read mobile phone data from JavaScript

    d. You need to ask for user's permission and over an HTTPS connection

5. What is true about Three.js controls:

    a. `OrbitControls` does not need to be updated every frame

    b. It is the only way to control Three.js cameras

    c. `PointerLockControls` works like a first-person shooter game camera

    d. `TransformControls` is a different type of camera control

Answers

1. d

2. a

3. c

4. d

5. c

Questions

1. On keyboard event listeners, what is the difference between `event.key` and `event.code`?

2. What is the difference between mouse and touch controls? Is it possible to use mouse controls on touch interfaces and vice-versa?

3. Why is it interesting to add inertia and gravity effects to interactive elements on a 3D scene?

4. Why does the raycasting algorithm need to read the camera position and a Vector2 point to work?

5. What is the difference between the methods `raycaster.intersectObjects` and `raycaster.intersectObject`?

6. Why does the mobile browser need user's permission and an HTTPS connection to read mobile phone data?

7. Which other mobile phone data can be read from a JavaScript code?

8. Could you suggest a different and new scene/camera control to be added to Three.js? Why should it be added to the library?

9. Why has `DeviceOrientationControls` been deprecated from Three.js? What is your opinion about it?

10. Which other features would you add to the Basic Game Concept boilerplate provided at the end of this chapter?

Key Terms

- **Quaternion**: Different from regular (*Euler*) rotation that uses only three dimensions (x, y and z), quaternions are a way to represent a rotation in four dimensions (x, y, z and w). It is a more precise way to represent rotations on 3D spaces because they do not suffer from the *Gimbal Lock* problem.

- **Gimbal Lock**: It is a rotation issue that happens on Euler (Vector3) angles where, depending on the sequence of rotations made on a 3D object, it loses the rotation on one of the axes. You can see it happening very clearly here on this example: https://gimbal-lock-quaternions.glitch. me. Rotate the cubes pressing the keys W,A,S,D and Q, and press R to reset. You will notice, after some operations, that the cube on the Euler quadrants will detach from the ones on the Quaternion quadrants.

- **Damping**: It is a parameter used to slow down a movement when no user input is being read. It acts like an inertia effect, making the object still moving after some time until the velocity reaches zero.

- **Delta**: We generally call `delta` a parameter to calculate the difference between the current value and a previous value of a variable. We can use it to calculate the difference between a clicked point on a screen (`deltaX` and `deltaY`) or to calculate a time difference between the current and the previous rendered frame.

- **Raycasting**: It is an algorithm used for detecting interactive 3D objects clicked on a 2D screen. It traces rays between an origin (generally the camera position) and the 3D point corresponding to the point clicked on a 2D screen. If a casted ray intercepts a 3D object, it returns the intercepted object and the position of the interception.

- **Gyroscope**: On mobile phones, it is a sensor that reads angular velocity changes on the device. The data can be used to calculate the direction the phone is pointed to, serving as a compass.

- **Google's MediaPipe:** It is a Machine Learning library/API from Google that contains very useful tools to interact with multimedia (audio and video) data. It can detect facial landmarks on the user's face, hand gestures, image classification and loads of interesting features.

CHAPTER 4

Adding Some Realism

Introduction

We have progressed a lot so far, building a scene from scratch with the internal resources that Three.js provides to us. Now it is time to make a big leap and start using 3rd party assets to improve our scene quality and realism. We will learn how to prepare 3D assets from Blender to Three.js (or any other 3D software), 3D model optimization, PBR materials export, and texture baking. After that, we will learn how to import and deal with GLTF files, and finally we will explain how to integrate your Three.js scene with a physics engine in order to build more interesting interactive 3D scenes.

Structure

In this chapter, we will discuss the following topics:

- 3D Export from Blender
- 3D Asset Optimization
- PBR Materials
- Texture Baking
- Loading 3D Objects Externally
- Integrating a Physics Library

Reasons to Use Blender

To start this chapter, let us explain why our choice is Blender instead of another 3D software:

- Blender is one of the best 3D softwares in the market.

- It is very powerful in 3D modeling and editing, animation and material editing.
- It is PBR native, with a very powerful native renderer (Cycles), so you do not need any 3rd party renderer (such as V-Ray or Corona) to render high-quality scenes.
- It has a real-time render engine that works similarly as Three.js renderer (Evee) and works very well to pre-visualize your scene before exporting the assets.
- It has a native and very powerful GLTF importer/exporter.
- Blender is used by loads of independent game studios that use the same workflows we are going to use to build and export assets for Three.js.
- It is 100% free.

However, all the lessons in this chapter are perfectly adaptable to any other 3D software, since they are based on the same principles.

3D Export from Blender

We will not go deep into Blender modeling capabilities, but we will focus on editing, optimizing, and exporting 3D assets for Three.js. Among the features that we mentioned in the previous section, is the native and powerful GLTF importer/exporter that Blender has. However, what is the GLTF file format?

GLTF stands for **GL Transmission Format,** and **GLB** is **GL transmission format Binary.** They are the same file type, except for some export settings, and we will talk about them soon. The GLTF file format was created by Khronos Group in 2012, in order to have a standard 3D file format extensible and compatible with several 3D software and real-time renderers. Well, Khronos Group are the people who created WebGL, so it seems very clever to use their own file format on WebGL projects!

GLTF file format really delivers it– version 2.0+ allows you to have, in the same file, geometry, PBR materials, textures, cameras, lights, animations, and more. There is also a possibility to compress the file to make it even smaller. So, it is no coincidence this file format is known as the "JPEG of 3D". So, the choice to use it is a smart one.

However, you can use other formats of 3D files too– Three.js has several file importers such as FBX (very common on Unity and Unreal Engine projects), OBJ, 3DS (both obsoletes), Collada, STL, USDZ (the standard 3D format for native iOS

AR applications), among others. But we strongly recommend that you rely on the GLTF file format, especially if you want to build web AR/VR applications.

In this section, we will investigate in depth four different GLTF files. Three of them are provided by Khronos Group on their amazing **GLTF Sample Viewer** (https://github.khronos.org/glTF-Sample-Viewer-Release/). Besides Khronos GLTF Sample Viewer, we use other two GLTF testers too:

- **Babylon Sandbox**: https://sandbox.babylonjs.com
- **Don McCurdy's GLTF Viewer:** https://gltf-viewer.donmccurdy.com

Even if Khronos Group's GLTF Sample Viewer looks much more complete, Babylon and Don McCurdy versions are more compatible with Three.js and will show you a more precise GLTF look, so use one of these two on your workflow. This book's GitHub repository includes the following three 3D model formats: the source Blender file, a GLTF Separate (non-binary with the separated texture files) file format and a GLB (binary self-contained) file format.

The first example is the DamagedHelmet, a futuristic sci-fi helmet, with very interesting reflections and a HUD with an emissive map, among other textures. If you open it on some GLTF visualizer, you will see this:

Figure 4.1: *Damaged helmet*

The DamagedHelmet file contains a GLTF file, a binary file, and five texture files:

- Base color (albedo or color map)
- Metal/roughness
- Ambient Occlusion

- Emissive
- Normal

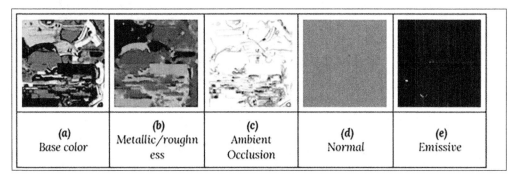

(a) Base color	(b) Metallic/roughn ess	(c) Ambient Occlusion	(d) Normal	(e) Emissive

Figure 4.2: *Texture files*

The second GLTF example is a candle holder, with tinted glass material that we would like to focus on to explain how the transmission (transparent material with true refraction) works:

Figure 4.3: *CandleHolder*

The glass material has very interesting properties: volume absorption (that adds a tint color to the glass material), transmission (that presents this true transparency look) and a thickness map to give the glass variable thickness depending on the map area.

Apart from it, the glass material has a metallic/roughness texture and a default base color texture:

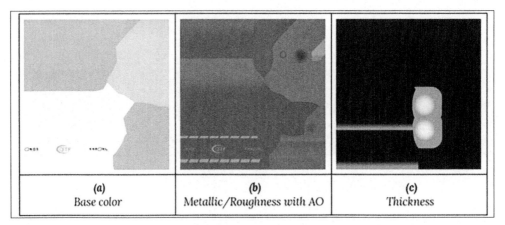

Figure 4.4: *Texture files*

Figure 4.5: *WaterBottle*

The other example (WaterBottle) is pretty much the same: a base color map for the entire mesh, a metallic/roughness/ambient occlusion map packed on a single texture, a normal map and an emissive map that renders the LCD display in front of the bottle holder:

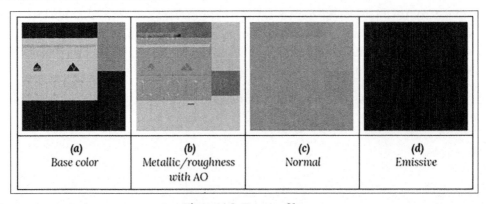

Figure 4.6: *Texture files*

However, we want to focus a bit more on the `AnimatedCharacter` example, because it has some different properties that we would like to discuss in detail. Let us ignore the materials and textures (they are basically the same metallic/roughness workflow) and focus on the animation properties. If you open it on Blender and go to the **Animation** tab, change the **Dope Sheet** to **Action Editor** and you will be able to see the animation actions that are present in the file:

Figure 4.7: *Example of GLTF file with animations*

Using **Animation Actions** is the best way to export animations from Blender to Three.js. This way you will have the possibility to control all your animations from Three.js very easily. You just need to set the animation actions and name them (very important) to be able to play each animation action on your scene. We will discuss more about it in the section titled *Loading 3D Objects Externally*.

Now the Blender scene is all set, it is time to export your GLTF file. These are the available options (all the marked-down items are the recommended values):

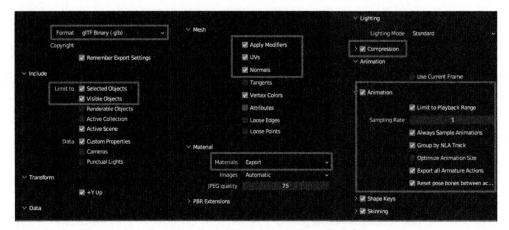

Figure 4.8: *Optimal export options*

- **Format:** Here you select if you want to export in standard mode (GLTF) or binary (GLB) mode. In standard mode, you have two options– GLTF separated and GLTF non-binary. The first format saves all the files separated– a GLTF file (which is an editable text file you can edit), a binary file (that contains the geometry, animations, materials, and so on, and cannot be editable) and the texture files used on the materials. Use it if you want to tweak the textures when you are seeing the scene on Three.js, or if you need to dynamically change the texture containers on the materials. Otherwise, just choose the GLB format that exports only one self-contained file.

- **Include:** select the objects you want to export and use it as you wish. If you want to export your lights and cameras, enable both options but be aware that you will need to deal with them inside Three.js (the exported camera will not be the default scene camera, for example).

- **Mesh:** if you added modifiers to your meshes, then enable **Apply Modifiers** option. Always enable **UVs** and **Normals.**

- **Material:** keep it enabled by default, and on **Images**, keep it as **Automatic** if you do not need to change the textures format or quality.

- **Animation:** if you are exporting animations, keep all these options on.

These are pretty much the most useful export options. It is a good idea to enable the option **Remember Export Options** too, so you will save your export setup to the Blender file. If you use 3D Max or Maya, do not forget to download and install the Babylon GLTF Exporter (https://doc.babylonjs.com/features/featuresDeepDive/Exporters), because GLTF is not a native format for these 3D softwares. The export workflow will differ a bit for them, but the concept remains the same. Remember that if you are using a third party renderer (such as Vray or Corona render), you need to bake the textures and/or convert these materials to 3D Max or Maya default (choose a PBR standard material to keep the PBR compatibility) before exporting the file:

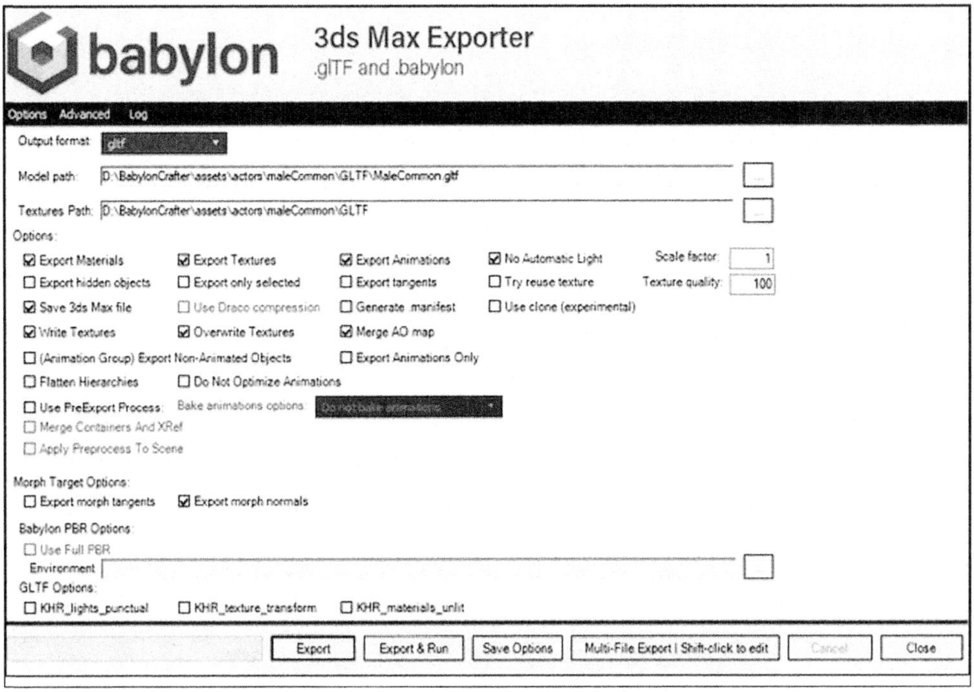

Figure 4.9: *3D Max/Maya Babylon GLTF exporter*

3D Asset Optimization

When exporting 3D assets to Three.js or any game engine, we need to be always aware of the file size– a heavy 3D file will take ages to load (if you are working on an online project), it can drastically reduce the performance (low FPS) and can even crash the browser if the textures are too heavy. You must not forget that Three.js runs through WebGL which runs through the web browser, so you do not have direct access to the GPU to control the performance and the memory load. Keeping this in mind, let us discuss the main aspects of 3D assets optimization. First of all, let us enable the Three.js **stats** in the scene to be able to track down the optimization. We are creating a new boilerplate for the GLTF import, and in this boilerplate, we need to add the Stats lib:

```
import Stats from "https://unpkg.com/three@0.153.0/examples/jsm/libs/
stats.module";
```

Then create two new global variables at the beginning of the script:

```
let stats1, stats2;
```

Right after the scene definition, let us add this code:

```
stats1 = new Stats();
stats1.showPanel(0); // Panel 0 = fps
stats1.domElement.style.cssText = "position:absolute;top:0px;left:0px;";
document.body.appendChild(stats1.domElement);


stats2 = new Stats();
stats2.showPanel(2); // Panel 1 = memory load
stats2.domElement.style.cssText = "position:absolute;top:0px-
;left:80px;";
document.body.appendChild(stats2.domElement);
```

And finally, in the animation loop:

```
stats1.update();
stats2.update();
```

When you refresh the page, you will notice two small panels on the top left of the screen:

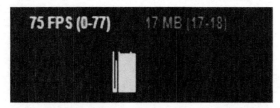

Figure 4.10: *Three.js Stats - FPS counter and memory load*

The first one is the FPS counter– it tells you the current FPS of your scene. The second panel is the memory load– it tells you the amount of megabytes the scene is occupying on the browser's memory. Note that your scene has basically nothing– only the Three.js renderer, the camera, and the animation loop. And even so, it occupies 15–30mb of memory! So, be nice and mindful about your 3D assets!

Now that you have the stats in place on your Three.js scene, it is time to jump back to Blender and see how to optimize a 3D model. The first step– mesh decimation.

Mesh decimation (or Mesh optimization in other 3D software) is basically the process of simplifying the 3D object geometry in order to make it less heavy. In other words, reduce the number of polygons. To be honest, the best decimation technique is **not decimating the mesh!** Since the decimation process is destructive and removes vertices arbitrarily, the results are unpredictable. In an ideal world, the 3D modeling task should consider low-poly modeling techniques, use normal maps instead of detailed geometry, and so on. But we are living in the real world, and you will for sure need to work on high-detailed super-heavy 3D models sometimes. In these cases, it is alright to decimate (among other optimization techniques) the mesh in order to get optimized 3D assets.

On Blender, you have two ways to decimate a mesh:

Figure 4.11: *Blender decimation modifier*

By adding a `Decimate Modifier`, you can select the decimation algorithm and the amount of decimation you want to be applied to your mesh. It works well for individual objects.

In `Edit Mode`, select the faces you want to optimize, then go to `Mesh/Clean Up/Decimate Geometry`. In the small window that shows up after you click `Decimate Geometry`, you can define the amount of decimation and some other parameters. It works better on 3D characters, with Armature applied on the objects:

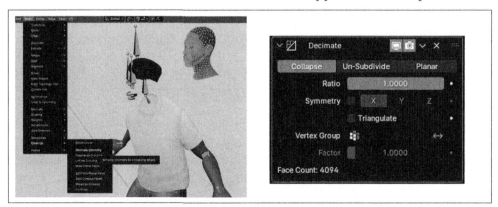

Figure 4.12: *Blender decimate geometry*

Especially, if you are optimizing 3D characters, *always* test the armature and the animations before exporting the GLTF file. The same for the UV maps. As explained earlier, it is a destructive process and can give you unpredictable results, so always be prepared (and with a mesh or file backup!) to roll the decimation back and try other parameters values. Also, be mindful that, if you are using the `Decimation modifier`, to export the GLTF with the `Mesh/Apply Modifiers` option on.

The second step is an easy one– turn `Draco Compression` when exporting the GLTF file. It is very straightforward– just turn it on the `GLTF Export` options. Do not mind the other `Compression` parameters, they will not change the file size too much. Please note that, if you are using `Draco Compression`, you will need to set up `Draco Compression` on your Three.js scene. We will learn more about it in the section titled *Loading 3D Objects Externally*.

Moving on, the next step is **optimizing the textures**. This step is very important not only to reduce the file size, but to avoid webGL memory issues that can even crash the browser. It is not only about the file size – you can have a 4096x4096 JPEG texture with 300kb of file size, but when uncompressed in the browser's memory, it can reach 2mb or even more! So it is more a balance between the size in pixels, the texture compression, and the file size. Really, in 90% of the projects you will not need a very detailed 4096×4096 texture to your 3D model. So it is a good idea to keep your textures up to 2048×2048, but we strongly recommend that you use 512x512 or 1024x1024 textures. Also, instead of using dozens of different textures for each 3D model material, try to combine them and bake the textures in order to have only one texture (or different textures, up to five, in case you are using the metallic/roughness workflow) for each 3D model. Less is more, always.

Also, the texture file format is important– always use JPEG with medium compression (60 to 80%), and for normal maps use PNG files (the JPEG compression can ruin your normal map and lead to bad results when applied on a 3D mesh). To optimize PNG files (or even JPEG files), you can use the amazing **TinyPNG** (tinypng.com). It has a special algorithm that compresses PNG files without loss, reducing the file size up to 50% or even more.

Finally, if you are using animated 3D files, it is a good idea to optimize the animations to reduce the file size. You can do it manually, removing unused keyframes, or on `GLTF Export` options, under `Animation/Optimize Animation Size.` As we advised earlier, it is always wise to check the exported file to make sure the animations are alright.

PBR Materials

In the beginning of this chapter, we had a quick look at the example file structure. They have basically the same structure, with a Base Color map, a Metallic/ Roughness (and sometimes with an Ambient Occlusion) map, a Normal map, and an Emissive map. In this section, let us deep dive on each one and show how they are integrated with the Blender materials:

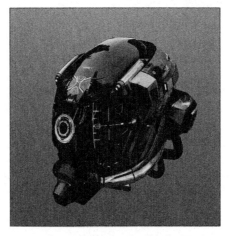

Figure 4.13: *Damaged helmet*

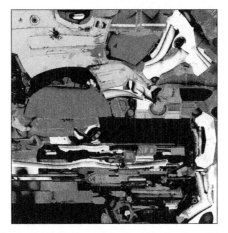

Figure 4.14: *Diffuse map (or Albedo/Base Map)*

It is the main texture map. It contains the 3D model colors.

It is a good example of Packed Texture (or Channel Packing) workflow. The Metalness map is a grayscale image on the blue channel, and the Roughness map is a grayscale image on the green channel. The red channel is absent (black) because this 3D model has a separated AO map texture file:

Figure 4.15: *Metal/Roughness map*

It contains the ambient occlusion map, an optimization approach that 3D softwares use to improve the render quality by rendering a map with internal shadows (also known as contact shadows) from the internal edges of a 3D object. It can be rendered in real time on PostProcessing stack too but it impacts on the render performance:

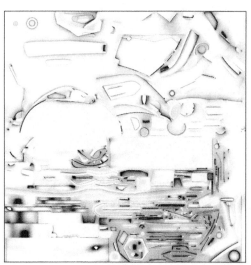

Figure 4.16: *AO (Ambient Occlusion) map*

Normal map is a RGB image that contains the bump details of the 3D model. Instead of adding more details to the mesh (impacting render performance and file size), you can render the details of the mesh on a normal map, and simplify the mesh to decrease the file size:

Figure 4.17: *Normal map*

It contains the parts of the 3D model that emit light. In this case, the HUD and the helmet lights are light sources and should be lit all the time. Please note that they will not emit real light, instead, they will be visible even with no lighting:

Figure 4.18: *Emissive map*

When opening the Blender file, we can see in detail the material setup:

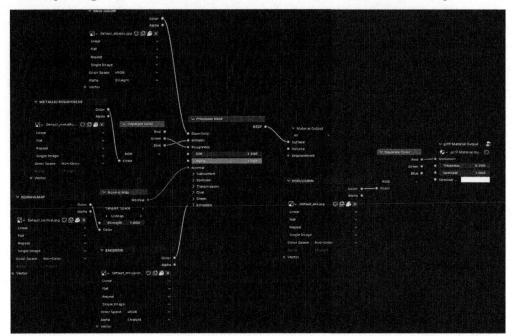

Figure 4.19: *Blender shader nodes*

- **Base Color**: The albedo image texture is connected directly to the **Base Color** parameter.

- **Metallic**: Gets the metal/roughness image texture, separates the image channels, and applies the blue channel to the **Metallic** parameter.

- **Roughness**: Gets the metal/roughness image texture, separates the image channels, and applies the green channel to the **Roughness** parameter.

- **Emissive**: Gets the emissive image map and applies it to the **Emission** parameter.

- **Normal**: Gets the normal image map and applies it to the **Normal** parameter, but through a **Normal Map node**, otherwise Blender will not use it as a normal map.

- **Occlusion**: Blender does not have a native **Ambient Occlusion** parameter, but you can enable it by adding a new node called **GLTF Material Output** and connecting the red channel of the AO image map to the **Occlusion** parameter. Please note that it works only for exporting GLTF files, it will not impact the Blender preview or render.

By the way, it is a good idea to install an Add-on called **Import-Export GLTF 2.0,** if it is not already installed. It will enable good GLTF 2.0 resources such as Shader Editor Add-ons and Material Variants.

The second GLTF example (the `CandleHolder`) has pretty much the same structure, with the difference that it has the **Ambient Occlusion map** packed with the **Metallic/Roughness** map and an additional **Thickness** map:

Figure 4.20: CandleHolder 3D model

The glass material has very interesting properties: a **volume absorption** node that adds a tint color to the glass material, a `transmission` property that works on the true transparency effect, and a `thickness` map to give the glass variable thickness depending on the part of the material:

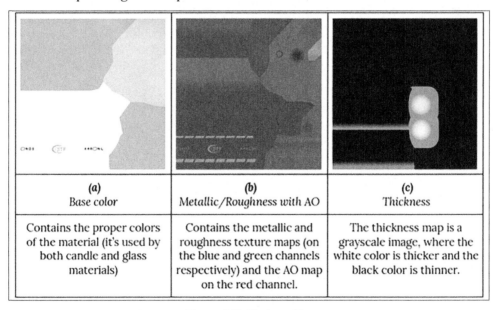

(a) *Base color*	*(b)* *Metallic/Roughness with AO*	*(c)* *Thickness*
Contains the proper colors of the material (it's used by both candle and glass materials)	Contains the metallic and roughness texture maps (on the blue and green channels respectively) and the AO map on the red channel.	The thickness map is a grayscale image, where the white color is thicker and the black color is thinner.

Figure 4.21: Texture files

Taking a deeper look in the glass material, we will see this:

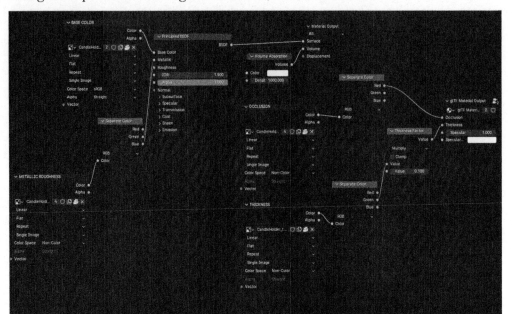

Figure 4.22: *Blender shader nodes*

- **Base color** and **metallic/roughness**: The normal albedo and metallic/ roughness workflow, as we saw in the previous example.

- **Volume absorption**: It is a special node that gives the material this bluish look. If you click the color, despite the fact that it is almost white, you will see it is a very light blue (R: 0.8, G: 0.95 and B: 1) color. Even this very light blue color can present this blue transparency effect. Try to play with this color to see how it impacts the transparency color.

- **Transmission**: It will give the realistic transparent aspect of the material. In this case, 1.0 is fully transparent, with the thickness map controlling the thickness of the transparent parts. Do not be confused with the **alpha** parameter, which basically works on the material's general transparency without considering the thickness, refraction, and other light distortion parameters. Try not to use both– if you are using transmission (1.0), keep alpha 1.0 as well, so you will not have side effects on it. Also, avoid transparent objects over other transparent objects– it will cause some weird effects on your material.

- **Ambient Occlusion**: Works in the same way we did in the previous example, but in this case, it works on a transparent material.

- **Thickness**: In this case, it has a specific texture for the thickness parameter– the same way we did in the metallic/roughness parameters, the green color is separated from the texture and added a **factor** node with the value of 0.1 and the `multiply` blend mode to smooth the transparency transition.

This PBR workflow will work for 90% of your 3D models. You can mix numeric values with texture maps– a metallic map that will be applied to parts of your 3D model and a 0.5 roughness value that will be applied to the entire 3D model.

Texture baking

You can find the code of this section in the folder: https://github.com/OrangeAVA/ Creative-Technology-with-Three.js/tree/main/chapter04/section05d_baking_ textures

Now that you know a bit more about the PBR workflow, let us introduce you to a well-known game production term – **texture baking**. In real-time 3D graphics, the tasks to render shadows, reflections, light effects, and so on cost a lot to the GPU to process. It is not a surprise that only very powerful videogames and PC GPUs are able to render high-detailed and hyperrealistic 3D graphics that would be impossible to render in real time on a low-end GPU or on mobile devices. The **texture baking** process is basically saving GPU resources by rendering previously (in the 3D software) some material or scene details directly to the textures. You can bake on your textures:

- Geometry details on normal maps
- Static shadows and shadow maps
- Static light effects and light maps
- Ambient Occlusion
- Indirect Lighting (global illumination)

You can even group and bake all the scene details in one map to save resources, if your scene is fully static (if it does not have dynamic elements on it).

For this section, we created a Blender template to show the basics of texture baking. It is just a 3D coin with a golden material on it, but it will allow us to show the main Blender texture baking features. You will be able to find all baking stages on this template, but for now let us focus on `coin_original` 3D model. It has quite a complex geometry, with something around 50k faces and almost 100k triangles, so it is a bit heavy for a single coin mesh. The exported file size is about 500kb: not so heavy, but the polycount could have a big impact on the scene performance if we, for example, want to render hundreds of coins. Also, maybe this coin will show up very tiny in the scene, so there is no point in having 50k+ faces in the mesh for it. But how can we optimize it? If we examine the mesh, the most detailed part of it is the dollar symbol ($) that is carved in the coin geometry. We could decimate it but probably it would destroy the mesh without reducing the polycount too much. The other solution would be baking the geometry details as a normal map and maybe an AO map to add more details to it. So let us do it!

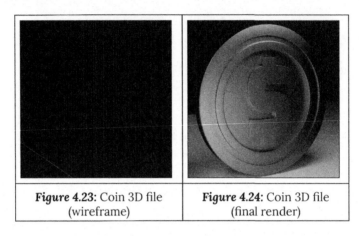

Figure 4.23: Coin 3D file (wireframe)	*Figure 4.24*: Coin 3D file (final render)

We created a rounded cylinder (cylinder + bevel modifier) with the same size as the coin mesh: it has only 450 faces, so it is a good start! We are going to use a Blender technique called **Cage Baking**, which is basically rendering a map from a detailed mesh to a simpler mesh, without worrying about complex UV map unwraps too much.

With the rounded cylinder selected, go to `UV Editing` tab, go to `Edit Mode`, select all faces then UV/Smart Project. It will create a simplified UV for the rounded cylinder. Move it exactly to the position of the original coin mesh and duplicate the 3D model, keeping the position. Then, go to `Edit Mode`, select all faces and use `ALT+S (Mesh/Transform/Shrink Flatten)` to scale it to cover the original coin mesh entirely. Rename it as `cage`.

Select the rounded cylinder and go to the `Shading` tab. Create a new material and name it as `coinBaked`. Then, add a new `Image Texture` node, and on this node click `New` and add a new empty image texture named as `normalMap`. Keep the size as 1024x1024px, then click `OK`. Keep the `Image Texture` node selected, then go to `Render Properties`, change the render engine to `Cycles`, scroll down to Bake properties, change the `Bake Type` to `Normal`. Enable the option `Selected` to `Active`. Now, click the original coin mesh, press, and hold the *Shift* key (if you are going to click the viewport) or *CTRL* key (if you are going to click the outliner) and select the rounded cylinder:

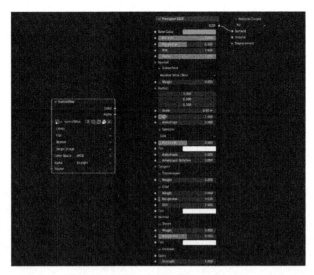

Figure 4.25: *Coin baked material*

On the bake options, enable the option **Selected to Active,** and in the option **Cage Object**, click it and select the cage object we created previously. You are now ready to bake it– click on the **Bake** button and wait for Blender to render the normal texture to the empty image node you created in the material **coinBaked.** Once it is rendered, you just need to create a **Normal Map** node, add the recently created normal texture to it as **Color** entry, and link it to the **Normal** parameter on the material. Now, you can use the same Metallic and Roughness properties from the original coin material, or you can create a completely new one if you want:

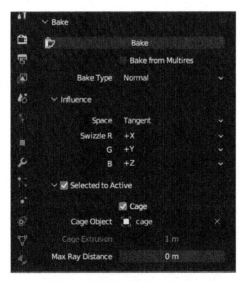

Figure 4.26: *Baking options*

You can do the same for the ambient occlusion map– go to the rounded cylinder material, create a new image texture node and a new image. Name it as `aoMap`, then click the original coin mesh, **Shift + click** (on the viewport) or *CTRL + click* (on the outliner) then select the rounded cylinder mesh. On the Bake options, change the `Bake Type` to `Ambient Occlusion` and click `Render`. To make it work on the viewport, you can mix it with a golden color and set a Multiply Mix to multiply the AO grayscale to the golden color. To export the AO map along with the GLTF file, do not forget to add a `GLTF Material Output` node and link the AO map to it:

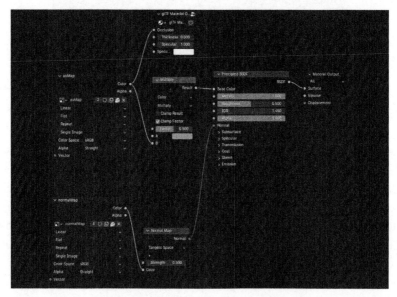

Figure 4.27: *Ambient occlusion material*

You can do the same process for baking other maps. In the Blender template, we created an additional example with a combined bake (AO + Diffuse + other maps) to bake into the texture all the available baking options. You can even bake the shadows and lighting to the floor– create a Floor material and a new image texture on it. Turn the `Selected to Active` baking option **off**, and in the `Baking Type` select `Combined`, and click the `Bake` button again. Then, link the recently created image texture to the `base color` parameter on the Floor material, and that's it! To see if it is working as intended, switch the Viewport Shading from Renderer to Material preview (that renders the viewport without shadows, reflections, and lighting) and you will be able to see the shadows and normals as they have been rendered in Cycles!

You can now export each one of these baked cylinders and see how they look in Three.js, with less than 500 faces!

Loading 3D Objects Externally

You can find the code of this section in the folder: https://github.com/OrangeAVA/Creative-Technology-with-Three.js/tree/main/chapter04/section05a_gltf_loader

This chapter has been all about 3D assets but let us go back to the code – now you know almost everything about 3D asset optimization and exporting, it is time to import them into a Three.js scene. We already added the Three.js stats code, so let us start the GLTF importer and add this line to the beginning of the script:

```
4   import { GLTFLoader } from
    "https://unpkg.com/three@0.153.0/examples/jsm/loaders/GLTFLoader";
```

Then in the variables definition section:

```
9   const loader = new GLTFLoader();
```

And finally right after the animation() call:

```
60  loader.load(
61      "../assets/models/DamagedHelmet/binary/DamagedHelmet.glb",
62      function (gltf) {
63        scene.add(gltf.scene);
64      },
65      function (progress) {
66        console.log((progress.loaded / progress.total) * 100 + "%
          loaded");
67      },
68      function (error) {
69        console.error(error);
70      },
71  );
```

We are loading the file DamagedHelmet.glb (binary version), but the process to load the GLTF file is exactly the same. The GLTF loader has three states:

- The first one is the on loaded method – it is called when the GLTF file is fully loaded, and it returns the GLTF object. Inside this object you can find some useful information, but what we want now is the scene object – it contains the 3D exported object we need to add into the Three.js scene.

- The second method is the on progress method – it is called while the GLTF file is being loaded, so you can create a fancy asset loader here.
- The last method is the on error method – of course, it is called when a loading error occurs.

After adding it to your code, you probably will see an error:

```
Error: THREE.GLTFLoader: No DRACOLoader instance provided.
```

It is because we exported the GLTF asset with the **Draco Compression** option enabled. To enable it in your code, you need to add this:

```
5  import { DRACOLoader } from
   "https://unpkg.com/three@0.153.0/examples/jsm/loaders/DRACOLoader.js";
```

Then, right after the GLTF loader initialization:

```
10  const dracoLoader = new DRACOLoader();
```

And finally right before the GLTF loader call:

```
55  dracoLoader.setDecoderPath(
   "https://www.gstatic.com/draco/versioned/decoders/1.5.6/");
```

```
58  loader.setDRACOLoader(dracoLoader);
```

Be aware that the Draco decoder path is different from the Three.js and libraries path. We are loading them directly from Google (gstatic) server, and it is normal to find compatibility issues between the Three.js Draco loader and the Draco decoder. The Three.js and libraries version we are using in this book (R153) is compatible with version 1.5.6 of Draco decoder.

After adding the Draco decoder path, you will be able to see the GLTF model on your scene. It is a bit dark, though, so let us add some HDRI background/ environment to make things more interesting. By the way, you are able to see something in the scene (even without any light or environment image) just because the 3D model has emissive maps– this is a good example of how they work. Now add this in the loaders section:

```
6  import { RGBELoader } from
   "https://unpkg.com/three@0.153.0/examples/jsm/loaders/RGBELoader.js";
```

And this code after the camera initialization:

```
44  const backgroundTexture = new RGBELoader().load(
45      "../assets/images/pisa.hdr",
46      function (texture) {
47        texture.mapping = THREE.EquirectangularReflectionMapping;
```

```
48          scene.background = texture;
49          scene.environment = texture;
50      },
51   );
```

Figure 4.28: *Externally loaded GLB/GLTF file*

And *voilá!* You can see this beautiful 3D model floating in your scene, with a nice HDRI illuminating it (without shadows, though) and nice reflections. You can add the other GLTF examples from this boilerplate in order to see them in the scene.

Interacting with children objects

You can find the code of this section in the folder: https://github.com/OrangeAVA/ Creative-Technology-with-Three.js/tree/main/chapter04/section05b_gltf_ loader_traverse

The next useful step in the GLTF asset loading workflow is the traverse method– it basically runs through all children of your 3D object to do something. Generally GLTF files have a complex hierarchy with different meshes inside one file, so it is a good idea to learn how to deal with them. You can change the material of the children's meshes, for example. Or you can enable shadows for your full 3D object (if you simply add gltf.scene.castShadow = true it will not work). Let us see how it works:

```
gltf.scene.traverse(function (child) {
});
```

It is pretty much like a forEach loop– it will iterate on the gltf.scene children and will return the child object you can work on:

```
90    gltf.scene.traverse(function (child) {
91        if (!child.isMesh) return;
93        child.castShadow = true;
```

In the preceding example, you are telling Three.js to enable shadow casting to all `gltf.scene` children objects. In line 91, we are making sure the children object is a mesh (and not a group or a light, for example) to avoid further errors.

Another important tip– try not to change the hierarchy of the children objects directly inside the `traverse` loop, or it will return an error too. Instead, create an array of objects, add each child object to this array, and after the `traverse` loop create another loop to iterate through the array. By the way, the traverse method works the same way if you need to look through all your scenes (and not only inside one object)– just use `scene.traverse`.

Now, let us say you want to change only one child object, what would you do? To do this, let us use the `CandleHolder` GLTF file. If you open it on Blender, you will notice that the file contains two objects: `CandleHolder-glass` and `CandleHolder-opaque`. We want to change the glass material to a Three.js `MeshStandardMaterial`. You can do it in this way:

```
gltf.scene.traverse(function (child) {
        if (child.name === 'CandleHolder-glass') {
          //do something
        }
});
```

But there is a much easier way to do that– Three.js has some methods to get children objects by its properties. In this case, we want to search by the children's name, so:

```
124   const candleHolderGlass = gltf.scene.getObjectByName('CandleHolder-
      glass');
125   if (!candleHolderGlass || !candleHolderGlass.isMesh) return;

126   const chromeMaterial = new THREE.MeshStandardMaterial({
126           color: 0xffffff,
127           metalness: 1,
128           roughness: 0,
129   });
141   candleHolderGlass.material = clearGlassMaterial;
```

Of course, we need to test if there is an object named `CandleHolder-glass` and if it is a mesh, otherwise it will return an error. You can also search by children's objects properties, using `getObjectByProperty(property, value)` or `getObjectsByProperty(property, value)`. The first method will return the first occurrence, and the second method will return an array of objects that matches your search. Unfortunately, there is no method to find objects by material, so in this case you will need to traverse between the object children and create an array of objects with the ones that have the material you want to find. You can check some examples of use of `traverse` and `getObjectBy` methods in the boilerplate of *Chapter 4, section 5b*.

Playing animations

You can find the code of this section in the folder: https://github.com/OrangeAVA/ Creative-Technology-with-Three.js/tree/main/chapter04/section05c_gltf_ loader_animation_mixer

Another important topic in this chapter is how to make the animations work in your scene. In the provided file called `AnimatedCharacter`, we can find some Animation Actions that were exported to the GLTF file. They are— Elbow punching, Fist fighting, Idle, Punch, Roundhouse kick and Thriller. This character was created on *Ready Player Me* and we imported some animations from *Mixamo*. If you open this file using Babylon GLTF Viewer or Don McCurdy's GLTF Viewer, you will be able to see them under the tab Animation and play them individually.

When you import a GLTF file which contains animations, you will need to create an Animation Mixer, which is the Three.js animation controller. Each animated object should have its own animation mixer (and not one animation mixer for the entire scene), and each Animation Mixer contains the Action Clips, that are exactly the same Animation Actions exported from Blender.

If you just load the `AnimationCharacter` GLTF file, you will be able to see the character standing in a static position— it is because there is no animation mixer on it, so let us add it. First of all, let us create an `animationMixers` array in the beginning of the code to store the scene animation mixers (remember that each animated object will have its own `animationMixer`, so it is clever to group them into an array to make it easier to access them):

```
8  let animationMixers = [];
```

Inside the GLTF on load method, add this:

```
91  const characterMixer = new THREE.AnimationMixer(gltf.scene);

92  animationMixers.push(characterMixer);
```

Now we need to find the available animations inside the GLTF object. They are stored inside the object gltf.animations (the geometry, materials, and so on are stored inside gltf.scene), so it is a good idea to group them in order to be more accessible in the future:

```
95  gltf.actions = {};

96  for (let i = 0; i < gltf.animations.length; i++) {

97       const clip = gltf.animations[i];

98       const action = characterMixer.clipAction(clip);

99       gltf.actions[clip.name] = action;

100       action.loop = THREE.LoopRepeat;

101  }
```

We have already created the object gltf.actions, so from now on, if you want to access any specific animation clip, you just need to look for gltf.actions[nameOfAnimationClip]. We also turned the animation action loop on (THREE.LoopRepeat, but we could set it as THREE.LoopOnce to play once and THREE.LoopPingPong to play it until the end and to make it run backwards to the beginning of the animation). Now it is time to set the animation clip we are going to play first, in this case it is the 'Idle' animation:

```
104  gltf.activeAction = gltf.actions["Idle"];
```

And finally play the animation (resetting the current animation, in case it is already playing something):

```
107  gltf.activeAction.reset();

108  gltf.activeAction

        .setEffectiveTimeScale(1)

        .setEffectiveWeight(1)

        .fadeIn(0.5)

        .play();
```

What this piece of code does is basically to set the time scale (animation speed) to 1 (original animation speed), then set the weight of the activeAction (Idle) to 1 (full weight, but you could set 0.5 to get half pose Idle and half pose of the previous action), then set the animation action fade in half second (0.5), and finally play the animation. And now we have the character playing the Idle animation in loop! Now, how about creating some buttons to play the other available animations?

In the boilerplate related to this section, we have added some UI buttons related to each animation clip available in the GLTF file. We have also added some styles to show the buttons over the Three.js canvas and prevent the buttons from showing up before the GLTF file is fully loaded. To trigger the buttons, we have added these lines inside the start() function:

```
122   const buttons = document.querySelectorAll("#ui button");
123     buttons.forEach(function (element) {
124       element.addEventListener("click", function (e) {
125         const animationClipName = element.dataset.animation;
126         fadeToAction(animatedCharacter, animationClipName, 0.5);
127       });
128   });
```

This loop reads the data-animation parameter on each button and uses it on the function fadeToAction(), that is basically what we did previously to play the Idle animation:

```
154   function fadeToAction(model, animationClipName, duration) {
155       model.previousAction = model.activeAction;
156       model.activeAction = model.actions[animationClipName];
158       if (model.previousAction !== model.activeAction) {
159         model.previousAction.fadeOut(duration);
160       }
162       model.activeAction.reset();
163       model.activeAction.setEffectiveTimeScale(1).
      setEffectiveWeight(1).fadeIn(duration).play();
168   }
```

The only difference here is that we need to have a previousAction in order to be able to play the transition. We created the first action here inside the GLTF on load function:

```
104   gltf.activeAction = gltf.actions["Idle"];
```

Figure 4.29: *GLB file with animation clips*

And now we use it as the previous action and play the transition between this action and the new action. If the new action has the same name as the previous action, it does nothing and keeps playing the current animation in loop.

Integrating a Physics Library

You can find the code of this section in the folder: https://github.com/OrangeAVA/ Creative-Technology-with-Three.js/tree/main/chapter04/section06_physics_ library

In this chapter, we have already discussed realistic 3D models, realistic PBR materials, realistic baked textures, and realistic animations. However, building a realistic interactive 3D scene is not only about visuals— we can take a step further adding some physics to make the scene objects react just like in the real world. Yes, we are talking about gravity, collisions, and other cool features that make everything much funnier. Of course, Three.js does not have a physics engine embedded in the library, but we can use some 3rd party physics libraries to do the job. There are some Three.js compatible physics libraries available on the internet but let us use one that is quite simple and straightforward: Cannon. js (https://github.com/schteppe/cannon.js).

To show how a physics engine works, how about revamping the *First Person Shooter* game we created in the previous chapter by adding some gravity, friction, and real collisions? Sounds interesting? So to start, let us add the library in the `index.html` file:

`(index.html):`

```
10  <script
    src="https://github.com/schteppe/cannon.js/releases/download/v0.6.2/
    cannon.min.js">
    </script>
```

We had to add some global variables to the beginning of the code:

`(./js/main.js)`

```
14  let world, sphereMesh, floorPhysicsMaterial, bulletObject,
    enemyObject;
15  let shootVelocity = 25;
16  let shootDirection = new THREE.Vector3();
```

Now, we need to initialize the Cannon.js physics world. To do it, we create a function called `physicsSetup()` that we are going to call right after the lights initialization:

```
75  await physicsSetup();
```

And the function itself, outside the `start()` function:

```
322  async function physicsSetup() {
323    world = new CANNON.World();
324    world.gravity.set(0, -9.82, 0);
325  }
```

It created the `Cannon.js` world (that will calculate all the scene physics) and set the gravity. The variable `world` will store the physics world, so we will use it to add the bodies (`body` is any object in the 3D scene that is affected by physics) and other scene components.

Now, we need to transform the floor object into a body. `Cannon.js` does not have a straightforward way to do it, but we can use the properties of the Three.js object to replicate it in the `Cannon.js` world:

```
86  floorPhysicsMaterial = new CANNON.Material();
87  const floorBody = new CANNON.Body({
88      shape: new CANNON.Plane(
89        floor.geometry.parameters.width,
90        floor.geometry.parameters.depth,
```

```
91        ),
92        mass: 0,
93        material: floorPhysicsMaterial,
94     });
95   floorBody.position.x = floor.position.x;
96   floorBody.position.y = floor.position.y;
97   floorBody.position.z = floor.position.z;
98   floorBody.quaternion.setFromAxisAngle(new CANNON.Vec3(1, 0, 0),
     -Math.PI / 2);
99   world.addBody(floorBody);
```

In the preceding code, we create a Cannon.js body with a shape of a plane, with the same width and depth of the Three.js plane, then we set the Cannon.js plane position to the same position of the original plane and finally add it to the world (with the method addBody). By the way, the floorPhysicsMaterial is not about the material of the object, but Cannon.js uses it to set some specific properties that are shared with other objects. We will show how to use it further in this lesson.

Remember in the *First Person Shooter* game that we created a function to draw the enemies and spread them through the scene? We need to create the Cannon. js body as well, so let us add to it:

```
238   let enemyBody = new CANNON.Body({
239        mass: 5,
240        shape: new CANNON.Box(
241          new CANNON.Vec3(
242            enemyInstance.geometry.parameters.width / 2,
243            enemyInstance.geometry.parameters.height / 2,
244            enemyInstance.geometry.parameters.depth / 2,
245          ),
246        ),
247        position: enemyInstance.position.clone(),
248   });
250   enemyBody.quaternion.setFromAxisAngle(
251     new CANNON.Vec3(
252       enemyInstance.rotation.x,
```

```
253        enemyInstance.rotation.y,
254        enemyInstance.rotation.z,
255    ),
256    -Math.PI / 2,
257  );
```

The principle is the same as we used in the Floor object— copy the position, rotation, and size from the original (enemy) object. Please note that Cannon. js creates the box body by its half extent (and not the full extent as Three.js does), this is why the new `CANNON.Box` method uses `enemyInstance.geometry.parameters.width / 2` to create it. Now we need to add this line:

```
259  enemyInstance.cannonRef = enemyBody;
```

Cannon.js creates the body, however it does not update the original object (the Three.js object) automatically, so we need to store the `enemyBody` object inside the enemy object in order to update the enemy object in the animation loop.

And finally we can add the `enemyBody` to the `Cannon.js` world:

```
260  world.addBody(enemyBody);
```

So we are done with the enemies. Time to do the same with the bullets in the `shoot()` function. To start, let us create the physics material that will tell how `Cannon.js` will calculate the interaction between the bullets and the floor:

```
272  const matPhysicsBullet = new CANNON.Material();
273  const matPhysicsBullet_ground = new CANNON.ContactMaterial(
274      floorPhysicsMaterial, matPhysicsBullet,
275      {
276        friction: 0.0,
277        restitution: 0.5,
278      },
279  );
280  world.addContactMaterial(matPhysicsBullet_ground);
```

The `restitution` parameter is about the bullet bounciness— change it to make your bullet bounce more or less when it hits the floor. And now let us add the `Cannon.js` bullet body:

```
282  const bulletBody = new CANNON.Body({
283      mass: 1,
284      position: bullet.position.clone(),
```

```
285        shape: new CANNON.Sphere(bulletObject.geometry.parameters.radius),
286        material: matPhysicsBullet,
287    });
```

As we did with the enemies, we created the bullet body copying the bullet geometry radius and position (we do not need to copy the rotation because the bullet is a sphere). Now we need to set the direction and the velocity the bullet is being shot. For it we created a function called getShootDirection(), that projects a ray from the camera to the infinite, in the forward (targetVector.set(0, 0, 1)) direction:

```
326   function getShootDirection(targetVector) {
327       var vector = targetVector;
328       targetVector.set(0, 0, 1);
329       vector.unproject(camera);
330       var ray = new THREE.Ray(
331           camera.position,
332           vector.sub(camera.position).normalize(),
333       );
334       targetVector.copy(ray.direction);
335   }
```

We call it right after the ballBody definition:

```
289   getShootDirection(shootDirection);
```

With the direction defined by the camera orientation, we set the velocity (shootVelocity) of the bullet:

```
291   bulletBody.velocity.set(
292       shootDirection.x * shootVelocity,
293       shootDirection.y * shootVelocity,
294       shootDirection.z * shootVelocity,
295   );
```

And finally add the bullet body reference to the Three.js object and add it to the Cannon.js world:

```
297   bullet.cannonRef = bulletBody;
298   world.addBody(bulletBody);
```

We have now everything done for calculating the physics of the scene, but we need to update the Three.js objects position according to the Cannon.js bodies. For this we modified the previous updateBullets() function and added an updateEnemies() function:

```
304  function updateBullets() {
305    if (!isReady) return;
306    [...bulletArray].forEach((bullet) => {
307      if (!bullet.cannonRef) return;
308      bullet.position.copy(bullet.cannonRef.position);
309    });
310  }

312  function updateEnemies() {
313    if (!isReady) return;
314    [...enemyArray].forEach((enemy) => {
315      if (!enemy.cannonRef) return;
316      enemy.position.copy(enemy.cannonRef.position);
317      enemy.quaternion.copy(enemy.cannonRef.quaternion);
318    });
319  }
```

These functions should be called in the animation loop, and they basically run through the arrays of bullets and enemy objects, updating their positions and rotations according to the **cannonRef** object stored previously. The **cannonRef** objects (for bullets and enemies) contain the updated positions and rotations calculated by Cannon.js.

And finally, we need to update the Cannon.js world in the animation loop:

```
148  if (delta > 0) {
149        world.step(delta);
150  }
```

The delta variable starts with zero (the first cycle of the animation loop), so we need to make sure the Cannon.js world will be updated if delta is higher than zero, otherwise it will throw an error:

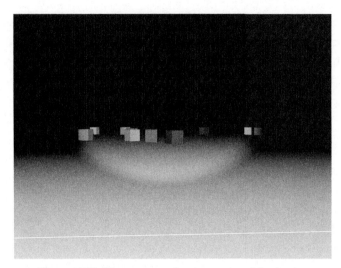

Figure 4.30: *First person shooter game with physics*

And that's it! We improved the *First Person Shooter* game a lot, right? Cannon.js has very cool features that you can use to simulate physics– cloth simulation, vehicle simulation, ragdoll simulation, object constraints, and much more. Take a look at their GitHub repository to be inspired and add more features to the game!

Conclusion

In this chapter, we improved our knowledge on how to add more realism to the scene, not only on the visual side, but also through adding animations and a physics engine. You now have everything in hand to build a realistic scene, using high quality animated 3D assets, and even adding some real physics reactions to it.

In the next chapter, we will talk about Post Processing, which is a different approach on how to add some visual effects to our scene.

Points to Remember

- Building a realistic Three.js scene is not just about visuals– everything that relates to the real world is welcome– high quality 3D assets, realistic environment, realistic lighting, real world-like interaction, sound effects and real-world physics.

- Blender is a very powerful 3D software, and it is FREE. Also, it is almost Three.js native– it exports natively to GLTF format, it is PBR native and does not need any 3rd party renderer.

- There are many 3D file formats available, but GLTF format is the perfect fit for Three.js.

- Always use Three.js stats on your more complex scenes to keep track of the scene performance. Not only the FPS count, but the memory load is very important, especially if you are building a mobile 3D experience.

- To reduce the poly count of your 3D objects use the **Decimation modifier** (or **Mesh Optimization** on other 3D softwares) but use it carefully– it can ruin your mesh, especially if it has UVs and animations.

- ALWAYS use Draco compression– it is free and can save precious megabytes of your 3D assets, without loss of mesh or texture quality.

- Pay special attention to the textures– you do not need to use a 4k texture map if the object will not be close to the camera or if the user will not be able to see it in detail. Try to keep it between 512x512 and 1024x1024 pixels. And always use the **'Power Of Two' Rule**– the image sides should be a power of two number of pixels– 2^3 (8), 2^4 (16), 2^5 (32), 64, 128, 256, 512, 1024, 2048, 4096, and so on.

- Do not forget to use **TinyPNG** to compress your textures, especially if you are using PNG images.

- **Channel Packing** technique– metalness map on the blue channel, roughness map on the green channel, and ambient occlusion on the red channel.

- Normal maps should be always exported in PNG format– the JPG compression algorithm causes image artifacts that will distort the 3D object appearance.

- Texture baking is a very useful tool to optimize 3D assets:
  - you can reduce the mesh complexity by rendering it to a normal map.
  - You can save render resources by baking the lighting, shadows, and global illumination to the 3D object.
  - You can improve the 3D object visual quality by adding an ambient occlusion and other beauty maps.

- Use `mesh.traverse` loop to iterate through your mesh children objects– add shadows, change materials or tweak some child object position, rotation, or scale.

- Create one **animation mixer** for each animated object on your scene. And do not forget to update all the mixers on the animation loop.

- Physics engines are very useful to add more realism to your scene– you can simulate gravity, collisions, inertia, object constraints, clothes, and so on.

Multiple Choice Questions

1. Which GLTF export options are available in Blender?

    a. GLTF binary and GLTF separated

    b. GLB (binary) and GLTF separated

    c. GLTF non-binary, GLTF separated and GLB (binary)

    d. None of them

2. Channel packing technique is:

    a. Zipping your textures to reduce the file size

    b. Save each texture type to a different file

    c. Compose your textures into one single file, side by side

    d. Save each texture type into an image channel– metalness map on the blue channel, roughness map on the green channel, ambient occlusion map on the red channel

3. Draco compression is:

    a. A compression algorithm that reduces your GLTF file size without messing up with your meshes and textures

    b. A destructive compression algorithm to reduce the GLTF file size

    c. A zip-like compression technique

    d. The algorithm used by TinyPNG

4. You are traversing a GLTF 3D file. What is the best way to change the meshes hierarchy?

    a. GLTF files do not have a 3D mesh hierarchy– they do not accept child objects

    b. You just need to change the hierarchy inside the traverse loop

    c. Use traverse to create an array of objects, followed by a loop through this array and changing the hierarchy

    d. You cannot change a 3D file hierarchy in any way

5. Which one is true about physics on Three.js:

   a. Cannon.js is one of the compatible physics engines

   b. Three.js has an embedded physics engine

   c. There is no way to add physics to Three.js

   d. You can use WebGL methods to simulate physics on your Three.js scene

Answers

1. c

2. d

3. a

4. c

5. a

Questions

1. Which 3D software do you like the most? Why?

2. What is the workflow to optimize 3D assets?

3. Why has the GLTF file format become the most popular 3D file format when building web applications? What are the other recommended options?

4. You have a 3D file with 100mb of file size, and even decimating it / Draco compressing does not help too much. What could you do to optimize this asset to be less painful for loading it on your Three.js scene?

5. Why is it recommended to use only textures / 2D assets with a **base two** size?

6. For some reason, your client provided you with only FBX (non-PBR) files and you are not allowed to convert them to GLTF format. What should you do to use the PBR workflow on your project?

7. What are the reasons people use the Channel Packing technique?

8. Why can't you change the 3D file mesh hierarchy inside the traverse loop?

9. On the physics boilerplate, we used simple spheres and boxes to build the scene. What could you do to use imported 3D objects instead of these primitives?

10. In your opinion, why powerful 3D software like 3D Max and Maya are not natively compatible with GLTF formats?

Key Terms

- **GLTF:** GL Transmission Format, 3D file format WebGL native created by Khronos Group.
- **FBX:** Filmbox 3D file format. It is very popular on Unreal Engine and Unity.
- **Draco compression:** open-source 3D file compression library created by Google.
- **FPS:** Frames per second, the most usual way to measure a 3D scene performance.
- **Mesh Decimation (or Mesh Optimization):** Technique to reduce the poly count by simplifying a 3D mesh. It is destructive, so use it with caution.
- **Power of Two Rule:** On game engines, the recommended image size should be power of two: 8, 16, 32, 64, 128, 512, 1024, 2048, 4096, and so on, for performance reasons.
- **TinyPNG:** Online service that compresses PNG and JPG images using a special algorithm that reduces the file size without (or almost without) loss of quality.
- **Texture Baking:** Technique that renders on the 3D object texture some complex material features, like normals, ambient occlusion, reflections, lighting, shadows, and so on. It is used to optimize the 3D file size/complexity and to save real time rendering resources.
- **Mesh Traverse:** Three.js loop that iterates through all the 3D file children objects.
- **Animation Mixer:** Three.js animation player that controls the animation actions from an animated 3D file.
- **Animation Clip:** Each animation piece comes on an animated 3D file.
- **Rigid Body:** On a physics engine, it is a body (a 3D object) that is affected by the physics simulation and does not deform when interacting with other objects.

- **Soft Body**: On a physics engine, it is a body that is affected by the physics simulation and deforms when interacting with other objects. Due to its complexity, Cannon.js does not have this feature (but you can find it on Ammo.js and other more complex physics engines).

- **Physics World**: All objects and properties that are considered by a physics engine on the physics calculations.

CHAPTER 5

Post Processing

Introduction

In the last chapter, we discussed how to improve scene realism by revamping materials using the PBR workflow, how to use high-quality 3D assets, and how to bake them to have photorealistic textures without making them more complex or costing render resources. This chapter will move on to this subject but add a complexity layer over the default Three.js render target. We will need more GPU resources because Post Processing uses the rendered image to add effects and improvements over it– all in real-time.

Structure

In this chapter, we will discuss the following topics:

- Post Processing Concept
- Filters and Effects
- Post Processing Stack
- Caveats

Post Processing Concept

First of all, let us conceptualize what **Post Processing** is– think about image layers in Photoshop or video layers in After Effects or Premiere. First, you have the original image (or footage) and you want to add visual effects over it– add some color adjustments, add a pixelated effect, and, finally, add some bloom effect to emphasize the lighting and give to your image (or video) a special look. Using one of these softwares, you just need to add effect layers and tweak the parameters to get to the desired look, building a pile of layers that will result in a final image.

The Three.js Post Processing works pretty much in this way– you add the Post Processing effects into the Post Processing Stack and finally add an Output layer to render the final look. The main difference is that on Three.js you do this over a real-time rendered image– this is the main reason we need a powerful GPU or need to be gentle with the Post Processing Stack to get your scene rendered with more than 30FPS.

On Three.js, we call each layer a **pass** over the main WebGL output, and they can be stacked up indefinitely as you wish, but of course, costing a lot of GPU and browser's memory resources. The last pass is, generally, the **OutputPass** which will collect all the calculated pixels from the previous passes and render them in the Canvas. We said generally because you do not need **OutputPass** on all occasions. You will be able to see how it works in the next sections and on the boilerplate of this lesson:

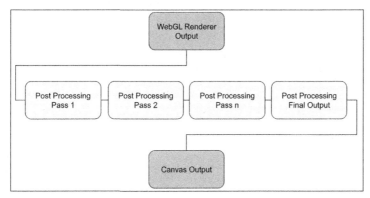

Figure 5.1: *Post Processing stack*

In the next chapter, we will talk about each effect available.

Types of Filters and Effects

We can divide the Three.js filters and effects into some categories:

- **Color adjustment/color grading**: Effects that correct or alter the way the colors are rendered/displayed on the screen.

- **Lens/light effects**: Effects that add lens effects (such as Depth of Field) or light effects (such as bloom and ambient occlusion) to the rendered image.

- **Image stylizing**: Effects that distort the way the image is rendered on the screen or add an artistic look to it.

- **Image composition**: Filters that allow you to combine one or more render targets/images into one output.

- **Image improvement**: Filters that improve the image quality or add more realism to the rendered image.

Post Processing Stack

Now you know more about each available Three.js Post Processing effect, and how to use them. We explained previously that on Three.js we "stack" the effect up, first of all, you get the rendered image (render target) and start adding the effects. Finally, you add an output to render the final result to your screen.

We split this lesson into two parts– the first part uses "regular" effects, such as Pixel or Outline filters, and the second part is focused on mask effects, which require a different scene setup.

In the first lesson (and its boilerplate as well), we will add all the effects to the scene in a way that you can turn them on and off to see the results in real time. However, be aware that some effects overcome the results of the previous ones (like the `PixelatedPass`), so you will not be able to compose the results (you can, of course, change the pass order in the code to see different outcomes) when you turn it off. Also, be careful when enabling all the effects– as we explained before, they are very heavy for the GPU and can cause some rendering issues or even crash your browser!

The second lesson (and boilerplate) contains the `maskPass` and its dependencies, and contains a different scene setup because it requires a different renderer and two or more scenes to present some result to the screen. We will talk more about it soon.

Another novelty that we are introducing here is the amazing `dat.gui`, which is a simplified GUI (Graphical User Interface) that helps us to create some UI elements to control some scene properties. Dat.gui is very straightforward and we will not spend much time talking about it, but you can see the full documentation here: https://github.com/dataarts/dat.gui.

Post Processing Caveats

Post Processing effects are very heavy for the GPU– they get all the rendered scene frame information, such as colors, depth buffer, pixel positions, and so on, to deliver a desired result on the screen. So, there are a lot of calculations going on, frame by frame, and you need to be gentle with your GPU.

Of course, if you have a high-end GPU such as a Geforce RTX 3060 or similar you will not need to bother about these limitations, but keep in mind that we are, mostly, building experiences for a general audience, which includes people with limited GPU, so it is a good idea to test your projects on low-end devices too.

A special note for mobile devices– even mobile phones and tablets with good GPUs are not comparable to good desktop GPUs, so if you are delivering your project to mobile devices, double the caution with Post Processing.

Some other caveats that you should take into consideration when using Post Processing effects:

- When using anti-alias passes, do not use too many AA samples otherwise it will drop your FPS or even crash your browser.
- Be careful with bloom effects over other effects– it increases the scene complexity, making your GPU struggle to render the scene.
- Try not to use more than three or four stacked effects.
- If you are targeting your project to desktop and mobile devices, it is a good idea to detect the device and deliver fewer effects to mobile ones.
- Post Processing effects depend on the screen resolution, so on screens with more resolution the GPU will be more challenged.

You can find the code of this and the next sections in the folder: https://github. com/OrangeAVA/Creative-Technology-with-Three.js/tree/main/chapter05/ section01a_post_processing

So, for the first lesson, let us load the main libraries into our boilerplate:

```
7  import { EffectComposer } from
   "https://unpkg.com/three@0.153.0/examples/jsm/postprocessing/EffectCom-
poser.js";
8  import { RenderPass } from
   "https://unpkg.com/three@0.153.0/examples/jsm/postprocessing/Render-
Pass.js";
```

These two libraries are responsible for the effects passes and the render target pass. Let us add the `OutputPass` now:

```
9  import { OutputPass } from
   "https://unpkg.com/three@0.153.0/examples/jsm/postprocessing/Output-
Pass.js";
```

For regular filters, this is a non-mandatory pass that you can add to the end of the stack to improve the visual quality of the result and perform a sRGB color space conversion. For `maskPass`, the `outputPass` is mandatory, otherwise you will not be able to see the final result rendered on screen.

After that, we need to add the libraries related to each effect we want to add to our scene. Here is the full path of all the filters we mentioned in the previous section:

```
11  import { HalftonePass } from
    "https://unpkg.com/three@0.153.0/examples/jsm/postprocessing/
    HalftonePass.js";

12  import { LUTPass } from
    "https://unpkg.com/three@0.153.0/examples/jsm/postprocessing/LUTPass.
    js";

13  import { SAOPass } from
    "https://unpkg.com/three@0.153.0/examples/jsm/postprocessing/SAOPass.
    js";

14  import { SSAOPass } from
    "https://unpkg.com/three@0.153.0/examples/jsm/postprocessing/SSAOPass.
    js";

15  import { UnrealBloomPass } from
    "https://unpkg.com/three@0.153.0/examples/jsm/postprocessing/
    UnrealBloomPass.js";

16  import { BokehPass } from
    "https://unpkg.com/three@0.153.0/examples/jsm/postprocessing/
    BokehPass.js";

17  import { DotScreenPass } from
    "https://unpkg.com/three@0.153.0/examples/jsm/postprocessing/
    DotScreenPass.js";

18  import { FilmPass } from
    "https://unpkg.com/three@0.153.0/examples/jsm/postprocessing/FilmPass.
    js";

19  import { GlitchPass } from
    "https://unpkg.com/three@0.153.0/examples/jsm/postprocessing/
    GlitchPass.js";

20  import { RenderPixelatedPass } from
    "https://unpkg.com/three@0.153.0/examples/jsm/postprocessing/
    RenderPixelatedPass.js";

21  import { OutlinePass } from
    "https://unpkg.com/three@0.153.0/examples/jsm/postprocessing/
    OutlinePass.js";

22  import { AfterimagePass } from
    "https://unpkg.com/three@0.153.0/examples/jsm/postprocessing/Afterim-
    agePass.js";

24  import { ShaderPass } from
    "https://unpkg.com/three@0.153.0/examples/jsm/postprocessing/
    ShaderPass.js";
```

```
25  import { SobelOperatorShader } from
    "https://unpkg.com/three@0.153.0/examples/jsm/shaders
    /SobelOperatorShader.js";

27  import { TexturePass } from
    "https://unpkg.com/three@0.153.0/examples/jsm/postprocessing/
    TexturePass.js";

28  import { SMAAPass } from
    "https://unpkg.com/three@0.153.0/examples/jsm/postprocessing/SMAAPass.
    js";

29  import { SSAARenderPass } from
    "https://unpkg.com/three@0.153.0/examples/jsm/postprocessing/
    SSAARenderPass.js";

30  import { TAARenderPass } from
    "https://unpkg.com/three@0.153.0/examples/jsm/postprocessing/
    TAARenderPass.js";

31  import { SSRPass } from
    "https://unpkg.com/three@0.153.0/examples/jsm/postprocessing/SSRPass.
    js";
```

You will find inside this chapter boilerplate, the respective code for each one.

After importing the right library for the effect you want to use, you need to initialize the effectComposer (do not forget to add the composer variable as global in the beginning of the code):

```
159  composer = new EffectComposer(renderer);
```

And add the renderPass, that will get the render target (render output) and turn it into a Post Processing pass:

```
160  const renderPass = new RenderPass(scene, camera);
```

The next step will depend on the filter you are going to use– each filter has specific parameters that you need to set up to make it look the way you want.

Halftone Pass

It adds a halftone effect to the image, which is this old-school print-like pattern (moiré). The color transitions are separated by RGB dots that blend according to the color gradient:

Figure 5.2: *Halftone pass*

```
163    halftonePass = new HalftonePass(window.innerWidth, window.innerHe-
       ight);
165    halftonePass.params = {
166       shape: 1, ///shape of dot
167       radius: 4, ///radius of the dot
168       rotateR: Math.PI / 12, ///rotation of the red dot
169       rotateG: (Math.PI / 12) * 3,  ///rotation of the green dot
170       rotateB: (Math.PI / 12) * 2, ///rotation of the blue dot
171       scatter: 0, ///scatters the R,G and B dots apart
172       greyscale: false, ///turn on/off grayscale mode
173       disable: false, ///enable/disable the effect
174    };
```

Add the `outputPass` to the stack (optional, but it increases the final render quality, especially the colors):

```
364  const outputPass = new OutputPass();
```

You will notice that, after adding the `outputPass`, the antialiasing of your scene has gone – this is because `outputPass` is not compatible with the regular Three.js renderer antialiasing, so you will need to add a Post Processing antialiasing pass to fix it, as we will explain in the next sections.

Finally, you need to build the Post Processing stack:

```
340  composer.addPass(renderPass);
341  composer.addPass(halftonePass);
363  composer.addPass(outputPass);
```

First add the render target pass (`renderPass`) then add the halftone effect over it and the `outputPass` at the end of the stack.

As you expected, we need to update it frame by frame in the animation loop:

```
375  composer.render(delta);
```

But one important detail— you need to remove the `renderer.render(scene, camera)` line from the animation loop, otherwise, it will render the original render target over the Post Processing stack and you will not see the final result. In the next section, we will talk about the other Post Processing effects.

LUT Pass

LUT stands for Look-up Tables, and it is basically a color remap table that alters the way the colors are shown on the screen. LUT is used especially in film post-production to give the film a special look that matches a specific art direction. You can find interesting LUT tables here: https://www.presetpro.com/ultimate-free-lut-lookup-table-collection-2020/:

Figure 5.3: LUTPass

To use `LUTPass`, you need first to import the LUT loader then load the LUT table you want to use and apply it:

```
5  import { LUTCubeLoader } from
   "https://unpkg.com/three@0.153.0/examples/jsm/loaders/LUTCubeLoader.js";
```

On the boilerplate of this lesson, we added different LUT tables so you can see different results on the screen:

```
181      lutMap = {
182          "Bourbon 64.CUBE": null,
183          "Chemical 168.CUBE": null,
184          "Clayton 33.CUBE": null,
185          "Cubicle 99.CUBE": null,
186          "Remy 24.CUBE": null,
187      };
```

After defining the LUT tables, we will run through this array of objects to load the LUT from the parameters defined on GUI.dat UI element:

```
189      Object.keys(lutMap).forEach((name, index) => {
190          new LUTCubeLoader().load(
191            "https://threejs.org/examples/luts/" + name,
192            function (result) {
193              lutMap[name] = result;
195              if (index >= Object.keys(lutMap).length - 1) {
196                setupGUI();
197              }
198            },
199          );
200      });
```

If you want to load a single LUT table file, just do it:

```
lutPass = new LUTPass();
new LUTCubeLoader().load(
    "https://threejs.org/examples/luts/Bourbon 64.CUBE",
    function (result) {
        lutPass.lut = result.texture3D;
    },
);
```

SAOPass

It stands for **Scalable Ambient Occlusion** and adds fake shadows to intersections, surfaces, creases, and holes that are close to each other:

Figure 5.4: *SAOPass/SSAOPass*

```
203    saoPass = new SAOPass(scene, camera);

205    saoPass.enabled = true;

207    saoPass.params = {
208    saoIntensity: 0.01, ///intensity of thee AO effect
209    saoScale: 5, ///scale of thee AO effect
210    saoKernelRadius: 20, ///increases the core of the AO effect
211    saoBlur: true,  ///blurs the AO result
212    saoBlurRadius: 50,   ///amount of AO blur
213    saoBlurStdDev: 5, ///AO blur spread
214    output: SAOPass.OUTPUT.Default
    // Default: original + AO // SAO: SAO only // Normal: only normals
215    }
```

SSAOPass

This stands for **Screen Space Ambient Occlusion**. Unlike Scalable Ambient Occlusion, it analyzes the scene depth buffer and computes the amount of occlusion from each pixel, so it depends only on the depth difference between the scene objects and not each object individually:

```
219    ssAOPass = new SSAOPass(scene, camera);

220    ssAOPass.enabled = true;
```

```
222  ssAOPass.kernelRadius = 8; // increase the core of the AO effect

223  ssAOPass.minDistance = 0.005;  // min distance to be considered
     when rendering AO

224  ssAOPass.maxDistance = 0.1; // max distance to be considered when
     rendering AO

224  ssAOPass.output = SSAOPass.OUTPUT.Default; // effect output
```

UnrealBloomPass

This adds a glow (bloom) effect over the scene. It calculates the color and position of the scene lights and highlights and adds a bloom layer over it. It does not consider the real light's properties, so do not expect accurate results with this kind of pass:

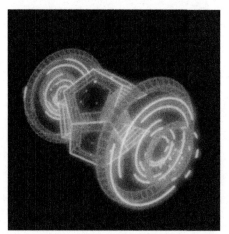

Figure 5.5: *UnrealBloomPass*

```
222  unrealBloomPass =

        new UnrealBloomPass(new THREE.Vector2(window.innerWidth, window.
        innerHeight),1.5, 0.4, 0.85);

224  unrealBloomPass.enabled = true;

225  unrealBloomPass.strength = 1.5;  ///strength of the bloom effect

226  unrealBloomPass.threshold = 0.85;  ///increases the effect threshold

227  unrealBloomPass.radius = 0.4;  /// increases the bloom radius
```

Depth of Field / BokehPass

In photography, the **bokeh** effect is an image distortion caused by camera lenses depending on the scene's Depth of Field. The amount of DoF depends on the camera lens, the lens aperture, and the camera focus, blurring the objects that are closer and/or farther from the camera:

Figure 5.6: *Depth of Field / BokehPass*

```
231  bokehPass = new BokehPass(scene, camera, {
232      focus: 1.0, /// moves the camera's focus point
233      aperture: 0.025,  /// increases the DoF distance
234      maxblur: 0.01,  /// limits the DoF blur
235      });
236  bokehPass.enabled = true;
```

DotScreenPass

This adds a black-and-white dot screen effect, similar to HalftonePass:

Figure 5.7: *DotScreenPass*

```
240   dotScreenPass = new DotScreenPass(
241       new THREE.Vector2(0, 0), ///center
242       0.5, ///angle
243       0.8, ///scale
244   );
245   dotScreenPass.enabled = false;
```

FilmPass

This adds a grain effect over the image to simulate old film grain and similar effects:

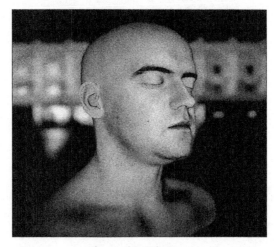

Figure 5.8: *FilmPass*

```
249   filmPass = new FilmPass();
250   filmPass.uniforms.grayscale.value = true;     ///turns grayscale mode
      on/off
251   filmPass.uniforms.nIntensity.value = 0.35;  ///increases grain in-
      tensity
252   filmPass.uniforms.sIntensity.value = 0.05;  ///increases vertical
      lines intensity
253   filmPass.enabled = true;
```

GlitchPass

Simulates a video/TV malfunction (glitch) over the image. It does not have too many useful parameters, but you can make it play continuously by adding the parameter goWild = true:

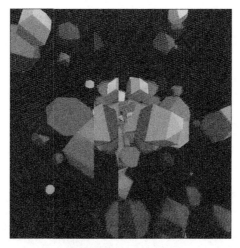

Figure 5.9: *GlitchPass*

```
257  glitchPass = new GlitchPass();
258  glitchPass.goWild = false;
259  glitchPass.enabled = true;
```

RenderPixelatedPass

This pixelates the scene to simulate a pixel art image. It can be used to simulate the look and feel of old-style isometric games:

Figure 5.10: *RenderPixelatedPass*

```
263  renderPixelatedPass = new RenderPixelatedPass(
     6, //pixel size
```

```
        scene, camera);
266   renderPixelatedPass.enabled = false;
267   renderPixelatedPass.normalEdgeStrength = 0.3;
268   renderPixelatedPass.normalEdgeStrength = 0.4;
```

OutlinePass

This adds an outline effect around your scene objects. It can be helpful for user interaction by adding this outline effect over selected objects:

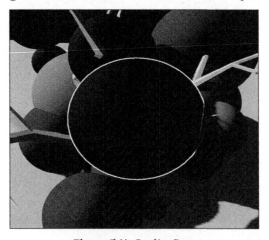

Figure 5.11: *OutlinePass*

```
272   outlinePass = new OutlinePass(
      new THREE.Vector2(window.innerWidth, window.innerHeight),
      scene,
      camera,
    );
277   outlinePass.enabled = true;
278   outlinePass.edgeStrength = 3;  /// strength of the outline
279   outlinePass.edgeGlow = 0; /// blur around the outline
280   outlinePass.edgeThickness = 1;  /// outline thickness
281   outlinePass.usePatternTexture = false;  /// turns on/off the inner
      pattern

    ///to enable the usePatternTexture option
285   const textureLoader = new THREE.TextureLoader();
```

286   textureLoader.load("../assets/images/tri_pattern.jpg", function
(texture) {

287   outlinePass.patternTexture = texture;

288   texture.wrapS = THREE.RepeatWrapping;

289   texture.wrapT = THREE.RepeatWrapping;

290   });

To make this effect work you need to add objects to the selectedObjects parameter. All the objects included inside selectedObjects parameter will present an outline effect:

    outlinePass.selectedObjects.push(object);

To remove the outline effect from some object, just remove it from selectedObjects parameter.

AfterimagePass

This adds a *ghost* image effect over your rendered scene. It can be used for interesting motion graphics effects on cut scenes and 3D UI effects:

Figure 5.12: *AfterimagePass*

293   afterimagePass = new AfterimagePass();

294   afterimagePass.uniforms.damp.value = 0.96; /// the amount of "ghostiness"

295   afterimagePass.enabled = true;

ShaderPass

This is not a filter of effect, but is used to build custom shaders using GLSL language. First of all, you need to import it to the scene:

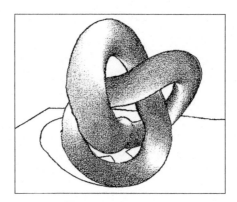

Figure 5.13: *ShaderPass*

```
24  import { ShaderPass } from
    "https://unpkg.com/three@0.153.0/examples/jsm/postprocessing/Shader-
    Pass.js";
```

This effect just transforms a GLSL shader into a Post Processing pass, so you will need a shader to do the effect you want. We are using a Sobel shader, which has a kind of edge detection algorithm that is applied over the rendered image:

```
25  import { SobelOperatorShader } from
26  "https://unpkg.com/three@0.153.0/examples/jsm/shaders/SobelOperator-
    Shader.js";
```

Then, add the imported shader to the `ShaderPass`:

```
299  sobelOperatorShader = new ShaderPass(SobelOperatorShader);
```

Set up the shader with the corresponding parameters (that will vary depending on the shader you are using). In this case, Sobel shader only accepts the rendered window size:

```
301  sobelOperatorShader.enabled = true;
       window.innerWidth * window.devicePixelRatio;
302  sobelOperatorShader.uniforms["resolution"].value.x =
       window.innerWidth * window.devicePixelRatio;
304  sobelOperatorShader.uniforms["resolution"].value.y =
       window.innerHeight * window.devicePixelRatio;
```

And finally, add it to the Post Processing stack:

```
364  composer.addPass(sobelOperatorShader);
```

You can experiment with different shaders from https://www.shadertoy.com, or you can even create your own GLSL shaders! Just remember you need to add the shader to the `ShaderPass` and add the shader parameters.

TexturePass

It adds an image texture (do not be confused with Three.js material's textures!) over the render target. The texture can be combined with the render target using blending modes and opacity values:

Figure 5.14: *TexturePass*

```
308   texturePass = new TexturePass();
309   texturePass.enabled = true;

311   textureLoader.load(
312       "../assets/images/background_image_1.jpg",
313       function (texture) {
314           texturePass.map = texture;
315       },
316   );

318   texturePass.opacity = 0.5;
319   texturePass.blending = 1;
```

Accepted blending values: `NormalBlending`: 1, `AdditiveBlending`: 2, `SubtractiveBlending`: 3, `MultiplyBlending`: 4.

SMAAPass/SSAARenderPass/ TAARenderPass

You already know what anti-alias is– a computer graphics technique that removes the jagged edges around rendered 3D objects. However, several different AA algorithms use different approaches to improve the render output quality. Inside the Three.js Post Processing stack you can find these:

- **SMAA** stands for **Subpixel Morphological Anti-Aliasing**: It results in high-quality anti-alias without being very heavy for the GPU. It blends the pixels on its borders, depending on the pixel pattern and position. It is the best cost x benefit AA algorithm.

- **SSAA** stands for **Supersampling Anti-Aliasing**: It is the most heavyweight anti-alias algorithm, but is the one that offers the highest quality of the available Three.js AA algorithms. It renders the image at a higher resolution and downsamples the image to the original resolution, resulting in a high-quality antialiased result.

- **TAA: Temporal Anti-Alias**: It combines information from past frames and the current frame to remove the image artifacts in the current frame. It works better on animated scenes:

Figure 5.15: SMAAPass/SSAARenderPass/TAARenderPass

SMAA:

```
329    sMAAPass = new SMAAPass(
330        window.innerWidth * renderer.getPixelRatio(),
331        window.innerHeight * renderer.getPixelRatio(),
332    );
333    sMAAPass.enabled = true;
```

SSAA:

```
337    sSAARenderPass = new SSAARenderPass(scene, camera);
339    sSAARenderPass.enabled = true;
340    sSAARenderPass.sampleLevel = 2 /// amount of supersampling
```

TAA:

```
343   tAARenderPass = new TAARenderPass(scene, camera);

345   tAARenderPass.enabled = true;

346   tAARenderPass.sampleLevel = 2;   /// amount of frames
```

Be aware that all the antialiasing effects only work on the OutputPass, so if it is disabled you will not be able to see any result. And, of course, if OutputPass is disabled you will depend on the new THREE.WebGLRenderer({ antialias: true }) setting to enable the anti-alias on your scene.

SSRPass

It adds **Screen Space Reflections** to your scene, which is a fake approach to calculate reflections without consuming too much GPU power on overcomplicated raytracing algorithms. It can be used to add more realism to the scene by calculating the natural reflections of non-reflective objects. It is much less expensive for the GPU than raytracing algorithms, but it is still very heavy for real-time rendering:

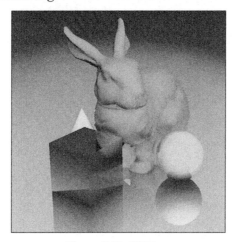

Figure 5.16: SSRPass

```
349   const groundReflector = null;

350   sSRPass = new SSRPass({

351       renderer,

352       scene,

353       camera,

354       width: innerWidth,
```

```
355        height: innerHeight,
356        groundReflector: groundReflector ? groundReflector : null,
357        selects: groundReflector ? selects : null,
358    });
360    sSRPass.enabled = true;
```

The groundReflector and selects parameters are used to create a fake floor that will reflect the objects that are over it.

MaskPass/ClearMaskPass/ClearPass

You can find the code of this and the next sections in the folder: https://github. com/OrangeAVA/Creative-Technology-with-Three.js/tree/main/chapter05/ section01b_mask

These filters are used to mask parts of one image (or render target) with another image (or render target). You can combine several different layers or simply use one image to mask parts of your scene:

Figure 5.17: *MaskPass/ClearMaskPass/ClearPass*

First of all, import the Mask effects:

```
10  import { MaskPass, ClearMaskPass } from
    "https://unpkg.com/three@0.153.0/examples/jsm/postprocessing/MaskPass.
    js";
11  import { ClearPass } from
    "https://unpkg.com/three@0.153.0/examples/jsm/postprocessing/Clear-
    Pass.js";
12  import { TexturePass } from
    "https://unpkg.com/three@0.153.0/examples/jsm/postprocessing/Texture-
    Pass.js";
```

The scene setup is a bit different from the other examples. You need to add a
WebGLRenderTarget right after adding the WebGLRenderer:

```
44    renderTarget = new THREE.WebGLRenderTarget(
45        window.innerWidth,
46        window.innerHeight,
47        { stencilBuffer: true },
48    );
```

In this example, we are using three composition layers, so we need to add three
different scenes and create the clearPass and ClearMaskPass passes:

```
49    scene1 = new THREE.Scene();
50    scene2 = new THREE.Scene();
51    scene3 = new THREE.Scene();


94    clearPass = new ClearPass();
95    clearMaskPass = new ClearMaskPass();
```

We will add the objects to different scenes so you can see the mask effect on
each one, and the final composition in the end. You can add different cameras
to it as well, but we want to simplify the process and show the same perspective
but with different objects.

```
70    scene1.add(plane);
77    scene2.add(cube);
83    scene3.add(sphere);
90    scene1.add(torus);


97    maskPass1 = new MaskPass(scene1, camera);
98    maskPass2 = new MaskPass(scene2, camera);
99    maskPass3 = new MaskPass(scene3, camera);
```

Now it is time to load the texture images that will be masked by the mask passes:

```
101   const texture1 = new THREE.TextureLoader().load(
102       "../assets/images/background_image_1.jpg",
103   );
104   texture1.colorSpace = THREE.SRGBColorSpace;
105   texture1.minFilter = THREE.LinearFilter;
```

```
107    const texture2 = new THREE.TextureLoader().load(
108        "../assets/images/background_image_2.jpg",
109    );
110    texture2.colorSpace = THREE.SRGBColorSpace;


112    const texture3 = new THREE.TextureLoader().load(
113        "../assets/images/background_image_3.jpg",
114    );
115    texture3.colorSpace = THREE.SRGBColorSpace;
```

And add the loaded texture to the corresponding texture passes:

```
117    texturePass1 = new TexturePass(texture1);
118    texturePass2 = new TexturePass(texture2);
119    texturePass3 = new TexturePass(texture3);
```

Now it is time to build the Post Processing stack, and the passes order is very important— it will be crucial to show the results the way you want to show them on the screen. In the following lines, we will explain each pass:

```
121    composer = new EffectComposer(renderer, renderTarget);
122    composer.addPass(clearPass); //clear screen
123    composer.addPass(maskPass1); //render the mask of texturePass1
124    composer.addPass(texturePass1); //render texturePass1
125    composer.addPass(maskPass2); //render the mask of texturePass2
126    composer.addPass(texturePass2); //render texturePass2
127    composer.addPass(maskPass3); //render the mask of texturePass3
128    composer.addPass(texturePass3); //render texturePass3
129    composer.addPass(clearMaskPass); //clear the masks and prepare for
       the next frame
```

The final pass needs to be the OutputPass, otherwise the mask passes will not work:

```
132    const outputPass = new OutputPass();
133    composer.addPass(outputPass);
```

On this lesson's boilerplate, you will be able to turn on/off the passes individually to see how they work and copy the example to your projects.

PMNDRS Post Processing library

We focused on the default Three.js Post Processing effects in this chapter, but there is an amazing library that makes all the Post Processing work easier, the pmndrs Post Processing library. It gathers all Three.js Post Processing effects in one single library. Also, `pmndrs` effects are more optimized and more organized than the original Three.js effects:

```
import { BloomEffect, EffectComposer, EffectPass, RenderPass } from "post-processing";
```

```
const composer = new EffectComposer(renderer);

composer.addPass(new RenderPass(scene, camera));

composer.addPass(new EffectPass(camera, new BloomEffect()));
```

You can find more details about this library here: https://github.com/pmndrs/postprocessing.

Conclusion

We finally have everything in our hands to deliver a high-quality 3D scene rendered in real-time on your desktop or mobile browser. The Post Processing technique is a very good way to increase the scene realism by adding special effects to your scene. Try to mix the techniques taught in the last three chapters to build realistic 3D scenes, but be careful with the GPU load.

In the next chapter, we will talk about webAR and webVR concepts and will introduce one of the most used 3D frameworks, Aframe.

Points to Remember

- The concept of Post Processing is very common in CGI and you can find it in 3D and composition software, and on other real-time 3D engines such as Unity and Unreal Engine.

- Post Processing passes add special effects layers over the rendered image, such as bloom, ambient occlusion, pixelization, and so on, but they are used to add embellishment passes such as anti-alias.

- You literally stack the Post Processing passes to get to the final result. The final result will depend on the order of the passes, and not all effects will consider the previous passes, so plan your passes order carefully.

- The `OutputPass` is not mandatory for several effects, but it increases the final render quality depending on the affects you are using on the previous passes, performing a sRGB color space conversion.

- For mask and anti-alias passes, the `OutputPass` is mandatory otherwise you will not be able to see the final result on your screen.

- Use `Dat.gui` to build a temporary UI and debug elements to your scenes. You can use it to present a previsualization of your project and allow your client to tweak the scene parameters and fine-tune the final result.

- Be gentle when building your Post Processing stack. Try not to use more than 3 or 4 effects over the same render target. Also, some effects are especially heavy for the GPU, such as `UnrealBloolPass` and some antialiasing algorithms.

- Use `ShaderPass` to build your effects. But you need to learn GLSL first (or tweak the examples from `ShaderToy`)!

- Anti-alias effects are rendered only over `OutputPass`, so if your `OutputPass` is disabled, you will rely only on Three.js renderer antialiasing.

- Mask passes are a bit difficult to understand, but they are very logical. Simply try to think about Photoshop layers and effects, and how the order of the layers affects the final result.

- Be careful when using Post Effects on mobile devices. Even the most powerful mobile GPU is not comparable to regular desktop GPUs.

Multiple Choice Questions

1. Post Processing is:

   a. A way to increase the rendered scene quality

   b. A way to fix the scene's imperfections

   c. A way to add special effects to the scene

   d. All of the alternatives above

2. About OutputPass:

   a. Is mandatory for any Post Processing stack

   b. Is mandatory for anti-alias and mask passes

   c. Is fully optional and can be used just to improve the scene quality

   d. Is mandatory only for PixelatedPass and GlitchPass

3. Antialiasing passes are:

   a. A way to improve the default Three.js render anti-alias

   b. Algorithms to improve and fix the scene colors

   c. Applied to the scene before Three.js render

   d. Different antialiasing algorithms are applied only on OutputPass

4. Why is it not a good idea to add more than four Post Processing passes into a scene?

   a. Post Processing passes are very heavy for the GPU to process

   b. They use a raytracing algorithm to calculate the effects

   c. We do not need to bother about it, our GPU will handle it

   d. If used with caution, we can use more than four Post Processing passes

5. Dat.gui is:

   a. A special class that comes with Three.js to build complex interfaces

   b. A third-party javascript library to render data on the screen

   c. A third-party javascript GUI library used to render simple UI elements

   d. An API to load external data from other websites

Answers

1. d
2. b
3. d
4. a or d
5. c

Questions

1. Why is Post Processing so powerful but so heavy for the GPU?

2. Why is the passes' order so important for the final result?

3. Which other Post Processing effects would you like to see that are not available on Three.js?

4. Could you explain how `ShaderPass` communicates with an external GLSL shader?

5. What are the pros and cons of using an ambient occlusion pass? And when using an ambient occlusion texture?

6. Why is `OutputPass` not mandatory to all Post Processing effects?

7. Why should you remove the `renderer.render(scene, camera)` line from the animation loop? What happens if you keep this line in the code?

8. Why does the screen resolution impact the Post Processing render performance? How to optimize it?

9. Thinking about the `UnrealBloomPass`, what is your approach to adding the bloom/glow effect to some objects only?

10. Why should you be careful when using Post Processing on mobile-targeted projects?

Key Terms

- **Bloom/Glow:** Special effect that adds a glow layer over scene objects highlights and lighting.
- **Screen Space Reflections**: Post processing technique that adds subtle reflections to a 3D scene using the scene depth and color buffer to calculate reflections.
- **Bokeh:** In photography, bokeh is the blur and dots effect caused by camera lenses depending on the scene's Depth of Field.
- **Film Grain:** In photography, film grain is the optical effect seen on photographic film due to the presence of metallic silver particles. In digital photography and filmmaking, we add a film grain effect to give the image a style of old-school movies and photos.
- **Glitch:** We call a glitch any video or TV malfunction effect over the rendered image.
- **Pixelated:** In computer graphics, a pixel is the smallest image component on a video screen. In the early times of CGI, the screen resolution was so low that you could see the pixels, so a pixelated effect uses this approach (enlarging the pixels without enlarging the image) to give this old-style game look.
- **Shader:** A code used to affect the appearance of 3D and 2D objects, affecting how the vertices, lights, reflections, colors, and more appear depending on the scene and materials setup. On Three.js we use GLSL (C++) language to write special shaders that will affect the appearance of the scene or its objects.

Chapter 6

Introduction to WebAR and WebVR

Introduction

We discussed Three.js in the previous chapters and we scratched the surface of making it work on your mobile phone. Three.js can do amazing things on your phone or even on your VR headset using webAR and webVR workflows. But the truth is that Three.js itself is not too optimized for running on mobile and VR devices. You can perform, of course, all functions that we are going to discuss in this chapter using pure Three.js, but it will require much more work. This is why we– and a big part of the webAR/webVR community– decided to embrace A-Frame as the main framework to build AR and VR experiences for the web. We will now introduce the concepts of webAR and webVR.

Structure

In this chapter, we will discuss the following topics:

- Understanding Virtual Reality
- Understanding Augmented Reality
- Importance of the Web for AR and VR
- Introduction to A-Frame
- A-Frame installation and Setup
- A-Frame Basics

Understanding Virtual Reality

First of all, let us define some useful terms that will follow us in this and the next few chapters.

VR stands for **Virtual Reality** and is a simulated 3D environment that overrides 100% of the user's field of view, immersing the user into a full virtual experience. To achieve this, we use a VR headset, an equipment that is attached to the user's head and covers 100% of the user's sight. It is generally composed of one high-definition LCD (or LED) screen, divided into two halves—one for each eye:

Figure 6.1: *VR Headset components (image originally published on https://www.makery.info)*

Right in front of the LCD panel, we find a pair of Fresnel lenses that force our eyes to focus on a more distant point, otherwise, we would struggle to focus the sight on something so close to our eyes. The screen and the lenses are the most recognizable parts of a VR headset, but taking a deeper look at the equipment electronics, we can find other interesting components:

- **Accelerometer**: Used to calculate the user's head position change in three dimensions.

- **Gyroscope**: Used to detect the user's head orientation and the angular acceleration, in three dimensions.

- **Microphone**: Used, of course, to capture the user's voice for VR communication or voice-activated commands.

- **Speakers**: Some VR headsets have built-in speakers to play the VR experience sound effects, background music, and more. Others have a headphone input jack where you can plug an external headphone.

- **Eye tracking sensor**: Not so common on consumer-level VR headsets, it is used for capturing the user's eye movement and his point of gaze to control scene objects or interact with the user interface.

- **Camera**: Used to capture the real point of view of the user (passthrough) and, depending on the VR headset (such as Meta Quest), to estimate the user position (inside-out tracking) in the real world.

- **IR sensors**: On some types of equipment (such as HTC Vive) they communicate with external trackers to estimate the VR headset position (outside-in tracking).

- **Hand controllers**: A different kind of game control used to get the user input, control the user interface, and so on. It is adapted for VR use since it needs to be very lightweight and provide user control for both hands. They generally have straps to attach to the user's wrist and avoid accidents.

The principle of a VR headset is quite simple− the accelerometer and the gyroscope read the headset orientation (rotation in three axes) and send the data to the headset hardware, which will decompose it and update the orientation of the virtual camera on a 3D space. The result− the user has a real feeling that what he/she is seeing in 3D corresponds to their head movement. This is why VR is so immersive. More sophisticated systems can read the headset translation in three dimensions, but we will talk more about it soon.

The first VR headsets were built at the end of the 80s for research and military use. At that time the 3D technology was very rudimentary, with very poor hardware and software resources even on desktop computers, so the researchers had to connect the VR headsets to powerful 3D workstations to have the 3D scene rendered in real-time. Apart from that, the LCD technology was very limited, the same for accelerometers and gyroscope sensors, so it was really hard to think about VR before the 90s:

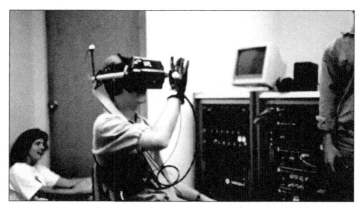

Figure 6.2: *First experiments with VR in the 80s (image published on https://virtualspeech.com)*

In the 90s we could see some consumer products that have been called VR, but they were far removed from what VR really is− SEGA VR-1 (for arcades) and Nintendo Virtual Boy (a Game Boy accessory). Only at the end of the 90s we could see some improvements in real-time 3D technology, with good desktop

GPU cards and game consoles capable of rendering real-time 3D graphics, such as Nintendo 64, Sega Dreamcast, and, of course, PlayStation:

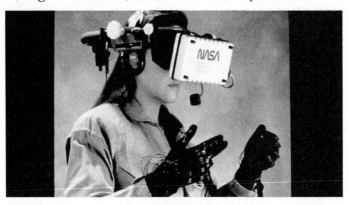

Figure 6.3: *Experimental VR headset from NASA to simulate spatial environments (image published on https://virtualspeech.com)*

But only in 2010, we could see the first real attempt at a real VR headset – the Oculus Rift prototype. The equipment took two years of development and a very successful Kickstarter campaign to get to a decent version of Oculus Rift: the DK1 and DK2 development versions and finally the first consumer version– the Oculus Rift CV1. After that, Facebook (now Meta) bought Oculus, HTC launched HTC Vive and some other companies launched their respective VR headsets. Even Google played around with VR with their (polemic) Google Cardboard.

By the way, we can use the Google Cardboard (and their cousins Samsung GearVR and other no-brand plastic VR headsets) to explain an important VR concept– 3-DoF and 6-DoF.

DoF stands for **Degrees of Freedom**. So, 3-DoF has three degrees of freedom, and 6-DoF has six degrees of freedom. But what is it about? When we say DoF we mean the directions in which the user can translate his position in a 3D space. 3-DoF talks about only rotational angles (pitch, yaw, and roll) in three dimensions, so the VR headset can read your head rotation in the three axes: x, y, and z, but not the head's translation. It is not capable of telling if you are moving up, down, left, right, forward, or backward. It is a standalone position.

On the other hand, 6-DoF talks about six degrees of freedom– the rotational angles of the 3-DoF (pitch, yaw, and roll) and the translation movement in the three axes x, y, and z. And it makes ALL the difference. With 6-DoF, the VR headset can tell if you are moving in any direction, apart from your head orientation, so you can avoid obstacles, get closer to objects, and even interact with them. It is a real immersion in VR.

The first VR headsets (and the simpler headsets like Google Cardboard and Samsung GearVR) were 3-DoF based, resulting in much simpler VR experiences: you are in a static position and interact with the 3D environment that is around you. If you stand up and move left or right, it will not result in any change in the 3D space. This limitation was sorted out when the researchers developed a way to read the headset position in 3D space– some prototypes in the 90s used cables for it, but the first decent VR headsets had infrared sensors that could read the headset position in three dimensions. Oculus Rift CV1 and HTC Vive had two sensors (or more), which should be positioned in specific places of the room and were used to triangulate the headset position and present a precise user's position tracking. This is called **outside-in tracking** and is still used on more precise VR systems and other kinds of equipment that need to read the user's position with more accuracy.

With Oculus Quest (Meta Quest now), Meta developed a new tracking system– the **inside-out tracking**. With cameras positioned on the VR headset surface and the motion sensors, the hardware is capable of estimating the user's position using **computer vision** algorithms. It is not as precise as the IR sensors available on outside-in tracking devices, but it is good enough for playing games and consumer applications. Also, it does not require annoying IR sensors placed in the room, with meters of cables around the user.

Another important concept regarding VR is **latency.** Latency is the time between the moment when the user changes his position and orientation and the moment it is updated in the 3D space. A system with high latency will take longer to update the 3D scene on the VR headset display, causing a discomfort called **motion-sickness**. High latency confuses the user's brain because the real user's position does not correspond to the image he/she is seeing, causing some dizziness and sickness in some users. It is known that a latency of more than 13 milliseconds (on 90Hz displays) could cause motion sickness in the users. Other factors that can cause motion-sickness are as follows:

- Displays with low screen refresh rates.
- 3-DoF experiences where the user is static but the environment changes very fast, just like on flight simulators and racing games.
- Slow 3D engines (or very heavy VR experiences) that cannot deliver a high frame rate, causing a *software latency*.

Nowadays, the available VR headsets are great in hardware and software, and the consumer-level headsets are available at a decent price so a general audience can afford to have one. Meta Quest 3 pricing is comparable to Xbox or PlayStation console prices. Apple has just launched their VR headset (Apple Vision Pro), with amazing hardware and software and a very promising VR operating system, but it is still very expensive and out of reach of the regular consumer.

Even though VR is not (yet) mainstream, it is a new amazing interactive platform that is evolving a lot. Apart from the failed attempts of Meta to create a private Metaverse!

What is the tech stack to develop VR applications? You can choose your path:

- Using Unity (C++) or Unreal Engine (Blueprint or C#) to develop and compile the application for VR stores or standalone (executables) apps for PC and Macs. It is the most common way to develop and deliver VR apps. Unity and Unreal Engine are capable of high-end 3D graphics, with sophisticated visual effects and other amazing features.

- Using native platforms (such as Java/Kotlin for Android and Swift/Objective-C for iOS) to build and compile standalone applications.

- Using a web stack (HTML, CSS, and JavaScript, and of course, Three.js) to develop webVR applications. It is the most simple and straightforward alternative– all the 3D scenes you created in this book can be easily ported to a VR environment and played on a VR headset. Even if the graphics are not so sophisticated when compared with Unity or Unreal Engine VR apps, you can create a very good webVR application that runs without the need to buy or download a regular VR app.

Understanding Augmented Reality

If Virtual Reality is all about immersing the user into an alternate, 3D-rendered, reality, Augmented Reality is all about mixing up reality with a virtual world – or as the name says – augmenting it. So, an AR application needs to use a camera (on mobile devices) or a transparent display + projection (on devices like Microsoft Hololens) to render a 3D scene over the real world.

The first AR applications came from military equipment back in the 70s, especially jet fighter helmets with **HUD (Head-Up Display)** that render, over the real world, visual aids and useful information to help pilots control the plane and seek/destroy military targets:

Figure 6.4: *Jet fighter helmet with digital HUD image from*
https://www.radiantvisionsystems.com

The first commercial AR applications were launched only around 2010 as virtual dressing rooms and virtual try-ons retail applications. After some years, medical and industrial AR tools started to be built on very specific applications, but only in 2016, AR started to own the spotlight with the launch of **Niantic's Pokémon GO**, an AR game that instantly hit millions of downloads and players. In this game, players should capture Pokemons in the real-world environment, making millions of people wander around the cities to capture virtual pets. This was the first time that the term Augmented Reality appeared in the headlines of hundreds of articles over the web, in newspapers, and in magazines.

From this point on, big players in hardware and software started to pay more attention to AR and started to launch specific tools for this new technology. In 2016, Microsoft launched their first version of the Hololens AR headset, and in 2017 Apple launched ARKit, an AR API that came embedded in iOS 11 and offered advanced AR resources for native iOS Apps. In 2018, Google launched ARCore, their own AR API integrated with Android OS. Yet in 2018, Unity launched their AR Foundation, a proprietary AR API built on top of ARKit and ARCode, giving the Unity developers the possibility to build native AR apps for iOS and Android using a single source code.

Even with Microsoft Hololens being a very powerful and amazing AR headset, their price and poor software resources confined it to a very specific niche. The thing that did not happen on mobile AR applications— with plenty of software resources and the mobile phone market as an audience, the AR apps started to be more and more present in the mobile app stores. The native AR applications had amazing features, such as:

- **Horizontal and vertical plane detection/world tracking**: A feature that allows the user to detect horizontal planes (such as floors and tables) or vertical planes (such as walls and picture frames) to place virtual objects on it and update the object position when the camera moves, even if the object is not visible to the camera:

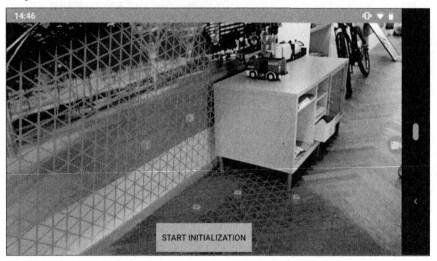

Figure 6.5: Horizontal and vertical plane detection – https://www.wikitude.com

- **Face tracking**: Detects facial features and allows the user to place 3D objects over them. For example, you can detect the user's nose and attach a fake nose to it or attach a pair of sunglasses over the user's face. You can also detect face movements such as eye blinks or mouth openness to trigger actions in the AR space:

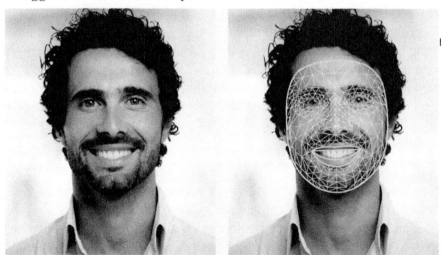

Figure 6.6: Face tracking and facial landmarks detection – image from Google

- **Hand tracking**: Detects hands and fingers, allowing users to interact with virtual objects or run commands from hand gestures.

- **Body tracking**: Detects body parts and creates a virtual skeleton that can be applied to 3D avatars and other 3D objects. It is capable of detecting specific body gestures and reacting to them:

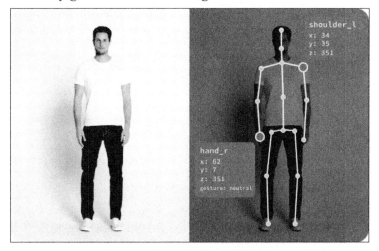

Figure 6.7: *Body tracking –image from https://www.deepar.ai*

- **Geotracking**: Detects the user's real-world location, allowing developers to attach virtual objects to real landmarks that can be shared with other users.

- **Image tracking**: Detects in the real world a previously registered image (image marker) and places virtual objects over it, considering its real-time position and perspective:

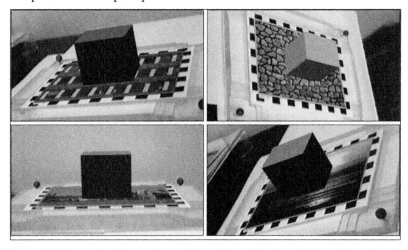

Figure 6.8: *Image tracking – image from https://www.vision.rwth-aachen.de*

- **VPS (visual positioning system)**: Detects previously scanned 3D objects and allows the user to place objects into it.

- **Lighting estimation**: Estimates the real-world lighting, allowing developers to use this information to set up and improve virtual scene lighting.

- **Object recognition**: Recognizes real-world objects based on their category, color, and more. It is very useful for learning AR applications.

- **Scene depth**: Detects the scene depth, resulting in a 2D grayscale depth map to enable environmental awareness and natural interaction with a virtual scene:

Figure 6.9: *Depth detection – image from https://engineering.monstar-lab.com*

- **Object occlusion**: Detects first-plane objects in the real scene and occludes virtual objects that appear behind them:

Figure 6.10: *AR Object Occlusion – image from https://grail.cs.washington.edu*

Even with such amazing resources, the native AR apps are stuck on a very simple fact– sometimes it is hard to convince the user to download a mobile app just to interact with an AR experience. We call it **app friction**. In physics, friction is a resistance that one surface suffers when moving over another surface. In our case, it has pretty much the same meaning– picture yourself watching a nice TV commercial or a newspaper advertisement talking about a very interesting

AR app. However, to use it, you need to capture a QR Code (or even worse, type the URL or look for it in the App Store), download it (which takes some time), then sign in to the app, and, finally, to be able to interact with the AR experience that you have seen 20 minutes ago. You will not do it unless the app has more interesting (and useful) features that will be worth keeping it installed on your mobile phone.

Importance of the Web for AR and VR

All these cases illustrate the **friction** problem– there is a huge resistance from the general audience to download a mobile app just to play around with an AR experience. So, the enthusiastic clients who were so excited about Augmented Reality started to get frustrated about the new technology. You could build interesting AR experiences to play inside already-installed apps (such as Snapchat, Facebook, Instagram, and TikTok) or mobile apps that have more than just a quick and simple AR experience, such as AR games and AR tools.

This friction problem on AR has been partially resolved by webAR, that is, AR tools built to run on mobile browsers, as simple websites that could run AR content using, of course, web 3D technology like webGL and Three.js. Even though the webAR apps are not so visually sophisticated or do not have the same AR resources as the native AR apps, webAR solved the friction problem giving the general audience the possibility to load AR experiences (almost) instantly and interact with it in (almost) the same way as in the native AR apps.

NOTE: The friction problem is even worse on VR– you need to get your VR headset, turn it on (if it has enough battery charge, of course), navigate through VR menus, find the VR app, download it, and so on. This (and the headset costs, apart from other reasons) explains why AR became much more popular than VR, despite VR being so rich and immersive.

To make the life of VR and AR developers and hardware manufacturers a bit less painful, the World Wide Web Consortium (W3C– the guys that created all the standards and guidelines of web development) created the WebXR Device API, a web protocol that gathers all input and output capabilities of XR (Extended Reality) devices– VR and AR:

- AR and VR headsets with opaque (Meta Quest, HTC Vive) or transparent (Hololens) displays.
- Mobile devices with positional tracking (all mobile phones and tablets with AR capabilities).

- Fixed displays with head tracking capabilities (desktop/laptop applications that have head tracking features).

The webXR API makes all the interaction with cameras, microphones, sensors, head tracking devices, pointing devices, and others easier, instead of building it from scratch on every new application. That sounds great, isn't it? Of course, it does, but not in the case of Apple. The iOS Safari browser lacks WebXR support, which means that any web browser that needs to run on iOS will not be able to run webXR.

This impacts other things – simple and crucial AR features, such as image tracking or surface tracking can't just work natively on iOS browsers, unlike Android Apps that can use Android AR features through native web browsers. This seriously delays all webAR innovation on mobile phones. The only way, for now, to use native AR resources on iOS web browsers is Apple's Quick Look, which has interesting features but has almost no integration with web pages and web resources.

To solve this issue, companies such as 8th Wall (recently bought by Niantic) developed a surface tracking software alternative based on a computer vision algorithm called **SLAM– Simultaneous Localization and Mapping**, a way to detect what the phone's camera is seeing. It integrates perspective, depth, horizontal, and vertical surfaces with an AR scene. 8th Wall and other companies such as Blippar, Zappar, and MyWebAR, among others, created software-based image tracking algorithms that mimic the native AR image tracking algorithm. In 2022, Google launched Mediapipe API– a series of computer vision features that allow developers to track facial landmarks, detect 3D objects, interact with voice, and other cool features. So, nothing is lost for webXR, we still have in our hands some interesting features that allow us to create immersive experiences using web resources, and it created a huge market demand for creative developers.

Talking about development resources, this is the stack for AR development:

- Native apps can be built by using Unity and Unreal Engine, or native languages such as Objective-C/Swift for iOS and Java/Kotlin for Android.
- WebAR apps can be built using a regular web stack: HTML, CSS, and JavaScript + a web 3D engine such as Three.js (and/or their frameworks A-Frame/React Three Fiber), Babylon, and PlayCanvas.
- To build webAR apps with more sophisticated AR resources, you can use 8th Wall for surface, image, and face tracking, or Blippar, Zappar, and others for image and face tracking.

In the next section, we will introduce you to A-Frame, a Three.js framework that has been adopted from the webAR community as one of the main webAR development tools.

Introduction to A-Frame

First of all, why has A-Frame become one of the main webVR/webAR development tools? It is hard to tell. A-Frame was launched in 2015 as an easy-to-use framework for those who do not have too much familiarity with pure JavaScript, Three.js, and webGL. With A-Frame, you can just work with HTML tags, but instead of <div>, <img> or <p> tags, you can use <a-sphere>, <a-box>, <a-plane>, among others. You can build an entire 3D scene just using A-Frame tags, without writing one line of JavaScript or Three.js code, but of course, you will be quite limited. This is why we recommend, first of all, a good knowledge of JavaScript and Three.js.

A-Frame was created with a focus on webVR, but little by little it has been adopted by the webAR community, and here lies one of the biggest advantages of this framework – it has pre-built elements and attributes that allow you to interact with XR input and output devices, such as cameras, motion sensors, VR controls, headsets, and so on without the need of writing any control class or function. It is compatible seamlessly with HTC Vive, Meta Quest, Windows Mixed Reality, mobile phones, and tablets.

Another big advantage of A-Frame is its **scene inspector**. By pressing CTRL-ALT-I, you can open the A-Frame inspector and see, graphically, the 3D scene, navigate through the objects, and even change its properties to see the result in real-time. It is a very powerful feature, especially when you are building complex scenes with dozens of objects and interactions.

This is what an A-Frame scene looks like:

```
<!doctype html>
<html>
  <head>
    <title>Chapter 6 - A-Frame boilerplate</title>
    <meta charset="utf-8" />
    <meta name="viewport" content="width=device-width, initial-scale=1.0,
          maximum-scale=1.0, user-scalable=no, viewport-fit=cover"/>
    <link rel="stylesheet" type="text/css" href="styles.css" media="all" />
```

```
  <script src="https://unpkg.com/A-Frame@1.4.2/dist/A-Frame-master.
  js"></script>
  <script type="module" src="js/main.js"></script>
</head>


<body style="touch-action: none">


  <a-scene>
    <a-box position="-1 0.5 -3" rotation="0 45 0" color="#4CC3D9">
    </a-box>
    <a-sphere position="0 1.25 -5" radius="1.25" color="#EF2D5E">
    </a-sphere>
    <a-cylinder position="1 0.75 -3" radius="0.5" height="1.5"
        color="#FFC65D"></a-cylinder>
    <a-plane position="0 0 -4" rotation="-90 0 0" width="4" height="4"
        color="#7BC8A4"></a-plane>
    <a-sky color="#ECECEC"></a-sky>
  </a-scene>


</body>
</html>
```

A-Frame considers that everything that comes inside the <a-scene> tag is an A-Frame element, so it is very easy to build scenes using it. Also, you can interact with A-Frame elements using pure JavaScript commands, change their properties, or even create A-Frame elements dynamically. Or, if you want more control, you can build the main scene using A-Frame and Three.js methods to work with the 3D elements in-depth.

A-Frame Installation and Setup

As Three.js, you can install A-Frame in several ways. You can simply import the framework into your code:

```
<script src="https://unpkg.com/A-Frame@1.4.2/dist/A-Frame-master.js"></
script>
```

```
<script src="https://unpkg.com/A-Frame-extras@7.1.0/dist/A-Frame-extras.
min.js"></script>
```

The second line (A-Frame Extras) loads some important features to use along with A-Frame, such as animation mixer and third-party controls, among others.

Alternatively, you can add it using NPM this way:

```
npm install --save aframe@1.4.2
npm install --save aframe-extras@7.1.0
```

Once it is added to your code, it is time to start developing.

A-Frame Basics

To explore all A-Frame possibilities we would need a full book for it because this framework is very rich, but we will try to resume this in the next chapters along with the main possibilities of it.

First of all, let us explain the A-Frame scene structure. As we said earlier, everything happens inside the <a-scene> tag. You can check the full code here:

https://github.com/OrangeAVA/Creative-Technology-with-Three.js/tree/main/chapter06/aframe_boilerplate

Scene Structure

By adding any A-Frame element inside the `<a-scene>` tag, you will be able to see something happening on your scene. But this tag controls all the scene settings. To add more properties to the scene, you just need to add the parameters inside the `<  >` in your code, as follows:

```
<a-scene
  renderer="antialias: true;
      colorManagement: true;
      sortObjects: true;
      physicallyCorrectLights: true;
      maxCanvasWidth: 1280;
      maxCanvasHeight: 1280;"
  fog="type: linear; color: #AAA"
  stats
>
```

These settings are the same as you would add to the `THREE.WebGLRenderer()`.

On A-Frame, all the 3D elements have the same basic properties, such as position, rotation, and scale, and, depending on the type of element, you can have more or fewer properties. To change them, just add the component inside the corresponding element tag:

```
<a-box position="0 1 0" rotation="0 45 0" scale="1 1 1" visible="-false"></a-box>
```

In the preceding example, the position is set to x: 0, y: 1, and z: 0, the rotation (in degrees, not radians) is set to x: 0, y: 45 and z: 0, and the scale is set to 1 for all the three axes. The `visible` parameter shows or hides the element and its `children` elements.

Some elements, such as A-Frame primitives, can have specific properties depending on their structure:

```
<a-box depth="2" height="2" width="2"></a-box>
```

You can set some material properties directly in the element tag:

```
<a-box color="#ff0000"></a-box>
```

```
<a-box src="./images/texture.jpg"></a-box>
```

We will discuss in detail the A-Frame primitives and materials in the next sections.

Apart from the A-Frame properties, we can add `components` to them. `Components` are, in short, just like JavaScript functions that can be applied to A-Frame elements. A-Frame comes with some useful components such as `animation` and `animation-mixer`, but you can build your components.

By using the `<a-entity>` tag you can create groups of elements, and you can use `position`, `rotation`, `scale`, and `visibility` the same way you would do with primitives:

```
<a-entity id="group">
  <a-box color="#ff0000"></a-box>
  <a-sphere color="#00ff00"></a-sphere>
</a-entity>
```

But be aware that the `<a-entity>` tag is not recursive, this is why some components (for example, `material` or `color`) will not have any effect on the children elements.

Primitives

As we learnt in the second chapter, Three.js has loads of pre-made 3D objects to help you out in building your 3D scenes. A-Frame uses the same primitives, just making it easier to add and set them up:

```
<a-box depth="2" height="2" width="2"></a-box>

<a-sphere radius="2"></a-sphere>

<a-plane width="10" height="10"></a-plane>

<a-cylinder height="2" radius="1" segments-height="18" segments-radial
="36" theta-start="0" theta-length="360" open-ended="false"></a-cylinder>

<a-circle radius="20"></a-circle>

<a-torus arc="270" radius="5" arc="360" radius-tubular="0.2" segments-radi-
al="32"        segments-tubular="36"></a-torus>

<a-cone height="1" radius-bottom="2" radius-top="0.5" segments-height="18"
segments-radial="36" theta-start="0" theta-length="360" open-ended="false"
></a-cone>
```

You can find a full list of primitives in the left side menu of the A-Frame documentation page: https://A-Frame.io/docs/1.4.0/primitives/a-box.html.

We have some special types of 3D objects that can be added the same way as the primitives:

```
<!-- default three.js camera -->

<a-camera id="camera" position="0 1 0"></a-camera>


<!-- loads an image and applies it into a plane -->

<a-image src="texture.png"></a-image>


<!-- loads an image and applies it into a 360 degrees environment -->

<a-sky src="environment_texture.jpg" radius="10"></a-sky>


<!-- text sprite - very useful! -->

<a-text value="Hello, World!" align="center" font="arial" col-
or="#ff0000"></a-text>
```

Some special kinds of elements require a JavaScript method to make them work, such as audio and video elements. First of all, you need to load them outside the `<a-scene>` tag:

```
<audio id="audio_element" src="./sound/sound_effect.mp3"></audio>
```

```
<video id="video_element" crossorigin="anonymous" preload="auto" webkit
-playsinline playsinline muted src="./video/video.mp4"></video>
```

Then, insert the element ID into the `src` property of the A-Frame element:

```
<!-- sound sprite, with positional audio feature -->
```

```
<a-sound id="A-Frame-audio" src="#audio_element" position="0 2 5" auto-
play="false" loop="false" volume="1"></a-sound>
```

```
<!-- loads a video into plane -->
```

```
<a-video id="A-Frame-video" src="#video_element" width="16" height="9"
position="0 0 -20"></a-video>
```

And finally, in your JavaScript code you need to play the HTML elements in order to make them work with A-Frame:

```
/// on audio elements, you play the A-Frame element, not the HTML element:
```

```
document.querySelector("audio-video").components.sound.playSound();
```

```
/// on video elements, you play the HTML element, not the A-Frame element:
```

```
document.querySelector("video_element").currentTime = 0;
```

```
document.querySelector("video_element").play();
```

Keep in mind that dealing with audio and video on A-Frame has the same privacy issues (especially on mobile phones) as Three.js: you can only play an audio or video asset with a user interaction.

Materials

Working with materials follows the same concept– adding a `material` component to the element and setting up the properties:

```
<a-box material="color: #ff0000; transparent: true; opacity: 0.5; side:
double; metalness: 1; roughness: 0.5; emissive: #ffffff"></a-box>
```

You can set all material properties up by adding them inside the `material` component. The same implements for textures:

```
<a-box material="map: ./images/texture.jpg; offset: {x: 0.5, y: 0.5};
repeat: {x: 0.25, y: 0.25};"></a-box>
```

```
<!-- For environment maps, you need to set up a cubemap:  -->
```

```
<a-box material="envMap: url(right.png), url(left.png), url(top.png),
url(bottom.png), url(front.png), url(back.png);"></a-box>
```

The good news is that you do not need to add a texture loader before applying it to a material– A-Frame deals with everything for you.

The default material shader on A-Frame is `THREE.MeshStandardMaterial`, which is PBR-ready. If you want to set a `THREE.MeshPhongMaterial` or a `THREE.MeshBasicMaterial`, you need to specify it using the parameter `shader`:

```
<a-box material="material="shader: phong;"></a-box>
```

```
<a-box material="material="shader: flat;"></a-box>
```

Of course, the parameters you are using inside the `material` component should respect the shader type, otherwise they will not give you the expected results.

Asset Manager

Another good feature of A-Frame is the **asset manager**: it deals with the loading of assets and makes them ready to use on your scene. You just need to add the `<a-assets>` tag right at the beginning of the `<a-scene>` tag:

```
<a-assets>
    <a-asset-item id="glb-asset" src="./models/3d_asset.glb">
    </a-asset-item>
    <img id="image-asset" src="./images/image_asset.jpg">
    <a-cubemap id="environment">
      <img src="right.png">
      <img src="left.png">
      <img src="top.png">
      <img src="bottom.png">
      <img src="front.png">
      <img src="back.png">
    </a-cubemap>
</a-assets>
```

In theory, you can preload video and audio assets inside the `<a-assets>` tag, but we have found some issues dealing with these kinds of assets when they are preloaded inside A-Frame. This way, we recommend that you load them directly outside `<a-scene>`.

Once they are preloaded, you can refer to them just by using their ID in the right place:

```
<a-box material="map: #image-asset;"></a-box>
<a-box material="envMap: #environment;"></a-box>
```

Importing 3D files

To import a GLTF file, you can use a `<a-entity>` tag along with the `gltf-model` property:

```
<a-entity gltf-model="#glb-asset"></a-entity>
```

If your GLTF file is DRACO-compressed, do not forget to add the DRACO loader path inside the `<a-scene>` tag:

```
<a-scene gltf-model="dracoDecoderPath:

https://unpkg.com/three@0.153.0/examples/jsm/loaders/DRACOLoader.js;">

...

</a-scene>
```

You can, of course, load other types of 3D models, such as FBX and OBJ, but we strongly recommend you use GLTF file format:

```
<a-entity fbx-model="#fbx-asset"></a-entity>

<a-entity obj-model="#obj-asset"></a-entity>
```

Lights and shadows

Light sources work in A-Frame pretty much the same way as the previously mentioned elements:

```
<a-entity light="type: point; color: #ffffff; intensity: 1"

position="-1 2 -5"></a-entity>
```

The light types are the same as Three.js: `point`, `spot`, `directional`, `hemisphere`, `probe`, and `ambient`, and they work with the same properties too. `Directional` and `spot` can have a `target` dependency that will act as the light target:

```
<a-entity light="type: directional; color: #ffffff; intensity: 1"

position="-1 2 -5" target="#directionaltarget">

  <a-entity id="directionaltarget" position="0 0 -1"></a-entity>

</a-entity>
```

To enable shadow casting, you need to enable it on your light element:

```
<a-entity light="type: point; color: #fffff; intensity: 1; castShadow:
true"
position="-1 2 -5"></a-entity>
```

The other shadow properties can be used in the same way as in Three.js:

```
<a-entity light="type: point; color: #fffff; intensity: 1; castShadow:
true; shadowMapWidth: 1024; shadowMapHeight: 1024; shadowBias: -0.001"
position="-1 2 -5"></a-entity>
```

And finally, enable the shadow casting/receiving on the corresponding elements:

```
<a-sphere shadow="cast: true; receive: false" position="0 1 0"></a-sphere>
```

```
<a-plane shadow="cast: false; receive: true" position="0 0 0" rotation="-90
0 0 "></a-sphere>
```

Inside the `<a-scene>` tag you can set the shadow map algorithm: `basic`, `pcf`, and `pcfsoft`:

```
<a-scene shadow="type: pcfsoft">
```

```
...
```

```
</a-scene>
```

Cameras and Controls

At the beginning of this chapter, we briefly mentioned the `camera` element. On A-Frame you can define the camera element in two ways:

- Using a `camera` `rig` to give you the possibility to move the camera around in the case of 6DoF devices, especially VR headsets. A camera rig allows you to update the virtual camera position when you walk in the real world, or when you interact with a controller to move the character around. Another interesting feature when using a camera rig is **teleportation**: you can set hotspots on your scene that will set a new position of the virtual camera:

  ```
  <a-entity id="rig" position="0 1 0">
          <a-camera id="camera"></a-camera>
  </a-entity>
  ```

- Using the camera directly, if the device camera is `static` (3DoF), In this case, A-Frame will consider only the device rotation:

  ```
  <a-camera id="camera"></a-camera>
  ```

The camera properties are, as expected, the same as Three.js: `near`, `far`, `fov`, and `zoom`, but you can add in the camera tag the `controls` components:

- `look-controls`: Updates the camera rotation reading the VR headset / mobile phone rotation or reading the mouse position. The parameters are:
  - `enabled` (boolean): Enables/disables the camera controls.
  - `reverseMouseDrag` / `reverseTouchDrag` (boolean): Reverse the up and down mouse drag position.
  - `touchEnabled` (boolean): Enables the touch controls on mobile phones.
  - `mouseEnabled` (boolean): Enables the mouse controls on desktop devices.
  - `pointerLockEnabled` (boolean): Enables the `pointerLock` feature, such as on `THREE.PointerLockControls`.
- `wasd-controls`: Updates the camera position by reading the WASD or arrow keyboard keys. The parameters are:
  - `enabled` (boolean): Enables/disables the WASD camera controls.
  - `acceleration` (integer): Controls the acceleration of the camera movement.
  - `adAxis` (x, y or z): Which axis that the A and D keys act upon.
  - `adInverted` (boolean): Inverts the A and D keys direction.
  - `wsAxis` (x, y or z): Which axis the W and S keys act upon.
  - `wsInverted` (boolean): Inverts the W and S keys direction.
  - `fly` (boolean): Restricts the camera movement to the camera's initial y value.

When using a VR headset with VR hand controllers, we need to attach to the camera rig the corresponding elements:

```
<a-entity id="leftHand" hand-controls="hand: left; handModelStyle: low-
Poly; color: #ffcccc"></a-entity>
```

```
<a-entity id="rightHand" hand-controls="hand: right; handModelStyle:
lowPoly; color: #ffcccc"></a-entity>
```

For the `handModelStyle` property, the options are `lowPoly`, `highPoly`, or `toon`.

Navmesh

You can find the code of this section in the folder: https://github.com/OrangeAVA/ Creative-Technology-with-Three.js/tree/main/chapter06/aframe_navmesh

Navmesh stands for **Navigation Mesh** and it is a 3D mesh created on a 3D software that can be used to restrict the player's movement on a 3D space. Instead of using a complex physics system and adding colliders to restrict the camera movement, you can use a navmesh to tell A-Frame where the camera can walk over.

To build a navmesh, you can draw a 2D shape over your map on Blender or any 3D software, and solidify or extrude it to transform the shape into a 3D mesh. You can fine-tune the mesh by moving the vertices and even give some elevation to parts of the mesh to act like a staircase or a hole. Then, export it as GLTF/GLB format and import the file inside A-Frame. First of all, preload it inside `<a-assets>`:

```
<a-asset-item id="navmesh-glb" src="./assets/models/navmesh.gltf"></a-asset-item>
```

Then, create the `navmesh` element:

```
<a-entity id="navmesh" gltf-model="#navmesh-glb" visible="false" nav-mesh></a-entity>
```

And finally activate it on the camera rig:

```
<a-entity id="rig" movement-controls="constrainToNavMesh: true" position="0 0 3">

   <a-entity camera="fov:75;" id="camera" position="0 2 0" look-controls>
   </a-entity>

</a-entity>
```

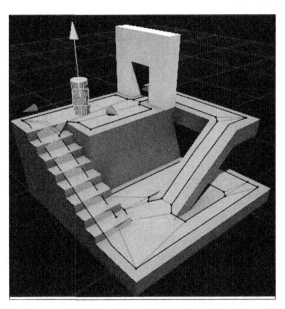

Figure 6.11: *Example of navmesh with elevation gain– image from https://www.donmccurdy.com*

With the `navmesh` activated, the camera will be able to walk only over the parts where there is geometry, and will be blocked by the empty spaces. Please be aware that when you are using a `navmesh`, you need to use `movement-controls` instead of `wasd-controls`.

Animation

You can find the code of this section in the folder: https://github.com/OrangeAVA/ Creative-Technology-with-Three.js/tree/main/chapter06/aframe_animation

A-Frame comes with a tween animation engine based on https://animejs.com that can be used in some useful ways. The simplest way to use it is adding an animation component this way:

```
<a-sphere position="0 0 -5"
    animation="property: position; from: 0 0 -5; to: 0 0 -10; dur: 1000;
    easing: linear; loop: true"
></a-sphere>
```

It performs a tween animation in the x-axis (from 0 to 2) in one second (1000 milliseconds), using a linear easing and looping it from the beginning when it ends. You can use any A-Frame property (position, rotation, scale, opacity, and so on), or sub-property such as a material color:

```
<a-sphere position="0 0 0"
    animation="property: material.color; from: #ff0000; to: #ffff00;
    dur: 1000; easing: linear; loop: true"
></a-sphere>
```

If you want to animate just one property of position, rotation, or scale, use `object3D.property.subproperty`:

```
<a-sphere position="0 0 -5"
    animation="property: object3D.position.x; from: 0; to: 2; dur: 1000;
    easing: linear; loop: true"
></a-sphere>
```

The easing parameter changes the value over time depending on the tween function– use it to create more natural animations. You can find all acceptable easing functions on `anime.js` documentation: https://animejs.com/ documentation/#pennerFunctions.

The `loop` parameter loops the animation. If it is `true`, it will repeat the movement forever, or you can set an integer value to repeat the animation **n** times. The default value is `false`.

There are some other parameters you can use along with the `animation` component:

- `dir`: Direction of the movement. The accepted values are `normal` (from -> to), `alternate` (from -> to -> from), and `reverse` (to -> from).
- `delay`: Milliseconds to start the animation.
- `autoplay`: Defines if the animation starts automatically. The default is `true`.

You can animate different properties on the same object, by adding a suffix in the animation component with double underscores (`__`) along with the animation name:

```
<a-box position="3 1 -5" color="#ff00ff"

       animation__rotation_animation="property: object3D.rotation.y;
       from: 0; to: 180;

       dur: 2000; easing: easeInOutCubic; loop: true; dir: alternate;"

       animation__scale_animation="property: scale; from: 1 1 1; to:
       1.5 1.5 1.5; dur:

       1000; easing: easeInOutElastic; loop: true; dir: alternate;"

></a-box>
```

The first animation (`animation__rotation_animation`) controls the rotation animation, and the second (`animation__scale_animation`) controls the scale animation.

If you want to start an animation via JavaScript (let us say, by a button click), you can use the property `startEvents` on the animation component, and the `emit` method in JavaScript:

`(./index.html)`:

```
<a-box id="interactive_box" position="6 1 -5" color="#0000ff"

   animation__scale_interactive="property: scale; from: 1 1 1; to: 1.5
   1.5 1.5;

   dur: 1000; easing: easeInOutElastic; loop: false; startEvents: click-
   ToScale"

></a-box>
```

```
(./js.main.js)
document.querySelector('#button_box').addEventListener('click', function() {
    document.querySelector('#interactive_box').emit('clickToScale');
})
```

In the preceding example, we add a listener to the HTML button (#button_box) to emit the clickToScale startEvent on the A-Frame element #interactive_box. You can set different startEvents by creating different animations using the double underscore method.

To end the animation subject, it is important to talk about the **animation callbacks**. You can use two kinds of callbacks– animationbegin and animationcomplete:

```
document.querySelector('#interactive_box').addEventListener
('animationbegin',
        function() { console.log('animation on blue box began'); }
)
```

```
document.querySelector('#interactive_box').addEventListener('animation-
complete',
        function() { console.log('animation on blue box is completed'); }
)
```

Do not forget that if you are using different animations with animation suffixes, you need to add it to the callback name as well, otherwise, the callback will be triggered from any of the A-Frame element animations:

```
document.querySelector('#interactive_box').addEventListener
        ('animationbegin__scale_interactive',
                function() { console.log('animation on blue box began'); }
)
```

Animation Mixer

You can find the code of this section in the folder: https://github.com/OrangeAVA/ Creative-Technology-with-Three.js/tree/main/chapter06/aframe_animation_ mixer

As we learnt in the previous chapters, you can use the Three.js **animation mixer** to deal with baked animations that come along with animated 3D files. The A-Frame's **animation mixer** works pretty much the same way, but with some advantages– A-Frame deals with different animation mixers on different objects and their respective loops. It comes with **A-Frame-extras**, so be aware that you need to load it in your HTML file first. To add the **animation mixer** to your 3D model you need to do this:

(./index.html)

```
<a-entity id="character" gltf-model="./assets/models/AnimatedCharacter.glb"
    position="0 0 0"
    animation-mixer="clip: Idle; loop: 'repeat'; crossFadeDuration: 0.5"
></a-entity>
```

The animation clips present on the GLB file are Idle, Elbow punching, Fist fighting, Punch, Roundhouse kick, and Thriller, so we created one button to play each animation clip. On the clip parameter, you add the animation clip name you want to play, or you can use * as a wildcard for all animation clips (it will play each animation clip one after another). The other parameters are:

- `loop`: Controls the loop of the animation clip that is being played. The options are `once`, `repeat`, and `pingpong`, and the default value is `repeat`.

- `repetitions`: If `loop` is set to `repeat` or `pingpong`, it will repeat the animation **n** number of times.

- `timeScale`: Sets the playback speed. 1 is the default playback speed that comes with the 3D file, 0.5 is half of the speed, and 0 is paused. A negative number will play the animation backwards, but it can produce unexpected results depending on the way the 3D file is animated.

- `duration`: If `timesScale` is set to 1, you can define the duration of the animation in seconds.

- `crossFadeDuration`: Transition duration (in `seconds`) between the current animation clip and the new animation clip.

- `clampWhenFinished`: Sstops the animation in the last frame if `loop` is set to `once`. The default value is `false`.

The available callbacks for the **animation mixer** are:

- `animation-loop`: If the `loop` parameter is set to `repeat`, it executes the callback function when the animation loops.

- `animation-finished`: If the `loop` parameter is set to `once`, it executes the callback function when the animation ends.

Adding/Removing Components via JavaScript

You can find the code of this section in the folder: https://github.com/OrangeAVA/Creative-Technology-with-Three.js/tree/main/chapter06/aframe_components

So far, we have shown you how to add components using only the A-Frame tags/elements, but you can add and remove components with JavaScript by using `setAttribute`/`removeAttribute` methods. To add a component, use `element.setAttribute('name_of_the_component', 'properties')`. To remove it, use `element.removeAttribute('name_of_the_component')`.

`(./js.main.js)`:

```
element.setAttribute('animation','property: scale; from: 1 1 1; to: 1.5
1.5 1.5;
dur: 1000;');
```

```
element.removeAttribute('animation');
```

As we learnt in the previous section, you can add/remove multiple components by using the double underscores (__) + animation name method.

You can use `setAttribute` to modify some component properties too. You just need to repeat the same command but with different parameter values:

```
element.setAttribute('animation','property: scale; from: 1 1 1; to: 2 2
2;
dur: 1000;');
```

If you try to scale the element to (1.5 1.5 1.5) when it is already running the same animation, A-Frame will simply ignore it. In this case, we recommend that you use the `startEvents`/`emit` method.

The `setAttribute` method will work to change any scene parameter or element that is accepted by A-Frame, such as `position`, `rotation`, `scale`, `visible`, and so on. To change sub-parameters, you can add the property name in the first parameter, and the sub-property + value in the second parameter, as it follows:

```
element.setAttribute('material','color:#ff0000');
```

```
<!-- for object sub-properties, such as offset or repeat →
element.setAttribute('position',{ x: 0.5, y: 0, z: 0 });
element.setAttribute('material','offset', { x: 0.25, y: 0 });
```

Apart from `setAttribute` and `removeAttribute`, we have `getAttribute` to get component values from A-Frame elements. It can be used to read elements property value:

```
const offsetX = element.getAttribute('material').offset.x -= 0.025;
element.setAttribute('material','offset', { x: offsetX, y: 0 });
```

A-Frame + Three.js

You can find the code of this section in the folder: https://github.com/OrangeAVA/ Creative-Technology-with-Three.js/tree/main/chapter06/aframe_interaction

It is good to know that you can change A-Frame component values using the `setAttribute` method, but there's a much more powerful (and faster) method to do it: by accessing Three.js properties directly. As A-Frame is built on top of Three.js, you can access all Three.js properties.

Let us start by looking into general A-Frame properties. If you just run `console.log(AFRAME)`, you will be able to see all A-Frame properties and core components. For example, inside `scenes` object, you will be able to find the scene's camera and even change its properties and see it updated in real-time on your screen. It is very good for debugging and fine-tuning your scenes. Inside `scenes.object3D. children` you will find all your scene elements, and change their parameters as well, and so on. We recommend you to go through these properties and parameters and play around with them. However, be aware that not all parameters will give you real-time feedback.

The same thing happens on A-Frame elements. You can do the same we did for the A-Frame object running `console.log(document.querySelector('#element_ id')`. At first sight, the console will show you the HTML element, but if you look for the property `object3D`, the magic will happen − it will return an object with all the element properties that you can revise and even change to debug:

```
document.querySelector('#element_id').object3D
```

Please note that, generally, the main A-Frame object is just a container (a Group object type actually). The real 3D object (a primitive, a light, an imported 3D object, and so on) will be found inside the `children` object. In the first level, you will find only the main element properties (position, rotation, scale, and some others), but will not find any `material` object, because it is a group and not a mesh. So, let us say you want to change the object rotation using Three.js directly:

```
///rotating the element y axis by 45 degrees
element.object3D.rotation.y = Math.PI/4;
```

We are using Three.js now and not A-Frame to perform the rotation, so the value is in radians, not in degrees. If you want to change the element's color and texture, remember that the material property is on the mesh, and not on the group, so you will need to find the mesh object first:

```
element.object3D.children[0].material.color.setHex( 0x0000FF )
```

A-Frame provides a useful method for finding the mesh object inside an A-Frame element: the getObject3D() method:

```
//use it on the A-Frame element, and not on the element.object3D
element.getObject3D('mesh').material.color.setHex( 0x0000FF );
```

You can do the same for light elements (getObject3D('light')), camera elements (getObject3D('camera')), and so on. However, be aware that, depending on how your scene is built, using getObject3D('mesh') can result in undefined because the element is not ready or not fully loaded into the scene. To avoid it you will need to wait for the element to be loaded:

```
//for primitives and A-Frame elements:
element.addEventListener("loaded", (e) => {
        element.getObject3D('mesh').material.color.setHex( 0x0000FF );
})


//for loaded 3D objects:
element.addEventListener("model-loaded", (e) => {
        element.getObject3D('mesh').material.color.setHex( 0x0000FF );
})
```

In the second example, we are expecting the element is a 3D object (a GLTF model for example) with just one mesh. If there are multiple meshes inside the 3D object, A-Frame will return the group that contains the sub-meshes. So, you will need to do what we did in *Chapter 3: Interacting with Our Scene*, using getObjectByName or running a traverse loop to find the right mesh you are looking for:

```
element.getObject3D('mesh').children[0].getObjectByName("name_of_the_
sub_object")
```

Building your Components

You can find the code of this section in the folder: https://github.com/OrangeAVA/ Creative-Technology-with-Three.js/tree/main/chapter06/aframe_components

So far, we have learnt how to add, modify, and remove A-Frame components, but A-Frame lets you build your own. The basic structure of a custom component is the following:

```
A-Frame.registerComponent('custom-component', {
  schema: {
    parameter1: {type: 'string', default: 'default property value'},
```

```
    parameter2: {type: 'number', default: 0},
    parameter3: {type: 'boolean', default: true},
  },
  init: function () {
    console.log(this.data.parameter1, this.data.parameter2, this.data.
    parameter3);
  },
  update: function () {
    console.log('It will run when you update the component parameters');
  },
  tick: function () {
    console.log('It will run on each frame');
  },
  remove: function () {
    console.log('It will run when you remove the component');
  }
});
```

One important thing to know– A-Frame requires you to load the components before the rest of the JavaScript code. If you are using only one JavaScript file, register the A-Frame components at the beginning of the file. If you are using different JavaScript files, create one for the components and read it before the others, inside the `<head>` section of your HTML file.

Where you find that `custom-component` is the component name, that will be used to add it to the A-Frame element. If the component has properties, you need to add them after the component name:

```
<a-entity id='element' position='0 0 0'
      custom-component='parameter: parameterValue'
></a-entity>
```

A component name is not case-sensitive and cannot start with a number or have special characters, such as &, *, %, and so on.

Inside the `schema` part, you define the component's parameters– here you define which parameters you will need to pass to the component in order to make it run. Properties can be `string`, `number`, `color`, or `boolean`, among other data types, and you can set (or not) a default value. You can add any parameters you need, separating them by commas (,) just like a JavaScript object.

```
schema: {
    parameter1: {type: 'string', default: 'default property value'},
    parameter2: {type: 'number', default: 0},
    parameter3: {type: 'boolean', default: true},
},
```

The `init` function is the function that will run the first time you add the component to an A-Frame element. Here you can initialize your variables and objects and load the elements needed.

The `update` function will run every time you update the component parameters. If you add (via JavaScript) a component without changing the current values, A-Frame will ignore the `update` function.

The `tick` function works pretty much like the Three.js animation loop: it runs frame by frame whatever is inside the function. Here you can update the element position dynamically or read some other element parameter to update the current one. You can reduce the tick update by using `throttleTick` method inside the `init` function:

```
this.tick = A-Frame.utils.throttleTick(this.tick, 500, this);
```

In this case, it will tell A-Frame to run the `tick` function every 500 milliseconds instead of the default speed of 60 frames per second.

Finally, the `remove` function will run when you remove the component from the A-Frame element. It is useful to clean up the element and prepare it to run the component in case it will be added again.

The component parameters defined inside the `schema` part can be accessed by `this.data` object:

```
init: function () {
    console.log(this.data.parameter);
},
```

Sometimes, when you are using a loop method, if you try to read `this.data` object you will probably get some errors. This is because JavaScript will consider the scope inside the loop, and not the A-Frame component scope. To avoid that, create a variable referring to `this` (A-Frame `this` scope) and read it inside the loop:

```
const scope = this;
this.el.addEventListener("model-loaded", (e) => {
```

```
    this.el.object3D.traverse(function(child) {
      if (child.isMesh && child.name === 'CandleHolder-glass') {
        child.material.color.setHex(scope.data.color)
      }
    })
  })
})
```

The element that the component is applied to can be accessed by reading this. el variable:

```
init: function () {
    console.log(this.el); /// it will return the A-Frame element
console.log(this.el.object3D); /// it will return the Three.js object
    this.el.object3D.position.x = 1;
},
```

In previous chapter, you will find different kinds of custom components:

- scene-environment: Already applied to <a-scene>, loads an HDRI image, and applies it to the scene.
- candle-holder-glass: It will change the candle holder glass color.
- helmet-float: It will add/remove a component to make the helmet float.
- look-ahead: Already applied to the camera, reads the camera rotation and shows a message if the y rotation is bigger than 45 degrees and smaller than -45 degrees.
- character-tshirt: It will change the character t-shirt color.

They use all basic custom component features: init, update, tick, and remove. Feel free to modify them and add more features to make the scene more interesting.

A-Frame Inspector

Our last topic about A-Frame will talk about another very useful feature – the A-Frame Inspector. When active, it will graphically show your scene, allowing you to see the scene elements, interact with them, and even change their parameters on the fly. To access the A-Frame Inspector, press the CTRL + ALT + I key and you will see this:

Figure 6.12: *A-Frame Inspector main screen*

The UI elements of the main **Inspector** screen are:

a. Closes the Inspector and goes back to the scene.

b. Creates a new element into the scene.

c. If your scene contains animated elements, this button will play/pause the animations.

d. Will gather all the elements from your entire scene and export it as a GLTF file.

e. Activates A-Frame-watcher (needs a special A-Frame setup, we will not discuss it in this lesson).

f. Will look for the typed element names and IDs.

g. On elements that have sub-elements, it will open/close the branch. It selects the element and opens the Element Inspector. Click twice on it and the scene view will focus on the selected element.

h. Shows/Hides the element.

i. Shows the available cameras and static views, allowing you to view the scene from other perspectives.

j. When an element is clicked, these three buttons change the behavior of the transform gizmo: translate/rotate/scale.

k. Toggle the local transform of the selected element.

When an element is selected (via **scene outliner** or via scene view), you will see the `Element Inspector` on the right side of the screen:

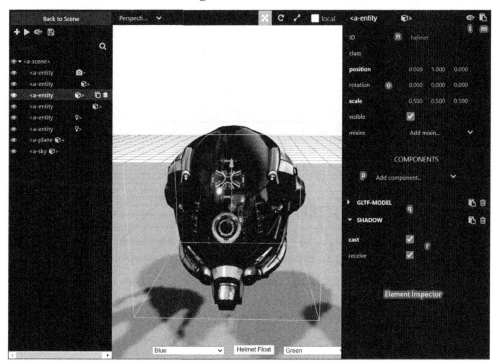

Figure 6.13: *A-Frame Element Inspector*

l. Exports the selected element as GLTF.

m. Copies the element tag to be pasted back into the scene code.

n. ID of the selected element.

o. Element's main properties: position, rotation, scale, and visibility.

p. Adds a new component to the selected element. The available components are the A-Frame defaults and the custom components you have available in your code.

q. Components that are applied to the selected element.

r. Current component properties. You can change these values to see the results on the screen for almost all component properties.

s.   Transform gizmo– depending on the selected transform type (item j), translates, rotates, or scales the element.

By graphically viewing your scene, you will be able to debug elements properties, arrange your scene elements, previsualize animations, and set up interactions between the elements. Getting used to A-Frame Inspector will save hours of scene building and scene debugging.

Conclusion

This chapter was a mix between history and development. We learned more about VR and AR technologies and why the web is so important for them. We introduced you to A-Frame, a Three.js framework that is the industry standard for building VR and AR projects for the web. We also understood in depth how to set up and install A-Frame and their main features. In the next chapter, we will move on with A-Frame and build our first webAR scene.

Points to Remember

- VR is all about immersing the user into a fully virtual scene. For that purpose, it takes over the user's view with a high-definition screen.
- AR is all about mixing the real with the virtual world. It captures the real world with a camera (in the case of mobile phones) and draws a 3D world over it, or it projects a 3D world over a transparent glass that will mix up with the real world.
- XR (eXtended Reality) is a generic term to talk about VR and AR experiences.
- 3-DoF is a standalone experience– the VR/AR device will read only the rotation of the user's head to update the virtual camera. In practical terms, you cannot walk towards virtual objects by walking in the real world.
- 6-DoF is a fully virtual experience– the VR/AR device can track the user's position and head rotation, allowing him/her to move around the virtual space by moving in the real space.
- App friction is a design or technical requirement that makes it harder for the user to run or interact with your app.
- Native VR or AR apps need a native compilation, whether through native tools (such as Swift or Kotlin) or software like Unity and Unreal Engine.
- Web VR or AR apps just need a web browser to run. Even though the experience is not so graphically sophisticated, the frictionless experience is much more appealing to the general audience.

- WebXR API has been created to allow native XR features on web and mobile browsers, but unfortunately, it is not (so far) compatible with iOS browsers.

- To workaround these difficulties, some companies such as 8th Wall, Blippar, and Zappar created web SDKs that mimic some native XR features by using computer vision algorithms.

- A-Frame is currently the industry standard for building webAR and webVR experiences because it has pre-built elements and attributes that allow you to interact with XR input and output devices without the need to write specific code for it.

- With A-Frame, you can write a full 3D scene without using any JavaScript line. But, of course, to build more complex scenes a good knowledge of JavaScript and Three.js is welcome.

- Mastering the A-Frame component system is a good way to start building complex and rich 3D scenes.

- A-Frame Inspector is a very useful tool and will save you hours of scene building and debugging. Get used to working with it!

Multiple Choice Questions

1. What is XR?

    a. A new technology that uses virtual and augmented reality altogether

    b. A generic term to talk about VR and AR technologies

    c. It is specific to the webXR API

    d. None of the alternatives above

2. 3-DoF is:

    a. A special algorithm to calculate the Depth of Field of 3D scenes

    b. A VR and AR concept that considers the user's head position and rotation

    c. A computer vision algorithm to estimate the user position on a 3D space

    d. A VR and AR concept that considers only the user's head rotation

3. Which of these features are not AR features?

    a. Image tracking and geo-tracking

    b. Face and body tracking

    c. Eye tracking and two-hand controllers

    d. VPS and light estimation

4. What is the friction concept when talking about app development?

    a. A parameter that can be used on physics engines to slow down a movement

    b. Is a design or technical requirement that makes it harder for the user to run or interact with an app

    c. A special requirement of user interaction on touch devices

    d. A design concept that considers the previous user navigation

5. Why A-Frame is considered one of the webVR and webAR standards?

    a. It is easier to code and more straightforward than Three.js

    b. A-Frame has pre-built elements and attributes that allow you to interact with XR input and output devices without the need to write any code for it

    c. You can extend A-Frame with Three.js code, so it is a good fit for experienced and non-experienced Three.js users

    d. All of the alternatives above

Answers

1. b

2. d

3. c

4. b

5. d

Questions

1. Why did VR technology take so much time to be available to end-users?

2. Why has AR technology become more accessible and popular than VR?

3. In your opinion, why is Apple still not allowing webXR to run on iOS devices?

4. In your words, explain the latency issue in VR headsets.

5. Which other features would you like to see on VR headsets and on AR devices?

6. Have you experienced the friction problem when trying to use a mobile app?

7. What would be your development choice when developing a 3D scene—pure Three.js, A-Frame, or React Three Fiber?

8. What are the advantages and disadvantages of using a framework such as A-Frame or React Three Fiber instead of pure Three.js?

9. If you could choose one, which AR/VR development stack would you prefer to use— native development with native tools, native development with Unity or Unreal Engine, or webAR/webVR?

10. Which technology do you think is more promising, VR or AR?

Key Terms

- **Inside-out tracking**: VR tracking system that uses cameras, sensors, and computer vision algorithms to estimate the user's position in a virtual space.

- **Outside-in tracking**: VR tracking system that uses external sensors (two or more) to triangulate the user's position, giving to the VR headset precise coordinates.

- **Computer vision**: A field of artificial intelligence that enables computers to get meaningful data from static or moving images. Specifically in VR and AR, it is used to estimate the user's position and orientation by reading the camera(s) feed(s) and crossing it with the sensor's data.

- **Motion sickness**: Visual discomfort caused by VR headsets with high latency (hardware or software), low 3D frame rates, or low-frequency displays.

- **Occlusion**: In AR, is a technique that allows virtual objects to be occluded by real objects, by reading the real scene depth.

CHAPTER 7

Creating Your First WebAR Experience

Introduction

In the last chapter, we introduced you to VR and AR concepts and explained about the importance of web technologies for immersive experiences. In conclusion to the chapter, we discussed why A-Frame is one of the standards for webAR development and explained to you the basics of this amazing framework. In this chapter, we will use all that we learned earlier to build our first webAR experience.

Structure

In this chapter, we will discuss the following topics:

- Basic webAR Scene Setup
- Project Concept
- A-Frame Interaction
- A-Frame Components
- Putting Everything Together

Basic webAR Scene Setup

You can find the code of this section in the folder: https://github.com/OrangeAVA/Creative-Technology-with-Three.js/tree/main/chapter07/aframe_webAR_template

Our webAR scene is based on the *Chapter 6 : Introduction to webAR and webVR*. However, with an important difference– it is integrated with the AR.js (https://github.com/AR-js-org) webAR library. This library allows the A-Frame scene to get your mobile phone camera feed and draws it into the scene background.

Also, it reads your phone gyro data and applies it to the A-Frame scene. The result is a 3D scene integrated with a real environment.

You already know how to make it work on your mobile phone– get your local server IP and open it on your mobile browser forcing the use of HTTPS. If you are using VSCode or NPM as a local server, you will need to generate an SSL certificate and set up the local server accordingly.

If you did it correctly, you will be able to see the scene as represented here:

Figure 7.1: *WebAR boilerplate*

With this scene you will be able to build any 3DoF webAR scene or, as we will explain further in this chapter, build any marker or image tracking scene. Next step– start building a webAR product showcase.

Project Concept

You can find the code of this section in the folder: https://github.com/OrangeAVA/ Creative-Technology-with-Three.js/tree/main/chapter07/aframe_webAR_ product_showcase

We will build in this chapter a product showcase in webAR. As a consumer, you will be able to place the AR scene into your real space, then interact with the products (three in total) and see more details about it. This little project will introduce you to some important AR concepts such as **tap-to-place, UI-to-AR interaction**, and **AR-to-UI interaction**.

We are not going to use any webAR SDK for features such as image tracking or SLAM/world tracking, so our project will be a 3DoF experience with no camera movement on the z-axis, but we will explain the path on how to integrate the scene with third-party webAR platforms.

HTML Code Overview

In order to make this scene work in AR, we had to add, apart from the usual A-Frame libs, the `ar.js` library in line 14:

```
11   <script src="https://unpkg.com/aframe@1.4.2/dist/aframe-master.
     js"></script>

12   <script

        src="https://unpkg.com/aframe-extras@7.1.0/dist/aframe-extras.
        min.js"></script>

14   <script

        src="https://raw.githack.com/AR-js-org/AR.js/master/aframe/build/
        aframe-ar.js"> </script>

16   <script src="https://unpkg.com/three@0.147.0/examples/js/loaders/RG-
     BELoader.js"> </script>

18   <script type="module" src="js/components.js"></script>

19   <script type="module" src="js/main.js"></script>
```

We also created a components.js file to gather all A-Frame components and keep them apart from the rest of the code. You can organize the structure even better if you want to gather all functions in one file, and all listeners in another file, but for clarity we decided to have them inside the `main.js` file.

From lines 24 to 45, we created the UI elements: message prompts and popups:

```
24   <div id="ui">

25     <div id="splash" class="popup fade show">

26       <span>Allow camera and gyro permissions to start</span>

27     </div>

28     <div id="tap_to_place_btn" class="message fade show">

29       <span>Tap on the screen to place the AR scene</span>

30     </div>
```

```
31    <div id="tap_product" class="message fade">
32      <span>Tap on a product to see more details</span>
33    </div>
34    <div id="product_info" class="popup fade">
35      <div class="container">
36        <button id="close_btn">x</button>
37        <h1></h1>
38        <p></p>
39        <div class="buttons">
40          <button id="btn_activate">Activate</button>
41          <button id="btn_deactivate"
                            class="disabled">Deactivate</button>
42        </div>
43      </div>
44    </div>
45  </div>
```

The most important is the product_info popup, which will show the product details.

Moving on, we started to add the A-Frame elements inside the <a-scene> tag:

```
47  <a-scene
48      renderer="logarithmicDepthBuffer: true;"
49      embedded arjs
50      loading-screen="enabled: true;"
51      scene-environment="hdrImage:./assets/images/pisa.hdr;hdrExposure:
        1;"
52      gltf-model="dracoDecoderPath:
    https://ar-libs.blippar.com/components/draco/1.4.1/;"
53      raycaster="objects: .clickable"
54      cursor="fuse: false; rayOrigin: mouse"
55  >
```

Here we have very important properties to add. First of all, in line 49 we added the ar.js components in order to make the scene work as a webAR scene— embedded and arjs. The arjs component comes with no parameter because we are not setting up any marker or image tracker for this scene.

In line 51, we added a `scene-environment` component to load an HDRI texture and add some light-based environment to the scene. And finally, importantly, in lines 53 and 54 we add the components to enable the interaction with A-Frame scenes. The `raycaster` component tells A-Frame that any object with a clickable class is clickable, and the `cursor` component will use the mouse (or touch) clicks as `rayOrigin`.

In lines 56 to 59, we preload the scene assets (placement marker and the product GLB file):

```
56  <a-assets>
57      <img id="tap-top-place-glb" src="./assets/images/tap_to_place.jpg"
        />
58      <a-asset-item id="product-glb"
    src="./assets/models/product.glb"></a-asset-item>
59  </a-assets>
```

In lines from 61 to 63, we create the `camera` element:

```
61  <a-entity camera="fov: 75; zoom: 2;" id="camera"
62    wasd-controls-enabled="false"
63    look-controls="enabled: true; touchEnabled: false;" >
      </a-entity>
```

And here is an important note— to make the scene camera read the phone gyro, you need to add and enable the component look-controls. The `touchEnabled:false` parameter will disable the camera rotation by clicking or dragging, but you can set it as true if you want the user to customize the camera rotation not only by rotating the phone.

In line 65, we create the scene container. All the A-Frame 3D elements should be inside this container, so it is important to create it at 0,0,0 position:

```
65  <a-entity id="ar-scene" position="0 0 0">
```

Then, we create the scene lighting— three-point lights to act as a key, fill, and backlights:

```
67  <a-entity light="type: ambient; intensity: 0.5;"></a-entity>
68  <a-entity light="type: point; color: #ffffff; intensity: 0.35;
        castShadow: true" position="1.5 3.3 2.4"></a-entity>
70  <a-entity light="type: point; color: #ffffff; intensity: 0.35;
        castShadow: true" position="-2.7 2.7 1.3"></a-entity>
```

```
72   <a-entity light=”type: point; color: #ffffff; intensity: 0.2;
         castShadow: true” position=”-0.09 1.4 -5.2”></a-entity>
```

From line 75 onwards, an important AR concept– the **Tap to Place** feature. It basically tells the user where he/she wants to place the scene. The user can rotate the camera on the y-axis (left/right) and on the x-axis (up/down) to choose which position the scene should be placed on. As we are building a 3DoF scene, the distance placement (z-axis) is merely visual, since the user will not be able to walk toward it. In case we were building a scene using SLAM/World tracking (that detects the placement surface), the user would be able to place the scene closer or farther from his position. For marker/image tracking scenes, the **Tap to Place** feature is not needed since the scene will be attached to the marker or image position in the real world:

Figure 7.2: *Tap to place the component*

In lines 75 to 77, we create the two containers that will receive all the scene contents:

```
75   <a-entity id=”placement-container” position=”0 0 0”
         tap-to-place=”enabled: true;”>
76   <a-entity position=”0 -1.5 -7” scale=”1 1 1”>
```

In line 75, we added the **tap-to-place** component, which basically rotates the **placement-container** element along with the camera, giving the user the impression that the scene is following his position. When the user taps on the screen, we disable this component, and the **placement-container** element will stay in the last placement position. The container in line 76 is placed in the position y: -1.5 to give the scene some height (since the camera is at y:0 position), and the z: -7 to push the scene back a bit, otherwise, the scene would be placed on top of the camera, and we do not want this.

In line 79, we created the placement marker, which is used as a visual cue for the scene placement:

```
79   <a-circle id="placement-marker" rotation="-90 0 0" opacity="0.7"
                    transparent="true" material="shader: flat" src="#tap-
                    top-place-img"

                    animation__scale_down="property: scale; from: 1 1 1;
                    to: 0 0 0; dur: 2000;

                    easing: easeInOutElastic; loop: false;

                    startEvents: placementMarkerScaleDown"

82   ></a-circle>
```

We are using a simple circle with a texture applied to it, but you could add an A-Frame primitive or a GLB model for it. We generally use a "ghost-like" GLB, a sort of semi-transparent duplicate of the main scene object, to tell the user how the scene will look after the placement.

From line 85 onwards, we started to add the following products:

```
85 <a-entity id="products-container" position="0 0 5" visible="true">
```

We pushed products-container a bit further to create the effect of having the products surrounding the user, instead of being in line. For it, besides pushing products-container a bit back, we created three more containers to contain each product. Each product GLB is z:-5 (to compensate for the products-container z position), and each container is rotated 30 degrees in each direction (except for the product02 which is right in front of the camera and does not need to be rotated). It is basically a way to move the pivot point of a 3D object using an A-Frame. Graphically speaking, we did this:

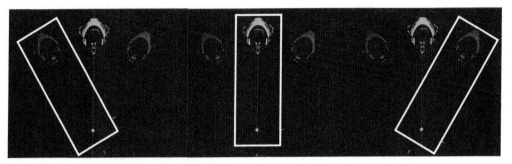

Figure 7.3: *Creating a fake pivot point using <a-entitiy> containers*

Of course, we could move the pivot point of the GLB model using Blender, but remember that it is always recommended to have your 3D models placed exactly in the center of the scene, so you can have better control over them and will not see unpredicted results when scaling them up or down.

The structure of each product is pretty much the same– we could even create them dynamically if we want, but for code understanding, we declared each product independently:

```
87   <a-entity id="product01" class="container" rotation="0 30 0">
88     <a-entity gltf-model="#product-glb" position="0 0 -5" scale="0 0 0"
89     class="product clickable"
90     product-component="color:0xff0000"
91     animation__scale_up="property: scale; from: 0 0 0; to: 1 1 1; dur:
       1000;
                   easing: easeInOutSine; loop: false; startEvents:
                   productScaleUp"
92     animation__move_up="property: position; from: 0 0 -5; to: 0 2 -5;
                   dur: 1000; easing: easeInOutSine; loop: false;
                   startEvents: productMoveUp"
93     animation__move_forward="property: position; to: 0 2 -2; dur:
       1000;
                   easing: easeInOutSine; loop: false; startEvents:
                   productMoveForward"
94     animation__move_back="property: position; to: 0 2 -5; dur: 1000;
                   easing: easeInOutSine; loop: false; startEvents:
                   productMoveBack"
95     >
96     </a-entity>
97   </a-entity>
```

As said previously, the container <a-entity> is rotated y:30 degrees and the product GLB entity is moved z: -5, to shift the pivot point of the GLB entity so the rotation will make it rotate around the central point, and not only on its initial pivot point. After that, we added two classes, product and clickable, the product is used to identify the GLB element further in the code, and the clickable is for enabling the raycasting on this element.

The product-component component was created to tint the 3D object color, so instead of having three GLB files with different colors, we have only one GLB file with dynamic colors.

The animations animation__scale_up and animation__move_up are used for the initial object animation. The scene starts with the objects with scale 0,0,0 and 0,0,-5 position, so when we play these two animations the products grow up from their initial position. The animations animation__move_forward and animation__move_back are used to move the products forward and backward when selected.

The other two products are exactly the same, so there is no need to explain their structure. You will be able to see this after the initial splash and permission popups:

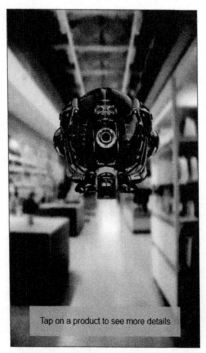

Figure 7.4: *Initial screen of the project*

Project Components

As explained earlier, we decided to create a different file for the project components. The main reason is to make the code more organized and understandable. The second reason is that the components should be loaded before all the other project code, so A-Frame can load them into the browser memory and make them ready in case you call the components in HTML or JavaScript code.

That said, let us analyze the three components we are using in this project:

- `scene-environment`: We used this in the previous chapter; it basically loads an HDRI image and uses it as a scene environment map for all materials that have some reflection. Also, it creates image-based lighting, tinting the scene with the HDRI texture colors.

- `product-component`: We are using this to tint the product GLB file with the color defined in the parameter color:

```
52  const elementMesh = element.getObject3D('mesh');

54  elementMesh.traverse(function(child) {

55    if (child.isMesh && (child.name === 'product_base' ||
                  (child.name === 'product_hood'))) {

56      child.material.color.setHex(color);

57    }

58  })
```

It basically iterates through the GLB file children objects, changing the original material color (white) to the `color` parameter. As the material map is premultiplied to the material color, the result is this tint effect that changes the material map color.

- `tap-to-place`: Applied to the placement-container element, it rotates the element along with the camera *x* and *y*-axis rotation, giving the user an impression the element is following the camera direction:

```
90  if (document.getElementById("camera") && this.data.enabled) {

91    let camrot =
                  document.getElementById("camera")
                  .getAttribute("rotation");

92    let ra = ((camrot.y % 360) + 360) % 360; // ra - Restricted
      angle

94    this.el.object3D.rotation.y = ra * (Math.PI / 180)

95  }
```

In line 92, we normalize the camera rotation y value to make sure it will never be higher than 360 degrees (if it is higher, we return the camera y rotation to zero), otherwise, it could cause some issues in the scene. To stop updating the element rotation, you just need to set the parameter `enabled` to `false` or remove the component.

Main Code

Now that we have explained the HTML structure and the components file, it is time to talk about the `main` project code, which is inside the `main.js` file. As we did in the previous examples, we created a load listener to run the `start()` function when the scene is fully loaded:

```
01  window.addEventListener("load", function () {

02      start();

03  });
```

Right after this listener, we declared another listener to read the `camera-init` state in order to remove the splash screen when the camera is ready. It can be used to hide the scene content before the camera is fully active and avoid some confusion of not having the full AR scene (real world + virtual world) ready:

```
06  window.addEventListener("camera-init", function () {

07      document.querySelector('#splash').classList.remove('show');

08  });
```

By the way, here we are using a cool CSS trick– we added a `fade` class to all the HTML elements (unfortunately we cannot use it with A-Frame elements, yet!) we want to show/hide dynamically:

```
(./styles.css):

43  .fade {

44      opacity: 0;

45      visibility: hidden;

46      transition:

47        opacity 0.5s ease-in-out,

48        visibility 0.5s ease-in-out;

49      -moz-transition:

50        opacity 0.5s ease-in-out,

51        visibility 0.5s ease-in-out;

52      -webkit-transition:
```

```
53        opacity 0.5s ease-in-out,
54        visibility 0.5s ease-in-out;
55   }
```

Every HTML element with the `fade` class will not be visible nor clickable, but if you add the `show` class, the element will be visible and clickable (if it is a button or `<a>` element). The `show` class basically sets the opacity to 1 and makes the element visible. The `hide` class has a transition property, it will fade in nicely:

```
57   .show {
58      opacity: 1;
59      visibility: visible;
60   }
```

To use it you just need to add/remove the `show` class in HTML or JavaScript:

```
document.querySelector('#element').classList.add('show');
```

```
document.querySelector('#element').classList.remove('show');
```

But do not forget the element needs to have the `fade` class applied to it in order to make this trick work.

We also created a very useful function to hold the scene playing for some time in order to align code functions to animation functions:

```
11  const Delay = (milliseconds) => {
12     return new Promise((resolve) => {
13        setTimeout(() => {
14           resolve();
15        }, milliseconds);
16     });
17  };
```

We are using here a very powerful resource of modern JavaScript versions—`async-await` functions. It basically tells JavaScript to wait until the function ends (with a `Promise` or a `Callback`) to proceed with the next command. In this case, the `Promise` is the `setTimeout` function that will wait for a number of milliseconds defined in the Delay function. We could use the `setTimeout` function directly, but it causes a bit of confusion when having timeouts inside timeouts. Also, the `setTimeout` function does not hold the code flow when it is running, so you can have unpredictable results if you are using several `setTimeout` on different parts of the code.

To use our `Delay` function, you just need to run it with an `await` method:

```
await Delay(milliseconds);
```

Due to some JavaScript restrictions, you always need to use `await` along with the `async` method, which means that you always need to include `async` before the function declaration, otherwise JavaScript will throw an error:

```
const testFunction = async function() {

   . . .

   . . .

      await Delay(1000);

}
```

Moving on with the code, we need to create an array of objects to store the product data:

```
20  const products = {
21      product01: {
22        name: 'Product 01',
23        description: 'This is the description of the Product 01'
24      },
25      product02: {
26        name: 'Product 02',
27        description: 'This is the description of the Product 02'
28      },
29      product03: {
30        name: 'Product 03',
31        description: 'This is the description of the Product 03'
32      },
33  }
```

In the `start()` function, we create all the interaction listeners:

```
41 document.querySelector('#tap_to_place_btn').addEventListener('click', async
                function() {
42        tapToPlace();
43  })
```

```
45 document.querySelector('#btn_activate').addEventListener('click', async
        function() {
46     activateProduct();
47 });
```

```
49 document.querySelector('#btn_deactivate').addEventListener('click',
   async

   function() {
50     deactivateProduct();
51 });
```

```
53 document.querySelector('#close_btn').addEventListener('click', async
   function() {
54   closeProductPopup();
55 });
```

The first function of this list is the `tapToPlace()` function. It is used to place the scene in the user's preferred rotation when the screen (actually the #tap_to_ place_btn element) is tapped. First of all, it will remove the #tap_to_place_btn to avoid further screen taps, then remove the `tap-to-place` component from #placement_container element to stop its rotation update (making it freezing on the last rotation value previously the screen tap). Finally, we remove the #placement-marker element because the scene is already placed, and we do not need it anymore:

```
63 document.querySelector('#tap_to_place_btn').classList.remove('show');
```

```
64 document.querySelector('#placement-container').removeAttribute
   ('tap-to-place');
```

```
65 document.querySelector('#placement-marker').emit('placementMarker-
   ScaleDown');
```

We need some time to wait for the animations to finish and be ready for the next sequence of commands, so we wait for 1.6 seconds:

```
67 await Delay(1600);
```

In this way, we have already placed the scene in the user's defined rotation. Now we need to start showing the products. To do this, we have the `productScaleUp` and `productMoveUp` animations previously defined on the HTML file. We do not want to show all the products at the same time, so we added a staggered animation to make them appear one after another:

```
70  document.querySelector('#product02 a-entity').emit('productScaleUp');
71  document.querySelector('#product02 a-entity').emit('productMoveUp');
73  await Delay(800);
```

As the `productScaleUp` and `productMoveUp` animations have a duration of 1000ms each, waiting 800ms will make the next product show up 200ms before the end of the previous product animation, resulting in a very fluid animation.

We are showing `product02` first because it is right in front of the camera, so it is a good way to catch the user's attention, otherwise, the user could miss the `product01` or `product03` animations because they are a bit out of the camera's field of view. Also, we could do a `forEach` loop to iterate through the `products` array and show/wait for each product after another, but we decided to show the complete code for better understanding.

After showing the three products, we are ready to interact with them. However, we need to tell the user about it first, so let us show the `#tap_product` message:

```
86  document.querySelector('#tap_product').classList.add('show');
```

And create the listeners for each product. Now we are doing this dynamically instead of declaring each listener individually, so you can see how it works.

First of all, let us get all the product elements that will be clickable. They are inside the `#products-container` element, but to avoid getting all the inner elements (the containers and the GLB elements), let us narrow our search only to the children elements that have the `container` class:

```
88  productList = document.querySelectorAll('#products-container
.container');
```

Which are, basically, these three elements:

```
<·  ▼ NodeList(3) [a-entity#product01.container,
      a-entity#product02.container, a-entity#product03.container] ⁝
   ▶ 0: a-entity#product01.container
   ▶ 1: a-entity#product02.container
   ▶ 2: a-entity#product03.container
     length: 3
   ▶ [[Prototype]]: NodeList
```

Figure 7.5: *Product list array*

Now we can iterate between these three elements and create one listener for each product:

```
91  productList.forEach(function(element) {
92    element.addEventListener('click', async function() {
```

For each clicked object, we need to get its ID:

```
93   activeProduct = this.id;
```

Then run `selectProduct` function to move the product forward/backward if needed:

```
94   selectProduct(activeProduct);
```

Now we show the product info popup:

```
97   document.querySelector('#product_info').classList.add('show');
```

Populate it by reading the product array of objects and, depending on the product ID (which is the same product object key), show the right product name and description:

```
98   document.querySelector('#product_info h1').innerHTML =
         products[activeProduct].name;
99   document.querySelector('#product_info p').innerHTML =
         products[activeProduct].description;
```

The product popup has also two buttons– `activate` and `deactivate`. They interact directly with the product 3D model, activating different **animation mixer** animations, which we will explain further in this chapter:

Figure 7.6: *Product popup*

The `tapToPlace()` function does 90% of all the interaction between A-Frame and UI. All the other functions are just accessories to interact with other elements:

- `activateProduct()`: Used to activate/deactivate the product interaction buttons and play the open animation on the GLB element:

```
107  document.querySelector('#btn_activate').classList.add
('disabled');

108  document.querySelector('#btn_deactivate').classList.
remove('disabled');

109  document.querySelector('#'+activeProduct + ' .product').

setAttribute('animation-mixer','timeScale: 3; loop: once;

clampWhenFinished: true; crossFadeDuration: 0; clip: open');
```

- `deactivateProduct()`: Used to activate/deactivate the product interaction buttons and play the close animation on the GLB element:

```
107  document.querySelector('#btn_activate').classList.re-
     move('disabled');

108  document.querySelector('#btn_deactivate').classList.ad-
     d('disabled');

109  document.querySelector('#'+activeProduct + ' .product').

       setAttribute('animation-mixer','timeScale: 3; loop: once;

       clampWhenFinished: true; crossFadeDuration: 0; clip: close);
```

- `selectProduct(product)`: Moves the selected product forward or backward depending on its state. If the product parameter is `null`, the loop runs through all the products and moves them back (if some of them are activated), leaving the function right after the loop ends:

```
124  if (product === null) {

125    productList.forEach(function(element) {

126      document.querySelector('#'+element.id + '

                  .product').emit('productMoveBack');

127    })

         return;

128  }
```

If the parameter is a product element, it will simply move the product forward:

```
132  document.querySelector('#'+product + ' .product')

       .emit('productMoveForward');
```

- `closeProductPopup()`: Resets the product states, resets the activate/ deactivate button states, and closes the product info popup. Here, if the selected product is open, the function closes it:

```
140   const animationMixer = document.querySelector('#'+active-
Product + '

.product').getAttribute('animation-mixer');

141   if (animationMixer && animationMixer.clip === 'open') {

142     document.querySelector('#'+activeProduct + ' .product')

        .setAttribute('animation-mixer','timeScale: 3; loop:
        once;

        clampWhenFinished: true; crossFadeDuration: 0; clip:
        close');

143   }
```

Now we need to reset the product states (move the selected product back) and set null to the `activeProduct` variable, to prepare for the next interaction cycle:

```
146   activeProduct = null;

147   document.querySelector('#product_info').classList.remove('show');

148   selectProduct(null);
```

We wait 500ms to wait for the `#product_info` `fade-out` animation to end, and show the Tap to the Product message again:

```
151   await Delay(500);

153   document.querySelector('#tap_product').classList.add('show');
```

And finally, reset the activate/deactivate buttons states:

```
156   document.querySelector('#btn_activate').classList.remove('disabled');

157   document.querySelector('#btn_deactivate').classList.add('disabled');
```

And now we have a product showcase in AR! You can try different things using this project as boilerplate:

- Load different GLB files
- Interact with more animations
- Add other UI elements into the AR space for a richer interaction

In the next chapter, we will try a different AR approach– marker/image tracking.

Using Image Tracking

You can find the code of this section in the folder: https://github.com/OrangeAVA/ Creative-Technology-with-Three.js/tree/main/chapter07/aframe_webAR_ image_tracking_mindAR

So far, we have used `ar.js` only for being able to use the camera stream along with the A-Frame scene. This AR framework takes all the complexity out of the code, dealing with camera and gyro permissions, AR cameras, and so on. Now we will take a step further and use image tracking to draw our AR scene. Even `ar.js` has image tracking features, it is not stable enough and we are going to use another good AR library: MindAR (https://www.mindar.org). You can ask why we did not use MindAR since the beginning of this chapter, and the answer is– MindAR will only show the A-Frame scene on detected image targets, so it will not work for 3-DoF AR projects. Also, MindAR has interesting face-tracking features which we will discuss in the next chapter.

So let us keep in mind the following:

- ar.js for 3DoF AR scenes
- MindAR for image and face tracking

This is for open-source projects, right? If you are planning to use a paid webAR library (such as 8th Wall, Blippar, Zappar, and so on), they are natively compatible with all the AR modes.

Image tracking is the technique of identifying a previously encoded image and placing a 3D scene over it, respecting the distance and the perspective distortion from the camera to the subject. Most of the open source (such as ar.js and MindAR) and paid AR frameworks use basically the same approach– a computer vision algorithm that recognizes the image and converts its position, rotation, and scale to 3D coordinates. The difference between open source and paid libraries is the tracking quality– paid SDKs such as 8th Wall SDK have a very sophisticated image tracking algorithm (among other good features) that basically sticks your 3D scene to the image target.

An **image target** can be any image– a photo, an illustration, anything. The AR image tracker will identify the **feature points** (distinctive points on the image) and calculate the position, rotation, and scale of the AR scene depending on what your phone camera sees. You can see in the following figure the feature points identified by the AR tracker:

Figure 7.7: *The red circles are the identified feature points – images from https://hiukim.github.io/mind-ar-js-doc*

Being open source or paid, the AR image trackers always rely on the image target quality. Not only the image quality, but the image itself should be very detailed and with a lot of contrast to generate a good number of feature points and provide a good tracking quality. You can see in these pages how to create a good image target here:

And here:

https://github.com/Carnaux/NFT-Marker-Creator/wiki/Creating-good-markers

Converting an Image into an Image Target

It is as simple as uploading a file to your server– just go to the link provided here and convert your image:

https://hiukim.github.io/mind-ar-js-doc/tools/compile

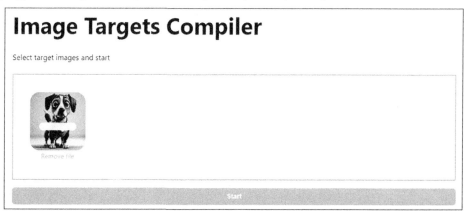

Figure 7.8: *Converting an image into an image target*

It will take some time to generate the image target file but eventually, it will finish the conversion and show the screen below. Here you can see the feature points the image tracker identified on your image– as more feature points it identifies, the better the tracking quality will be:

Figure 7.9: *Feature points of your image*

Now you can download the .mind file and save it into your ./assets/images folder.

Running the AR Image Tracker

Let us now prepare our boilerplate to read these files and place the AR scene over the image target. First of all, we need to change the **ar.js** library link to the **MindAR** library:

(./index.html):

```
13      <script
src="https://unpkg.com/mind-ar@1.2.3/dist/mindar-image-aframe.prod.js">
</script>
```

Then, on the <a-scene> tag, we need to remove the ar.js components and add the MindAR ones:

```
20      <a-scene
21        renderer="logarithmicDepthBuffer: true;"
22        loading-screen="enabled: false;"
```

```
23      device-orientation-permission-ui="enabled: false"
24      mindar-image="imageTargetSrc: ./assets/images/image_target.mind;"
25   >
```

In line 24 comes the path to the .mind file you downloaded in the previous step:

```
24      mindar-image="imageTargetSrc: ./assets/images/image_target.
mind;"
```

In line 29, you need to change the camera element since MindAR cannot read the camera component from an `<a-entity>` element:

```
29   <a-camera id="camera" position="0 0 0" look-controls="enabled:
false;
touchEnabled: false;"></a-camera>
```

Finally, we need to change the scene container to this:

```
31   <a-entity id="ar_container" mindar-image-target="targetIndex: 0">
...
```

MindAR will consider anything that is inside this container as your 3D scene. If you are using more than one image target (yes, you can upload several image targets to the converter), you can set up different A-Frame containers for each target:

```
<a-entity mindar-image-target="targetIndex: 1">
...
</a-entity>

<a-entity mindar-image-target="targetIndex: 2">
...
</a-entity>
```

Each container will show different 3D objects depending on the elements you added inside it. You can add as many targets you want, but be aware that it will increase the project size and complexity, so it's not recommended to add too many image targets.

That is all for showing the image target contents, you can make your AR scene work just by adding the HTML and A-Frame elements. If you need more control over your scene, you can use MindAR listeners. The first one is the arReady listener, triggered when mindAR library is fully loaded and ready to start tracking an image:

```
(./js/main.js)
13    sceneEl.addEventListener("arReady", (event) => {
14       messageBox.innerHTML = "MindAR is ready";
15    });
```

The listeners `targetFound` and `targetLost` are used to trigger events when an image target is found or lost:

```
18    document.querySelector('#ar_container').addEventListener("target-
Found", event => {
19         messageBox.innerHTML = "AR target found";
20    });


23    document.querySelector('#ar_container').addEventListener("target-
Lost", event => {
24         messageBox.innerHTML = "AR target lost";
25    });
```

After running the code, you will be able to see something like this:

Figure 7.10: *Image tracking example*

MindAR Image Tracker Caveats

As you can see, you will not be able to run it on your desktop browser. For some reason, MindAR cannot detect the desktop camera the same way ar.js does, so you will only be able to see it working when running on your mobile phone.

Also, the tracking quality is not perfect– depending on your image target, the tracker struggles to find and align the 3D scene, or sometimes it loses the position and the right perspective. You will notice that the tracking is a bit unstable, with the 3D scene shaking a bit. But for this issue we have a solution– MindAR comes with some parameters to improve the tracking and smoothen the movement:

- `filterMinCF`: Cutoff frequency. The default value is 0.001, but you can decrease it to reduce the shaking issue.

- `filterBeta`: Speed coefficient. The default value is 1000, and increasing it helps to reduce the shaking issue too.

- `warmupTolerance`: It is the delay time (in seconds) between the image tracker finding the image and showing it on the screen. A smaller value could give you false positives, so it is good to work with values between 3 and 6 seconds. The default is 5.

- `missTolerance`: It is the opposite of `warmupTolerance`; it is the delay time (in seconds) between the image tracker losing the tracking and hiding the 3D content. The default value is 5.

These parameters are set into the <a-scene> element, the same way you added the image target path:

```
<a-scene mindar-image="imageTargetSrc:image_target.mind; filterMinCF:0.1;
filterBeta: 10; warmupTolerance: 3; missTolerance: 3"/>

...

</a-scene>
```

Using Face Tracking

You can find the code of this section in the folder: https://github.com/OrangeAVA/ Creative-Technology-with-Three.js/tree/main/chapter07/aframe_webAR_ face_tracking_mindAR

Now that we know how to use MindAR image tracking, let us experiment with its cool face-tracking feature. It uses your front-facing camera to detect your face and attach objects to it. So let us start changing our HTML file. MindAR has a different library file to enable the face-tracking feature:

(./index.html):

```
13      <script
src="https://unpkg.com/mind-ar@1.2.3/dist/mindar-face-aframe.prod.js">
</script>
```

In the <a-scene> element, let's change the component from image tracking to face tracking:

```
20      <a-scene
21        renderer="logarithmicDepthBuffer: true;"
22        loading-screen="enabled: false;"
23        device-orientation-permission-ui="enabled: false"
24        embedded
25        mindar-face
26      >
```

Instead of using a boring cube, let us turn things more interesting by adding a jade mask GLB file into the scene, first loading it on <a-assets> area:

```
28      <a-asset-item id="mask-glb"
   src="./assets/models/jade_mask_low_poly.glb"></a-asset-item>
```

Then we will add it to our AR scene. However, now we need to change the container component to be able to read the user's face and add the mask GLB element:

```
28      <a-entity id="ar_container" mindar-face-target="anchorIndex: 1">
```

```
44      <a-entity id="mask" gltf-model="#mask-glb" position="0 -0.18 -0.58"
   scale="3.341 3.341 3.341"></a-entity>
```

In the boilerplate code, we added some lights and other stuff. On saving it and running it on your desktop (yes, this one runs on your desktop!) or mobile browser you will be able to see this:

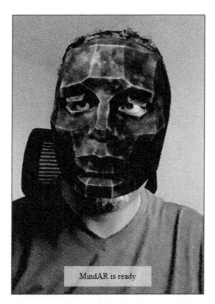

Figure 7.11: *Face tracking example*

*"Jade Mask low poly" (https://skfb.ly/oOz6o) by **uv15o6** is licensed under CC Attribution-Non-Commercial-NoDerivs (http://creativecommons.org/licenses/by-nc-nd/4.0/).*

If you rotate your face or get closer or farther from the camera, the mask will follow the position, rotation, and scale of your face. Differently from the image tracker, the face tracker uses **Google's TensorFlow** technology which is very powerful and accurate. If you go back a bit and read the code line 28, you will find this parameter: anchorIndex. MindAR (actually, Google's TensorFlow) is able to find up to 486 anchor points on the user's face. The number 1 is relative to the noise tip, so it's a good idea to attach the mask (or a fake nose, or a pair of sunglasses) to it. But you can use any of the other 485 anchor points to attach 3D objects to it:

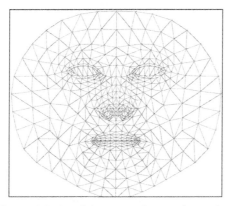

Figure 7.12: *Google's TensorFlow anchor points*

You can find a complete list of anchor points in high res on **Google's TensorFlow** GitHub:

https://raw.githubusercontent.com/tensorflow/tfjs-models/master/face-landmarks-detection/mesh_map.jpg

In line 28, we attached the mask:

```
28     <a-entity id="ar_container" mindar-face-target="anchorIndex: 1">
... </a-entity>
```

However, we could add other objects to different face anchors, for example, in the right eyebrow (anchor point #52):

```
<a-entity id="ar_container2" mindar-face-target="anchorIndex: 52"> ...
</a-entity>
```

Or on the user's chin (anchor point #199):

```
<a-entity id="ar_container2" mindar-face-target="anchorIndex: 199"> ...
</a-entity>
```

Adding a 3D Occluder

In AR terminology, an occluder is a 3D object that masks part of the scene (or parts of it). When working on face-tracking projects, we usually use a simplified 3D mesh of the head to mask out parts of the 3D model that should not be visible (or occluded) by the face.

In the following image, we can see how a head occluder should be positioned in order to occlude the inner parts of the mask that should be occluded by the real head:

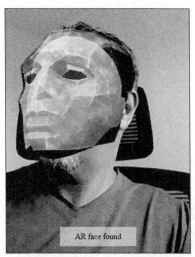

Figure 7.13: 3D occluder object

The `occluder` object should be added on top of all the objects that should be occluded. Its syntax is exactly the same as a GLB element, but we need to add the `occluder` component to make it work:

```
41    <a-entity id="head_occluder" mindar-face-occluder
  gltf-model="#head-occluder-glb"
        position="0 -0.00999 0.1299" scale="0.05987 0.05987 0.05987">
        </a-entity>
```

It is a good idea to remove the `mindar-face-occluder` component when you are moving and scaling the head occluder object until it gets to the right position and scale. Once it is in the right position, put the component back and watch the results!

Face Tracking Listeners

The way we have useful listeners for the image tracker, we have them on the face tracker too:

(`./js/main.js`):

```
13    sceneEl.addEventListener("arReady", (event) => {
14      messageBox.innerHTML = "MindAR is ready";
15    });


18    sceneEl.addEventListener("targetFound", event => {
19      messageBox.innerHTML = "AR face found";
20    });


23    sceneEl.addEventListener("targetLost", event => {
24      messageBox.innerHTML = "AR face lost";
15    });
```

The only difference is that `targetFound` and `targetLost` listeners are attached to the `<a-scene>` element for the face tracking feature, instead of the AR container (`#ar_container`) when using the image tracker.

Third-Party AR Libraries

In the previous chapters, we focused on open-source webAR libraries, such as `ar.js` and `MindAR`. Considering the fact that they are free to use, they are very good and provide us a good tracking quality at zero cost. However, if you are looking for better tracking quality or more powerful resources, you should look at some third-party webAR libraries. In this section, we will talk about the three main webAR libraries available, but there are lots more.

8th Wall

8th Wall (https://www.8thwall.com) is, nowadays, the most used webAR library in the AR market. The reason for this success is their very powerful SLAM/World tracking feature, which basically allows the AR developer to detect horizontal surfaces and place objects into them. The tracking is very stable and can keep objects in the AR space even if you are looking in a different direction.

The webAR library has other good features, such as image tracking (very stable and powerful) and VPS (Visual Positioning System), that allow you to capture real objects using a mobile app and track them in the real world, allowing the developer to attach virtual objects to it. 8th Wall has a very good face tracker.

The main caveat of the 8th Wall is its license cost– the subscription values are quite reasonable, but it is very expensive to publish commercial projects. It makes it very difficult for small (and even medium) clients to use the platform.

Blippar

Blippar's webAR SDK, available at https://www.blippar.com, offers a robust and reliable Image Tracking feature, along with a functional version of Surface Tracking, although not as precise and stable as 8th Wall. Despite this, the subscription and licensing costs make it a viable alternative to 8th Wall. Additionally, Blippar provides a user-friendly webAR authoring tool called Blippbuilder. This tool empowers AR enthusiasts to craft simple AR experiences directly within the web interface, eliminating the necessity of writing a single line of code.

Zappar

Zappar's webAR SDK, available at https://www.zappar.com is a comprehensive toolkit designed to empower developers in creating immersive AR experiences. With its wide range of features and capabilities, the Zappar SDK enables developers to build interactive and engaging AR content for various platforms and devices. With support for image recognition, face tracking, and surface detection, developers can easily build interactive AR content that seamlessly integrates with the real world. Zappar has a webAR authoring tool called

ZappWorks that uses a no-code approach and enables AR developers to build webAR experiences directly into the tool.

Other Options

These are, nowadays, the most used webAR libraries but we can find other interesting options in the AR market, such as AWE, MyWebAR, among others.

Conclusion

This chapter was all about code– with the learned lessons from this chapter you are now able to build a webAR scene from scratch– a product showcase using AR 3-DoF, an AR image tracking scene, and an AR face tracking scene. You now know a bit more about open-source webAR libraries and the main third-party webAR libraries too. In the next chapter, we will start developing VR headsets and more.

CHAPTER 8

Creating Your First WebVR Experience

Introduction

We are finally at the end of our journey through creative technology, Three.js, and A-Frame. Our last chapter with commented code examples will focus on one of the most promising technologies in the current days– Virtual Reality. It will focus more specifically on webVR, since we are using only web technologies to build our lessons. We are going to use some of the lessons learned in the previous chapters to build a cool web VR Art Exhibition– a VR experience that can run on VR headsets through VR browsers such as Meta Quest Browser, Firefox webVR, Vive Browser, or Supermedium with fully VR support (VR controllers also) or in an adaptive way on regular desktop and mobile browsers.

Structure

In this chapter, we will discuss the following topics:

- Basic webVR Scene Setup
- Art Exhibition Project Concept
- JSON File Structure
- HTML File Structure
- Main JS file
- Scene Components

Basic webVR Scene Setup

You can find the code of this section in the folder: https://github.com/OrangeAVA/Creative-Technology-with-Three.js/tree/main/chapter08/aframe_webVR_template

A-Frame was, initially, developed with a focus on webVR, and not webAR, so the scene setup for webVR scenes is much simpler and straightforward. Any scene with the basic A-Frame setup will work seamlessly on VR or desktop/ mobile browsers. The main differences between these two different platforms are, of course, the immersive view on VR headsets and the UI interaction– VR controllers on VR browsers and mouse/touch devices on desktop/mobile browsers.

You will notice, also, a small icon that should show up in the bottom right of your screen:

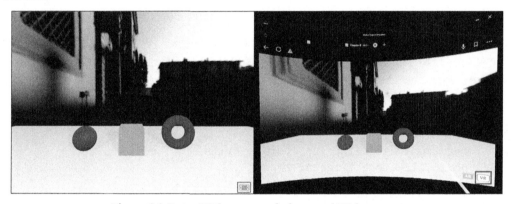

Figure 8.1: *Enter VR button on desktop and VR browsers*

This button has different behaviors depending on the device you are using. On VR browsers, you will be able to enter into the VR space at the click of the button– the scene will take over your VR headset screen and you will be fully immersed in it, being able, also, to interact with the scene using the VR controllers, walk around the scene, rotate the camera with the VR headset movement, hear positional audio, and so on. On desktop/mobile browsers, by clicking this button the scene will go full screen and you will be able to interact with it with your mouse/touch to rotate the camera, and your keyboard (using arrow keys and WASD keys) to walk around.

You can, of course, walk around your real space and update your virtual position inside the VR space but you will need a huge empty space to walk towards the scene objects and interact with them, so we recommend that you use the VR controller thumbstick to walk around the VR scene– on Meta Quest the left thumbstick will move you left/right/forward/backward, and the right thumbstick will rotate the camera (apart from the VR headset rotation). To interact with the VR scene objects, just point your VR controller pointer to the desired object and press the trigger button.

The A-Frame webVR scenes we are creating in this chapter are compatible with the following VR headsets:

- HTC Vive
- Oculus Rift
- Oculus Quest, Oculus Quest 2 and Oculus Quest 3
- Oculus Go
- Valve Index
- Vive Focus
- Windows Mixed Reality compatible devices

Now let us take a look into our boilerplate HTML file. We are essentially using the same HTML code from all the other examples, loading A-Frame libraries, and starting with the `<a-scene>` element to initialize A-Frame:

(./index.html)

```
25   <a-scene
26     renderer="antialias: true; colorManagement: true;
       physicallyCorrectLights: true;"
27     xr-mode-ui="enabled: true" shadow="type: pcf"
       light="defaultLightsEnabled: false"
28     loading-screen="enabled: true;"
29     scene-environment="hdrImage:../assets/images/pisa.hdr; hdrExposure: 1;"
30     gltf-model="dracoDecoderPath:
       https://ar-libs.blippar.com/components/draco/1.4.1/;"
31     raycaster="objects: .clickable"
32     cursor="fuse: false; rayOrigin: mouse"
33   >
```

The only difference from a regular or webAR A-Frame scene in line 27 is:

```
27     xr-mode-ui="enabled: true"
```

Here, we tell A-Frame to add the AR/VR buttons we presented in *Figure 8.1*. You can disable them, or you can set custom buttons. Just add the element ID on `enterVRButton` and `enterARButton` parameters to use the custom version:

```
xr-mode-ui="enabled: true; enterVRButton: #myEnterVRButton; enterARButton:
#myEnterARButton"
```

You will notice some important differences in the camera definition on a VR scene:

```
39   <a-entity id="rig" movement-controls position="0 0 0" rotation="0 0 0">
```

```
41    <a-entity camera="near: 0.005; fov:75;" id="camera" position="0 2 0"
      look-controls="pointerLockEnabled: false"></a-entity>

43    <a-entity id="leftHand" windows-motion-controls="hand: left"
      oculus-touch-controls="hand: left" vive-controls="hand: left"
      raycaster="objects: .clickable; far: 100" ></a-entity>

44    <a-entity id="rightHand" windows-motion-controls="hand: right"
      oculus-touch-controls="hand: right" vive-controls="hand: right"
      raycaster="objects: .clickable; far: 100"></a-entity>


46   </a-entity>
```

First of all, we use a camera rig to group the camera element and the VR controller elements. This way you can position the rig around the scene and still be able to move the player using a VR controller or simply by walking through your real space (when using roomscale/6-DoF devices). We have, also, the left and right controller elements with the respective components that read different kinds of controllers, such as, Oculus (Rift and Quest), Vive, and Windows Mixed Reality devices:

```
43    <a-entity id="leftHand" laser-controls="hand: left"
      windows-motion-controls="hand: left"
      oculus-touch-controls="hand: left" vive-controls="hand: left"
      raycaster="objects: .clickable; far: 100" ></a-entity>

44    <a-entity id="rightHand" laser-controls="hand: left"
      windows-motion-controls="hand: right"
      oculus-touch-controls="hand: right" vive-controls="hand: right"
      raycaster="objects: .clickable; far: 100"></a-entity>
```

On the controllers sections, we set up the raycaster objects, just like we did on AR scenes. The difference here is that we apply the raycaster component to each controller, pointing to some specific ID or class that will be used to trigger the events. You can even use different IDs or classes on left and side controllers, allowing some elements to interact only with the left or the right controller. Finally, the component `laser-controls` will read the controller's direction and use it to track the raycasting– this way you can point to objects in the scene and interact with them.

The next code part is about the scene itself. We have three elements that work as a "menu"– a sphere, a cube, and a torus. We have a plane too, to work as a floor and catch the shadows. Finally, we have an element called `popup`, which groups the elements that will work as a popup when the "menu" elements are clicked. Inside this menu, we have a button to close it (`close_btn`), and a plane with an `a-text` element that will get the text from the menu elements:

```
49   <a-entity id="container" position="0 0 0">
50     <a-entity id="scene_container" rotation="0 0 0">

52       <!-- menu elements -->
53       <a-sphere id="sphere_btn" class="clickable left menu"
         position="-2 0.5 -5" radius="0.5" color="#ff0000"
         shadow="cast: true"></a-sphere>
54       <a-box id="box_btn" class="clickable menu" position="0 0.5 -5"
         color="#00ff00" shadow="cast: true"></a-box>
55       <a-torus id="torus_btn" class="clickable menu" position="2 0.75 -5"
         radius="0.5" radius-tubular="0.1" color="#0000ff"
         shadow="cast: true"></a-torus>


57       <!-- floor -->
58       <a-plane rotation="-90 0 0" scale="20 20 1"
         shadow="receive: true"></a-plane>


60       <!-- popup -->
61       <a-entity id="popup" position="0 1 -1.5" visible="false">
62         <a-circle id="close_btn" position="0.5 0.25 0.01"
           scale="0.1 0.1 0.1" color="#000000" material="shader:flat"
           class="clickable">
63           <a-text position="0 0.166 0.01" value="x"
             text="anchor: center;align: center; wrapCount: 5"
             material="shader:flat"></a-text>
64         </a-circle>

65         <a-plane width="1" height="0.5" material="shader:flat">
66           <a-text id="popup_text" position="0 0 0.01" value="x"
             text="color: #000000; anchor: center;align: center;
             wrapCount: 50">
67           </a-text>
68         </a-plane>
69       </a-entity>
71     </a-entity>
72   </a-entity>
```

The popup group is initially hidden (visible="false") because the menu elements will control its visibility. All the popup elements have a flat shader material (material="shader:flat") because as it is an UI element, we do not want them to react with the scene lights.

And finally, we have the scene lighting:

```
75  <a-entity light="type: ambient; color: #fff; intensity: 1" ></a-entity>
76  <a-entity light="intensity: 5; type: point; castShadow: true"
    rotation="" position="2 3 2"></a-entity>
77  <a-entity light="intensity: 3; type: point; castShadow: true"
    rotation="" position="-4 3 1.5"></a-entity>
78  <a-entity light="intensity: 0.5; type: point; castShadow: false"
    rotation="" position="1 3 -2"></a-entity>
```

We had to increase the light intensity because they react a bit differently on VR scenes.

Now let us jump to the `main.js` file. It is very simple since A-Frame takes care of all the VR headset interfaces and deals with all the controller's interactions. First of all, we run the `start()` function when the HTML is fully loaded:

(./js/main.js)

```
1  window.addEventListener("load", function () {
2    start();
3  });
```

Then we initialize the variables and attach them to the scene elements:

```
5  const closeBtn = document.querySelector('#close_btn');
6  const popup = document.querySelector('#popup');
7  const popupText = document.querySelector('#popup_text');
```

And now we define the `start()` function:

```
9   async function start() {
10    const menuBtns = document.querySelectorAll('.clickable.menu');
```

In line 10, we read all the elements that have the classes `clickable` and `menu`. As explained previously, the `clickable` class makes the A-Frame elements readable by the raycaster. In other words, they will be clickable. The `menu` class is just to separate them from the other clickable elements (the popup close button, for example). Now we can loop through these elements and add the respective listeners to each menu button:

```
13    menuBtns.forEach(function(element) {
14      element.addEventListener('click', function() {
15        popup.setAttribute('visible','true');
16        popupText.setAttribute('value', element.id);
```

```
17        })
18      })
```

On each menu button click listener, we need to do two things– make the popup visible:

```
15    popup.setAttribute('visible','true');
```

Next, we need to change the popup text. In this case, we are reading the button ID and adding it to the popup text:

```
16    popupText.setAttribute('value', element.id);
```

And, finally, the close button– we just need to set the popup visibility to off:

```
20      closeBtn.addEventListener('click', function() {
21        popup.setAttribute('visible','false');
22      })
23    }
```

And it is done! It is a very simple project, just to build the foundations of a VR scene. It has the basic elements you will need to use on any other VR scene. Now let us move on with a much more complex project– a VR Art Exhibition!

Art Exhibition Project Concept

You can find the code of this section in the folder: https://github.com/OrangeAVA/Creative-Technology-with-Three.js/tree/main/chapter07/aframe_webVR_exhibition

Our Virtual Art Exhibition will be available to any art enthusiast with a web, mobile or VR browser, but of course, the impact of the experience will be much more intense if experienced on VR headsets.

Our art exhibition venue is a two-storey building, with a staircase connecting them. In the building entrance, you will find the **spawn room.** Here, you will be able to see more details about the art exhibition and see some special buttons that we will explain further. The art pieces are, mostly, placed over the building walls, but you will be able to find some sculptures placed in special spots. Also, you will be able to see the details of each art piece by clicking them:

Figure 8.2: *Art Exhibition spawn room*

Technically speaking, our art exhibition scene has some GLB files– the building 3D file is made from three GLB files, the spawn room, the first floor, and the second floor. We also have a GLB file for the spawn room buttons to make it easier to detect clicks on them. Finally, we have the navmesh 3D file that will tell A-Frame where the user can walk over. This way we avoid the user crossing through walls and blocking elements. Also, the navmesh will make it possible to go up to the second floor using the staircase, without the need for any more sophisticated physics library or special component. The other 3D files are related to third-party assets we need to load, such as sculptures and other elements:

Figure 8.3: *Art Exhibition first floor*

In the spawn room we will find some buttons that have `teleportation` functions— by clicking any of them, you will be moved instantly to the desired point, without the need to walk to each spot. It is an interesting approach when you have a huge scene and do not want your user to walk to each point. Even for smaller scenes it could be useful and save your user's time. The added two buttons to the spawn room— one to teleport the user to the first floor, and one to the second floor:

Figure 8.4: Art Exhibition second floor

The art pieces are created dynamically on the scene— we created a JSON file that contains references to all the art pieces, with their name, artist, date, file name, placement inside the building, and orientation (to match the wall orientation). It will allow us to keep the code organized and will make it easier to change any art piece asset, info, or placement in the future:

*The art room 3D model was created specially for this chapter by the 3D artist and Three.js developer **Felipe Matos** (https://sketchfab.com/felipeomatos) and licensed under Creative Commons Attribution (http://creativecommons.org/licenses/by/4.0/).*

*Art piece "African Masks" (https://skfb.ly/6EsE8) by **FletchTech** is licensed under Creative Commons Attribution (http://creativecommons.org/licenses/by/4.0/).*

*Art piece "The Thinker by Auguste Rodin" (https://skfb.ly/6YwPH) by **Rigsters** is licensed under Creative Commons Attribution (http://creativecommons.org/licenses/by/4.0/).*

*Art piece Nataraja, Shiva as the Lord of Dance (https://skfb.ly/o8MrI) by **clevelandart** and modeled by **Dale Utt**: https://sketchfab.com/turbulentorbit under Creative Commons Attribution (http://creativecommons.org/licenses/by/4.0/).*

So, let us get started!

JSON File Structure

The JSON file that populates the Art Room has the following structure:

```
2   "mona":{
3           "name":"Mona Lisa",
4           "author": "Leonardo da Vinci",
5           "date": "1503-1506",
6           "type":"paint",
7           "dimensions": [0.77,0.53],
8           "customScale": 2,
9           "position": [3.65,1.5,5],
10           "rotation": [0,0,0],
11           "src": "./assets/images/art-pieces/mona.jpg"
12  },
```

From line 2 to line 5, we have the basic art piece entry information– name, author, and date. This information is used to fill the art piece popup when the user clicks it. The parameter type is used to differentiate between paints and sculptures. For paint art pieces, the parameter dimensions are related to the real art piece size (used to keep the proportions), and customScale multiplies the values of the dimensions to make the art piece bigger or smaller. The position parameter tells the x, y, and z position of the art piece, and rotation is used to give the right orientation to it, depending on the wall position the art piece is placed on. Finally, the parameter src contains the path of the art piece file– a JPG file for paints or a GLB file for sculptures.

For the sculptures and art pieces, we have the following JSON structure:

```
183  "nataraja":{
184           "name":"Nataraja, Shiva as the Lord of Dance",
185           "author": "Tamil Nadu",
186           "date": "900-1200",
187           "type":"sculpture",
188           "dimensions": [],
189           "customScale": 0.75,
190           "position": [1.15, 1.15,-1.15],
```

```
191        "rotation": [0,0,0],
192        "src": "./assets/models/art-pieces/natajara.glb"
193    },
```

The main difference between the two art piece types is that `paint` art pieces read essentially a JPG file, and `sculpture` art pieces read a GLB file. Also, sculptures do not need to have the `dimensions` parameter set, since the GLB file contains its own scale values.

HTML File Structure

The HTML file starts with the A-Frame scene definition:

(index.html):

```
21  <a-scene
22    renderer="antialias: true; colorManagement: true;
      physicallyCorrectLights: true;"
23    xr-mode-ui="enabled: true" shadow="type: pcf"
    light="defaultLightsEnabled: false"
24    loading-screen="enabled: true;"
25    gltf-model="dracoDecoderPath:
      https://ar-libs.blippar.com/components/draco/1.4.1/;"
26    raycaster="objects: .clickable; far: 5"
27    cursor="fuse: false; rayOrigin: mouse"
28  >
```

It is pretty much the same of the previous A-Frame AR and VR examples, but with two important differences:

```
23    xr-mode-ui="enabled: true"
```

It is used to enable/disable the Enter AR / Enter VR buttons. You can disable it if you want to use your own buttons. In this case, you need to add the HTML ID to the button parameter:

```
xr-mode-ui="enterVRButton: #myEnterVRButton; enterARButton: #myEnterAR-
Button"
```

The second main difference is in line 26:

```
26    raycaster="objects: .clickable; far: 5"
```

Along with the `objects` parameter (used to make the A-Frame elements with the `clickable` class interactive), we added the parameter `far`— with this parameter, we can control the maximum click distance from the object to the camera. In short, objects that are farther than 5 units from the camera will not be clickable. This will prevent the user from clicking the objects that are far away, for example, if the user is in the spawn room, he/she will not be able to click any art piece that is in the art room. You can use the parameter `near` for the same reason– avoid clicks on objects that are nearer than the parameter value.

In the `<a-assets>` section, we preload all the GLB files that will be used to build the Art Exhibition building:

```
31  <a-asset-item id="spawn_room"  src="assets/models/spawn_room.glb"></
a-asset-item>
32  <a-asset-item id="spawn_room_btn"
    src="assets/models/spawn_room_btn.glb"></a-asset-item>
33  <a-asset-item id="art_room_1f"
    src="assets/models/art_room_1f.glb"></a-asset-item>
34  <a-asset-item id="art_room_2f"
    src="assets/models/art_room_2f.glb"></a-asset-item>
35  <a-asset-item id="navmesh_glb"
    src="./assets/models/navmesh.glb"></a-asset-item>
```

After that we start to define the camera rig element– it will include the A-Frame camera and the VR controllers. It will contain, also, an important element that we will explain soon:

```
40  <a-entity id="rig" movement-controls="constrainToNavMesh: true" po-
sition="14 0 0" rotation="0 -90 0">
```

In the camera rig element, we added a special parameter on the `movement-controls` component– the `constrainToNavMesh` parameter. It will be used to tell A-Frame that the camera rig needs to constrain the movement to the navmesh that we will define in the following lines.

The user starts his navigation inside the spawn room, which is positioned 14 units on the x-axis from the art room. The rotation **0 -90 0** faces the user to the navigation buttons and to the initial scene description.

Following the camera rig element, we define the camera itself:

```
42  <a-entity camera="near: 0.005; fov:75;" id="camera" position="0 1.4 0"
    look-controls="pointerLockEnabled: false">
```

The y position moves the "head" of the user to 1.4 units from the ground level, that is, in reference to the art room 3D object, a bit above the height of the art pieces, just like it would be in the real world. The `pointerLockEnabled` parameter, set to false, disables the pointer lock feature when the screen is clicked (in desktop mode) and will not affect the VR mode.

After the camera element, we have an important element of our scene– the info popup. It will be used to show the art piece information when it is clicked:

```
45    <a-entity id="popup" position="0 0 -0.5" scale="0 0 0" visible="false"
46      animation__scale_up="property: scale; to: 0.3 0.3 0.3; dur: 1500;
        easing: easeOutElastic; startEvents: scaleUp"
47      animation__scale_down="property: scale; to: 0 0 0; dur: 500;
        easing: easeInBack; startEvents: scaleDown"
48   >
49      <a-circle id="close_btn" position="0.5 0.25 0.01" scale="0.05 0.05
        0.05"

        color="#000000" material="shader:flat" class="clickable">
50        <a-text position="0 0.166 0.01" value="x" text="anchor: center;
          align: center; wrapCount: 5" material="shader:flat"></a-text>
51      </a-circle>
52      <a-plane width="1" height="0.5" material="shader:flat">
53        <a-text id="popup_name" position="0 0.13 0.01" value="x"
          text="font: roboto; anchor: center; width: 0.85; color: #000000;
          align: center; wrapCount: 22.25"></a-text>
54        <a-text id="popup_author" position="0 -0.009 0.01" value="x"
          text="font: roboto; anchor: center; width: 0.85; color: #000000;
          align: center; wrapCount: 22.25"></a-text>
55        <a-text id="popup_date" position="0 -0.150 0.01" value="x"
          text="font: roboto; anchor: center; width: 0.85; color: #000000;
          align: center; wrapCount: 22.25"></a-text>
56      </a-plane>
57    </a-entity>
```

Why is it placed inside the camera element? As you noticed in our previous example, we are not able to see non-A-Frame elements in VR space. So, any HTML div, button, span, and other elements will not be visible when the user is interacting with the scene with a VR headset. We could build the info popup outside A-Frame, but only desktop and mobile users would be able to see it.

The solution: Create a popup in VR space using A-Frame elements– entities, planes, circles, and text elements. We also want the popup element to act like a UI element fixed in the screen so it will not move when the user moves as we did in the previous VR example. The only way to do it is by creating the UI element inside the camera object. This way it moves and rotates along with the camera, whatever the position or orientation the camera is facing.

The popup container starts invisible (we just want to see it after the user clicks some art piece) and with a scale of **0 0 0**. Also, it contains two animations that will be called when we want to show or hide it– animation__scale_up and **animation__scale_down**.

Still talking about the A-Frame popup, we have four important elements inside it– the close button, which is basically an <a-circle> element with an <a-text> (the **X** text inside the circle) inside it. This <a-circle> element has a clickable class, so it can be visible by the A-Frame raycaster. The next elements are the **<a-text>** elements that will receive the clicked art piece data– popup_name, popup_author, and popup_date. By changing the parameter value of each one, we can update the <a-text> values dynamically.

Finally, all the popup internal elements are set with a flat material– we do not want the scene lighting to affect the popup look.

The last elements of the camera rig are the VR controls, just like we learned in the previous VR example:

```
60   <a-entity id="leftHand" laser-controls="hand: left"
     windows-motion-controls="hand: left" oculus-touch-controls="hand: left"
     vive-controls="hand: left" raycaster="objects: .clickable;" ></a-entity>

61   <a-entity id="rightHand" laser-controls="hand: right"
     windows-motion-controls="hand: right" oculus-touch-controls="hand:
     right"
     vive-controls="hand: right" raycaster="objects: .clickable;"></a-entity>
```

By using different selectors inside the raycaster objects parameter, we can differentiate between elements that can be clicked by the left controller and the right controller. In our case, we want both controllers to interact with objects with the class clickable, so there is no need to use different selectors now. If you are using two controllers, the left thumbstick will move the camera left/right/forward/backward, and the right thumbstick will rotate the camera. You can, of course, walk around your real space to update your virtual position, but you will need a lot of space to do it!

The last element of the first part of this section is the navmesh– the 3D model that will constrain the camera rig movement it:

```
66   <a-entity id="navmesh" nav-mesh position="0 0 0" scale="1 1 1"
     gltf-model="#navmesh_glb" visible="false"></a-entity>
```

The navmesh is basically a 3D plane that tells the 3D engine which parts of the 3D model the user can walk over or not. In practical ways, the user can walk where there is some geometry, and will be blocked by the empty parts. In our navmesh, we created a single plane and stretched it, and extruded the faces until we got the desired shape. For the holes, we refined the mesh and deleted the faces that would block the user from walking over it. We also added a plane to connect the two floors to act as a staircase. Finally, we joined all the different planes (first floor, second floor, and spawn room) to a single mesh, and exported the GLB file. You can check the final result in the following image:

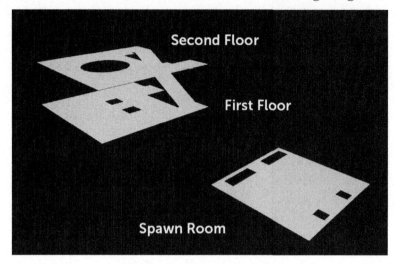

Figure 8.5: *Navmesh structure*

To tell A-Frame this 3D model is a `navmesh`, we added the component `nav-mesh` to the element but be aware that we can have only one `navmesh` on our scene. If you add more than one, A-Frame will consider the last `navmesh` as the valid one. Also, the `navmesh` element does not need to be visible in the scene, so it is a good idea to set `visible` to `false` when publishing your scene.

After defining the `navmesh` element, we will start building our art exhibition building structure. For this, we created two containers, one to contain all the scenes and another one to contain all the building structures:

```
68    <a-entity id="container">
69      <a-entity id="building_container">
```

The building container will have only the building structure (first and second floors and the spawn room), and the full container will have the building container, the lights, and any other element we need to add to the scene that is not part of the building structure.

Our first building element is the spawn room– the user will be positioned in this area to choose to go to the first or second floor, by clicking one of the red buttons. The spawn room element reads the `spawn_room` GLB file and we are applying the component `art-room-material` to add textures to it. We will explain the reason for it further in this chapter:

```
71   <a-entity
72     id="spawn_room"
73     gltf-model="#spawn_room"
74     position= "15 0 0"
75     art-room-material="map: ./assets/models/spawn_room.jpg"
76     shadow="cast: true; receive: true"
77     >
```

The two red buttons have a `clickable` class in order to make them interactive for the user:

```
78   <a-entity
79     id="btn_first_floor"
80     class="clickable"
81     gltf-model="#spawn_room_btn"
82     position= "2.18 1.02 -1.09"
83     art-room-material="map: ./assets/models/spawn_room.jpg"
84     shadow="cast: true; receive: true"
85   ></a-entity>

86   <a-entity
87     id="btn_second_floor"
88     class="clickable"
89     gltf-model="#spawn_room_btn"
90     position= "2.18 1.02 1.11"
91     art-room-material="map: ./assets/models/spawn_room.jpg"
92     shadow="cast: true; receive: true"
93   ></a-entity>
```

And finally, in the spawn room, we have a quick explanation about the Virtual Art Exhibition. These are just simple `text` components (you can use an `<a-text>` element as well) with no shadow casting or else whether:

```
95   <a-entity id="intro_title" text__intro_title="side: front; value:
     Welcome to our Virtual Exhibition!; color: #000000; width: 7.44;
     wrapCount: 83.81; zOffset: 0; align: center" scale="" rotation="0
     -90 0" position="2.75 1.735 0" shadow="cast: false; receive:
     false"></a-entity>
```

```
96    <a-entity id="intro_copy" text__intro_copy="side: front; value:
      Tap on the left button to go to the first Exhibition Floor, and on
      the right button to go to the second floor.; color: #000000; width:
      2.39; wrapCount: 29.67; zOffset: 0; align: center" scale="" ro-
      tation="0 -90 0" position="2.75 1.29 0" shadow="cast:false; re-
      ceive:false"></a-entity>
```

After setting up the spawn room, let us add the first and second floors. Here, we are just loading the GLB files and applying the textures on them by adding the `art-room-material` component:

```
99   <a-entity
100      id="art_room_1f"
101      gltf-model="#art_room_1f"
102      position= "0 0 0"
103      art-room-material="map: ./assets/models/art_room_1f_baked.jpg"
104      shadow="cast: true; receive: true"
105   >
106   </a-entity>

108   <a-entity
109      id="art_room_2f"
110      gltf-model="#art_room_2f"
111      position= "0 0 0"
112      art-room-material="map: ./assets/models/art_room_2f_baked.jpg"
113      shadow="cast: true; receive: true"
114   >
115   </a-entity>
```

By the way, why are we loading three different GLB files for the Art Exhibition building instead of having only one file with everything? The first reason is for optimization's sake– three files load faster than one big file. The second reason is to have more control over the element's position and materials– this way we can fine-tune the position, rotation, and other parameters instead of having only one GLB file, which would need us to tweak it on Blender for every single adjustment, and export again and again.

After setting up the Art Exhibition building, it is time to populate the art pieces over the rooms. We could, of course, add art pieces one-by-one directly in A-Frame, but this is a good opportunity to teach how to create A-Frame elements dynamically. Additionally, it makes the code much more flexible and organized:

```
118   <a-entity id="art-pieces-container"
      art-pieces="path: js/art-pieces.json"></a-entity>
```

It is just an A-Frame element with the art-pieces component applied to it. The component parameter path contains the path for the art piece's JSON file. We will explain this component in the next section.

To end the HTML section, we have the scene lighting setup:

```
123   <a-entity light="type: ambient; color: #fff; intensity: 3" ></a-entity>
125   <a-entity id="light_spawn_room" light="type: point; castShadow:
      true; intensity: 2" rotation="" position="15 2.9 0"></a-entity>
127   <a-entity id="light_1st_floor" light="type: point; castShadow: true;
      intensity: 2" position="0.05 2.42 -0.09"></a-entity>
129   <a-entity id="light_2nd_floor" position="0 6.4 0" light="type: point;
      castShadow: true; intensity: 2" position="0.05 2.42 -0.096"></a-en-
      tity>
```

The first light is an ambient light— we used it to make the scene clearer and increase the overall scene lighting. The other three lights are point lights, one for each room, each one casting shadows. We could add spotlights for every spot on the GLB file, but it would be very bad for the scene performance, so we decided to bake the scene lighting and ambient occlusion on Blender and export a single texture for each room. The A-Frame lights we defined here are just to cast some simple shadows and add some highlights to the objects since the art piece elements are fully dynamic and could not be baked previously.

Main JS file

We decided to use the main.js file only to control the event listeners and other UI interactions, and the A-Frame component system to control the specific scene functions, as the GLB material component and the art pieces populating function. Inside the main start() function we added the interface click listeners. The first one is the popup close button:

```
(./js/main.js):
19   closeBtn.addEventListener('click', function() {
20       closePopup();
21   })
```

The following ones are the spawn room buttons:

```
23   btnFirstFloor.addEventListener('click', function() {
24     navMesh.removeAttribute('nav-mesh')
25     rig.setAttribute('position','4.2 0.2 0');
26     rig.setAttribute('rotation','0 90 0');
```

```
27      navMesh.setAttribute('nav-mesh', true)
28    })
30    btnSecondFloor.addEventListener('click', function() {
31      navMesh.removeAttribute('nav-mesh')
32      rig.setAttribute('position','-3.78 3.33 -4.8');
33      rig.setAttribute('rotation','0 180 0');
34      navMesh.setAttribute('nav-mesh', true)
35    })
```

They just move the rig's current position to the desired (first or second floor) position and rotate the camera rig in order to make the user face the right direction when arriving at the new location. We are also removing the nav-mesh component temporarily to avoid positioning issues when defining the new values.

Outside the main start() function we added the functions to open and close the info popup. The openPopup function makes the popup element visible and plays the animation scaleUp which is defined directly on the A-Frame element. In this section, we also have the methods to update the text elements received from the data function parameter:

```
39    const openPopup = function(data) {
40        popup.setAttribute('visible','true');
41        popup.emit('scaleUp');
42        popupName.setAttribute('value', data.name);
43        popupAuthor.setAttribute('value', 'Artist: '+ data.author);
44        popupDate.setAttribute('value', 'Date: '+ data.date);
45    }
```

To close the popup, the function is a bit more simple– it emits the scaleDown animation (also defined on A-Frame element), and hides the popup after the animation is completed:

```
47    const closePopup = function(data) {
48        popup.emit('scaleDown');
49        popup.addEventListener('animationcomplete___scale_down',
          function() {
50          popup.setAttribute('visible','false');
51        })
52    }
```

Scene Components

For this scene, we have only two components– one to deal with the GLB materials, and another one to read the art piece's JSON file and populate it to the scene.

The component `art-room-material` is used to apply the material and the baked textures to the GLBs models. As explained earlier, we decided for this approach to have more control over the scene materials and textures, but you could just export the GLB file with the embedded texture in case you do not need to tweak it in code.

The component initially reads the parameter `map`, which contains the file path of the texture we want to apply to the object:

(`./js/components.js`):

```
1  AFRAME.registerComponent('art-room-material', {

3    schema: {

4      map: {default: ""},

5    },
```

After reading the texture file and setting up the texture map (fixing up the Y orientation and color space), we will run through all the GLB children elements to apply a `THREE.MeshStandardMaterial` material and a texture map to it. As we previously baked the entire scene on Blender, all the scene objects have the same material and texture, and the UV map of the GLB file will take care of the correct positioning of each texture area.

As said earlier, we want to have more control over our materials– we could, for example, increase the metalness or roughness of it, or simply ignore all the shadows and lighting by adding a `THREE.MeshBasicMaterial` material. We decided to use a `THREE.MeshStandardMaterial` to be able to use the scene lighting to add more or less lighting, and cast more defined shadows:

```
7    init: function() {

8      let el = this.el;

9      let mapSrc = this.data.map

10     let texture = new THREE.TextureLoader().load(mapSrc)

12     texture.flipY = false;

13     texture.colorSpace = THREE.SRGBColorSpace

15     el.addEventListener("model-loaded", e =>{
```

```
16          el.object3D.traverse(function(child){
17              if (child.isMesh){
18                      child.material = new THREE.MeshStandardMaterial({
19                          map: texture
20                      })
21                      child.material.needsUpdate = true;
22                  }
23              });
24          });
25      }
26  });
```

As we are creating and changing the materials dynamically, we set the material.
needsUpdate parameter to true, just to make sure it will be updated.

The next component is the one that creates the art pieces dynamically on the
scene, the art-pieces component. It has only one parameter, which is the path
to the JSON file that contains the art pieces:

```
29  AFRAME.registerComponent('art-pieces', {
31      schema: {
32          path: {default: ""}
33      },
```

Inside the init() function, we initialize the el variable, which is related to
the element to which the component is applied. In this case, the art-pieces-
container element will contain all the art piece elements:

```
37      const el = this.el;
```

In line 40 onwards, we start reading the JSON file and populating the art pieces.
The fetch JavaScript method reads the JSON file and executes the then callback
after reading it correctly:

```
40  fetch(this.data.path)
41      .then((response)=> response.json())
42      .then((json) =>
43      {
```

We have different ways to run through the JSON elements, such as a for...each
loop. However, we can use a more sophisticated approach by using the map

method. Here, we are telling JavaScript to run through the keys from the object json, since it is an array of objects:

```
45  Object.keys(json).map((artPieceKey, index) => {
```

To make the code more organized and understandable, we are creating a variable to store the data of the current art piece in the loop:

```
47  const currentArtPiece = json[artPieceKey]
```

And now we can start populating the art pieces into the scene. But wait, remember we have two types of art pieces, paints, and sculptures? So, we need to create two different situations for each one since they are completely different elements. First of all, we need to detect which kind of art piece the current object is. If it is a paint, we need to create an <a-box> element and apply a texture to it:

```
50  if (currentArtPiece.type === "paint") {
51    el.innerHTML += `
52      <a-box
53        material="src: ${currentArtPiece.src}"
54        scale= "${currentArtPiece.dimensions[1] *
        currentArtPiece.customScale} ${currentArtPiece.dimensions[0]
        * currentArtPiece.customScale} 0.08"
55                position="${currentArtPiece.position[0]}
        ${currentArtPiece.position[1]}
        ${currentArtPiece.position[2]}"
56                rotation="${currentArtPiece.rotation[0]}
        ${currentArtPiece.rotation[1]}
        ${currentArtPiece.rotation[2]}"
57                data-index="${index}"
58                class="clickable artpiece"
59                shadow="cast: true; receive: true"
60            >
61            </a-box>
62      `;
```

In line 53, we read the src parameter from the JSON, which is the texture path, and apply it to the <a-box> material. In line 54, we deal with the scale of the <a-box> element. Since the paints have different width and height sizes, we need to consider the parameters dimensions[0] (height) and dimensions[1] (width) to create a box with the correct paint size. We also have the customScale parameter, which is used to tweak the object size without messing up with the original art piece proportion. So, we just need to multiply `customScale` by both width and height parameters to have the correct box size.

For the position and rotation parameters, we just read the corresponding JSON values (position and rotation) and apply them.

In line 57, we created a `data` parameter (`data-index`) that stores the current object index that will be used further in the code to open the art piece popup with the correct data. In line 58, we added two classes, `clickable` and `artpiece`. The `clickable` class makes it clickable, and the `artpiece` class will be used to add event listeners only for these kinds of objects (art pieces).

Finally, in line 59, we add the `shadow` component since we want the art pieces to cast and receive shadows.

But what if the art piece type is not a paint? In this case, it is a sculpture, which means we need to load a GLB file and add it to the scene:

```
68   el.innerHTML += `

69     <a-entity

70       gltf-model="${currentArtPiece.src}"

71       rotation="${currentArtPiece.rotation[0]}
       ${currentArtPiece.rotation[1]} ${currentArtPiece.rotation[2]}"

72       position= "${currentArtPiece.position[0]}
       ${currentArtPiece.position[1]} ${currentArtPiece.position[2]}"

73       scale="${currentArtPiece.customScale}
       ${currentArtPiece.customScale} ${currentArtPiece.customScale}"

74       data-index="${index}"

75       class="clickable artpiece"

76       shadow="cast: true; receive: true"

77     >

78     </a-entity>

79   `;
```

In line 70, we simply load the GLB file by reading the `src` parameter (in the case of sculptures, the GLB file path) and applying it to the `gltf-model` component.

In lines 71 and 72, we position and rotate the object according to the JSON position and rotation parameters, and in line 73 we scale it, but now just using the `customScale` parameter, since the GLB files come with their original scale values, so we will not have the stretch issue.

The following lines are exactly the same as the paint art pieces type— the `data-index`, the classes, and the `shadow` components.

Have you noticed that we are creating A-Frame elements dynamically exactly the way we would do with HTML elements? The `innerHTML` method concatenates the elements inside the `el` container, making the process of building dynamic scenes very easy when using A-Frame. We could use the methods `insertAfter`/`insertBefore` or `appendChild` to create dynamic elements and add them to A-Frame as well.

Now that we have populated all the art pieces into the `art-pieces-container` element, it is time to set up the clicks on them. For this, we need to run through the recently created elements and add event listeners to each one:

```
85   const artPieces = document.querySelectorAll('.clickable.artpiece');
```

The array `artPieces` will store all the elements that contain the `clickable` and the `artpiece` classes, in other words, all the art pieces we want the user to interact with. Now we can run a loop through this array and set the listeners up:

```
87   artPieces.forEach(function(element) {
```

We need to know the art piece order, so we will be able to read the right data when the popup opens:

```
88      const index = element.dataset.index;
```

And now we can add the click listener to the current art piece element:

```
90      element.addEventListener('click', function() {
```

We can know the art piece data by crossing the clicked object index through the JSON data, and storing this data inside the object `artPieceData`:

```
91      const artPieceData = Object.entries(json)[index][1];
```

With the clicked art piece data stored in the `artPieceData` object, we can now open the popup object with the correct data:

```
92      openPopup(artPieceData);
```

Once it is clicked, the art piece will trigger the popup to open with its details. Nice and easy!

And that is it! We completed our last chapter about webVR using A-Frame. We can think about some improvements you could try using this scene as boilerplate:

- You can randomize the order of the art pieces to create a new exhibition every time the user opens it.

- You can add hotspots to the scene to show special content when the user is near them.
- What would you do to add more stores to this building?
- Besides paints and sculptures, how about adding videos, sound clips, and animations to your Art Exhibition?

Conclusion

We have finished our last lesson of our Three.js and A-Frame journey. You now have all the understanding and experience to build your own 3D scenes that will run on desktop, mobile, and VR browsers. We encourage you to duplicate all the examples given in this book to tweak the code lessons and learn different ways to accomplish different results. Moreover, we want you to use our code examples as boilerplates for your future projects and build your own boilerplates for different use cases.

In the next chapter, you will find good and useful boilerplates that you can use and tweak to your own projects.

CHAPTER 9

Useful Boilerplates to Start Your Projects

Introduction

As a bonus for you, brave reader, we provide here some useful boilerplates you can use to start your own projects. Some are variations of lessons we found in this book– but with a more "commercial" approach. Others are completely new ideas but use the lessons learned and the goals adopted in this book as starting points for commercial projects that you can adapt and, hopefully, sell to your clients. Feel free to duplicate and adapt them, or create totally new projects!

Structure

In this chapter, we will discuss the following topics:

- Best Practices
- T-Shirt Configurator App
- Isometric 3D Platform Game
- VR Travel App
- AR Product Showcase
- Animated Portfolio
- Home Design App
- Infographic

Best Practices

We have tried, during this book, to use development best practices in all our lessons, but there are many more points to talk about that are related not only to development itself. As a Creative Developer, you need to keep your mind open to other areas, such as 3D, animation, illustration, and even project management. In the next sections, you will find best practices that will help you on your Creative Development path.

General

- As a Creative Developer, you do not need to master 3D modeling or shading, animation, sound effects, or design, but you need to know the basics of these (and other) areas that have an impact on a creative development project.

- That said, even if you are able to tweak 3rd party assets (such as 3D models), it does not mean you need to do so. If you are working among a bigger team with 3D artists, animators, designers, and others, let them do their jobs. It will save you time and avoid stress with other team members.

- Be open and mindful about feedback on your work– the worst thing on a creative development project (or on any project!) is dealing badly with the feedback of team members (or clients). Respect is everything! We are generally part of a bigger team, so it is very important to keep the harmony and the morale of the team high to deliver successful projects.

- But never accept bad criticism, and harassment and never let other team members or clients diminish you and your work. Give respect and be respected! If it happens, try to keep things clear with the person who treated you badly and, if it does not help, escalate it to higher management.

- It is valid even for clients– sometimes it is better to end a project in the beginning to avoid further stress and drama than to keep accepting bad behavior from your client because he/she is paying.

- No matter how brilliant you are in development, always be mindful of project timelines and deliveries. The worst thing about a project is not being able to deliver the milestones on time. If there is any blocker or something happens that will make you delay a delivery, let your project manager or client know with some anticipation. Manage the expectations: it is much worse if you try hard to solve a problem but let your project manager know it at the last minute of the delivery.

- Be active and visible– if you work among a team or if you have your own clients, be always visible, even if it is only virtually. Collaborate on team channels, give (and ask for) feedback, let your managers or clients know what you are doing, and share interesting news and useful information.

Development

- Document your code as much as possible, especially if it is part of a bigger project or system. Some people argue about adding comments in the code, but you can write side notes on a shared document that will guide your team members, or even yourself, to understand the code and collaborate with it.

- Gather useful functions and methods into your own library– reusable code is useful and will save you a lot of development time.

- Always use good naming practices for your variables and functions– it will help you (and your team members) to understand the code in the future.

- Even if you are a freelancer and do not work with a bigger team, always use Git to store your projects. There are some free (but limited) solutions, such as BitBucket, but it is very important to keep your projects updated on repositories and not rely on hard drives, SSDs, or pen drives. Also, Git is an important version control system that will save you in case you break something and don't remember exactly when the problem started.

- Still about Git– there are people who push new code on any new feature or ticket, and they do it once a day– you should be in the middle ground. One push for any new feature would waste a bit of your time on this process and pushing once a day is quite risky in the case of losing information due an electrical failure or something. Try to do a new push every four or five features or tickets.

- Find a tech stack that you are comfortable with– and stick to it. Avoid jumping from one framework to another, just because it is "the best framework" of the week. It is interesting to learn new tools, but it is much more important to be consistent with a tech stack that works for you.

- By the way, one of the most important things in development (or even in life!) is consistency– a thing that you learned today will start to give you a return over time– never expect quick results for good things. Avoid the feeling of wasting time on something you believe in– a new language, a new framework, a new software– and jumping to something else before getting solid results about it. Consistency pays off!

- Do an extensive test before delivering a project, even if you have a QA professional working in your team. It will save you a lot of time (and stress) fixing simple bugs that you could easily catch with a quick test.

- ChatGPT, GitHub Copilot, and other AI tools are useful for quick things, but never rely entirely on these tools to do your work. Use them for what they are– just tools. You are the developer.

- Try, if possible, using staging and production environments, to avoid conflicts with what your PM (or client) is revising and what you are working at the moment.

- Never forget about **friction**– plan your project (especially AR and VR projects) in a way you can create a more frictionless experience as possible. Do not make your user struggle to open your experience by creating too many barriers such as required plugins, special software or devices. Your user will thank you and you will be able to reach more people.

- And if you need to, create a fallback version of your project where the users can interact with it without matching the requirements.

Three.js and A-Frame

- Try to understand (at least the basics) of object/scene matrix and quaternions– this knowledge will save you on more complicated projects.

- What to use on a project– pure Three.js or A-Frame? It depends totally on you, but in this book, we used the following approach– for general interactive 3D scenes we decided to use pure Three.js and for webAR and webVR scenes we opted to use A-Frame. We explained the reasons in *Chapter 6: Introduction to WebAR and WebVR*.

- We did not talk about it in this book, but **ReactThreeFiber** is an amazing framework and needs to be considered too, especially if you are familiar with React.

- Always be aware of your scene performance– heavyweight 3D assets and textures, too many post-processing effects, and too many animations happening at the same time, can ruin your scene performance especially if you need to run it on mobile browsers.

- Keep your A-Frame components organized. If possible, create your own component library where you can use it on different projects loading from a single location.

- We decided, in this book, not to stick to WebXR Device API to build webAR experiences because it does not run (yet) on Apple devices and there is no sense on building a commercial AR experience that runs only on Android devices, but we recommend that you learn it because sooner or later Apple will need to allow it on WebKit. When it happens, we will be able to use advanced AR features on any webXR-compatible mobile browser without the need of 3rd party plugin libraries.

- When creating a web VR scene, always be mindful of the devices you want to target when developing. And never leave the desktop version– it will be a fallback version in case your user does not have a VR headset around or does not want to charge it only for interacting with your experience!

- WebVR and webAR are still in the early days and you can find some limitations in them. Be patient because the future passes through these technologies!

Useful Boilerplates for Your Projects

In the next sections, we will share with you seven boilerplates based on this book's lessons and common commercial projects that will allow you to start building and selling Creative Technology projects to your clients. They are just a starting point– always have a good list of common ideas (with code, if possible) that you can easily adapt and offer to your clients. They will be your Swiss Army Knife and will keep you constantly busy with interesting and creative projects!

IMPORTANT NOTE: The assets (images, 3D models, and videos) on these templates are just for learning purposes and cannot be used in any commercial projects or redistributed.

Use your own assets on your projects!

T-Shirt Configurator App

You can find the code of this section in the folder: https://github.com/OrangeAVA/ Creative-Technology-with-Three.js/tree/main/chapter09/01_t_shirt_ configurator

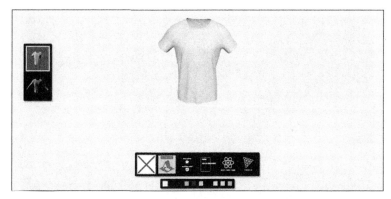

Figure 9.1: *T-Shirt configurator app*

With this T-Shirt configurator app, your customer can choose between two types of t-shirts– long or short sleeves, ten colors, and ten different designs. And you can even upload your own art!

3D Platform Game

You can find the code of this section in the folder: https://github.com/OrangeAVA/Creative-Technology-with-Three.js/tree/main/chapter09/02_platform_game

Figure 9.2: 3D platform game

This platform game is a revival of old-style platform games, such as Super Mario and Sonic but in 3D. It is a good starting point to build more complex levels and interactions.

VR Travel App

You can find the code of this section in the folder: https://github.com/OrangeAVA/Creative-Technology-with-Three.js/tree/main/chapter09/03_vr_travel_app

Figure 9.3: VR travel app

How about allowing your customer to try a travel destination before getting there? With this VR travel app, you can offer your customers the opportunity to be immersed into a destination in VR before buying a travel package.

(Note: Sea scent and wind blowing effect are not included in the experience)

AR Product Showcase

You can find the code of this section in the folder: https://github.com/OrangeAVA/ Creative-Technology-with-Three.js/tree/main/chapter09/04_ar_product_ showcase

Figure 9.4: *AR product showcase*

We revamped the Chapter 7 lesson and built an AR product showcase that allows your customers to try the products out.

Animated Portfolio

You can find the code of this section in the folder: https://github.com/OrangeAVA/ Creative-Technology-with-Three.js/tree/main/chapter09/05_animated_ portfolio

Figure 9.5: *Animated portfolio*

It does not mean that your portfolio needs to be this way, but it is a good starting point if you need a more appealing online website. Works well for consumer products websites too.

Home Design App

You can find the code of this section in the folder: https://github.com/OrangeAVA/ Creative-Technology-with-Three.js/tree/main/chapter09/06_home_design_ app

***Figure 9.6**: Home design app*

How about designing your own living room in 3D before buying the furniture? You can do this on Blender of course, but how about your customer? With this Home Design App your customer has a chance to pre-visualize, build, and experiment with different furniture types.

Infographic

You can find the code of this section in the folder: https://github.com/OrangeAVA/ Creative-Technology-with-Three.js/tree/main/chapter09/07_infographic

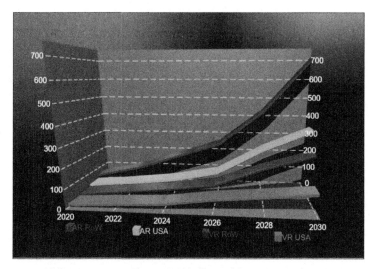

Figure 9.7: *Infographic*

This one is a good call for editorial content– instead of boring static infographics, how about showing them in 3D and spicing it up with some interaction?

Conclusion

We hope you had a nice journey through Creative Development using Three.js and A-Frame. As we have said earlier, this book is a starting point for developers who have some JavaScript and HTML knowledge and want to explore more creative possibilities using code, images, videos, and 3D assets. With the lessons and templates in this book, you will be able to start doing personal and commercial creative development projects. Feel free to modify them and add more features and functionalities. Good luck and have a good journey!

Index